SECOND LANGUAGE READING
RESEARCH AND INSTRUCTION

Crossing the Boundaries

SECOND LANGUAGE READING
RESEARCH AND INSTRUCTION

Crossing the Boundaries

ZhaoHong Han and Neil J. Anderson, Editors

Ann Arbor
THE UNIVERSITY OF MICHIGAN PRESS

∞ Printed on acid-free paper

ISBN-13: 978-0-472-03350-8

2012   2011   2010   2009   4   3   2   1

ACKNOWLEDGMENTS

This volume could not have been put together without the participation of a good number of people, and we are deeply indebted to them all. The contributing authors have displayed an extraordinary collaborative spirit and patience in the production process, and it has been a genuine pleasure to work with each of them. We are also grateful to the ESL editor, Kelly Sippell, and her team at the University of Michigan Press whose feedback and assistance have helped to elevate the book to a new level. We also wish to acknowledge Joo-Kyoung Jung at Teachers College, Columbia University, for her assistance.

CONTENTS

Introduction: Crossing the Boundaries

ZhaoHong Han, Neil J. Anderson,
and David Freeman

History has witnessed numerous transformations of second language (L2) teaching. Nonetheless, the teaching of reading has hitherto remained a central component of any L2 curricula, communicative or non-communicative. Accordingly, in comparison with the teaching of other aspects of language use—such as grammar, listening, speaking, and writing—reading has received the most attention from applied linguists (see, e.g., Aebersold & Field, 1997; Anderson, 1999; Bell, 1995; Bernhardt, 1991; Carrell, 1983a, 1984, 1991; Carrell, Devine, & Eskey, 1988; Carrell & Eisterhold, 1983; Nuttall, 1996; Urquhart & Weir, 1998) and ESL/EFL teachers.

To date, however, research and instruction on L2 reading have pursued three disparate approaches: whole language, skills, or acquisition. While both the whole language approach and the skills approach treat reading as a literacy skill, focusing thereby on the role of comprehension, the former emphasizes knowledge-based processes in discourse comprehension and interpretation and the latter, on the other hand, stresses micro and macro comprehension skills and strategies that may lead to better comprehension. Neither is similar to an acquisition approach that takes account of reading as a source of input for L2 acquisition (i.e., construction of linguistic competence). Importantly, the difference separating the three approaches goes beyond their respective domains of concern; rather, due to their epistemological differences, the three approaches offer conceptions and practical suggestions that are oftentimes contradictory. This scenario not only prevents a coherent understanding of L2 reading but also breeds lack of efficacy for instruction. This issue is becoming acute both in the United States, as more and more English language learners are placed in mainstream subject-matter classes in K–12 schools, and in many countries where communicative language teaching moves toward being content-driven. Teachers who operate in these settings often feel the tension between a focus on content and a focus on language. An urgent question that therefore needs to be addressed is to what extent reading can (be facilitated to) allow L2 learners to achieve multiple goals rather than one single goal. This question is complicated by second language acquisition (SLA) research findings suggesting that neither are comprehension and acquisition synonymous (Gass & Selinker, 2001) nor are meaning-based and grammatically based use of language (Swain, 1985).

Thus, in response to the complexity of the issue, and also in the spirit of promoting a symbiotic relationship between diverse conceptual and pedagogical practices, this volume attempts to cross the boundaries, so to speak, by bringing together the three perspectives on L2 reading research and instruction. Contributors to this volume are seasoned researchers who have examined reading from one of these angles and who, collectively, will tackle the following questions, among others: Should L2 reading instruction be comprehension-oriented, or should it be language-oriented? What types of knowledge and skills are necessary for improving reading comprehension? What elements of language can be learned through reading? Is it possible to integrate grammar training into comprehension training? If so, how may that be achieved in the classroom? As a secondary goal, this volume seeks to bridge the oft-noted gap between research and practice. This book is intended for L2 reading researchers, teachers, curriculum developers, materials writers, and graduate students of second language education interested in L2 reading.

THE CONTEXT

Reading plays a pivotal role in the life of L2 learners; reading is not only an important literacy skill that must be acquired for functional purposes, but it is also a necessary (if not sufficient) means by which learners develop a linguistic competence in an L2 (cf. Krashen, 1993), a competence that can subserve all other communicative skills, including, but not limited to, listening, speaking, and writing. This dual purpose sets L2 reading apart from L1 reading and underscores the complexity of L2 reading and instruction. Compounding this complexity are also two noteworthy facts about L2 learners: First, most learners, as Shiotsu (this volume) notes, "start to read in the second language before achieving the kind of grammatical maturity and the level of oral vocabulary that L1 readers attain before they begin to read" (p. 16). Second, they have varying experiences in reading in a prior language whose writing systems might bear unequal similarities to that of the target language (TL). Both realities have implications for the process and outcome of L2 reading and, hence, for instruction.

L2 reading instruction has traditionally been focused either on the literacy dimension (i.e., is comprehension-oriented), influenced largely by L1 research, or on the language dimension, as has research. To date, the two research paradigms have shown little crossover (cf. Grabe, 2005a; Horst, this volume). Nevertheless, it is becoming increasingly clear that a separation in instruction and research of the otherwise two interrelated dimensions is counterproductive to L2 learning: A focus on reading as a literacy skill dictates a functional emphasis on reading for efficient and effective textual comprehension. A focus on reading as a vehicle of language development, on the other hand, treats reading as a source of input for learners to intake linguistic information about the target language and calls for instructional attention to the psycholinguistic processes of representation and access. These two foci are not always compatible and may result in conflicting pedagogical recommendations (Han & D'Angelo, this volume).

The two foci need not be separate, however, at least as far as instruction is concerned. Indeed, in the history of L2 instruction, there have been attempts to fuse them. Krashen has recommended since the early 1980s that learners be exposed to large numbers of L2 comprehensible written texts as the means for achieving both goals, comprehension and acquisition. He argues that comprehension-based reading may *ipso facto* lead to language acquisition. However, this view, known as the Input Hypothesis (Krashen, 1982), has been the target of an array of criticisms from nearly all quarters of SLA research (see, e.g., Sharwood Smith, 1986; Swain, 1985; White, L., 1987). Evidence has been brought to bear that comprehension and acquisition are not synonymous (e.g., Genesee, 1987; Harley & Swain, 1984; Lightbown & Spada, 1990; Swain & Lapkin, 1982, 1989) and that learners have a natural tendency to prioritize semantic processing over syntactic processing (Kowal & Swain, 1997; VanPatten, 1996; Williams, 2001). Therefore, a comprehension-exclusive approach, in some sense, reinforces the learner's propensity to read for comprehension and not to read for acquisition. Observations have shown that learners trained with a comprehension-exclusive approach typically develop superior comprehension skills but little linguistic knowledge (Harley & Swain, 1984).

Amendments have subsequently been sought to the comprehensible input model. Researchers have found, among other things, that a focus-on-form approach (Long, 1991), which integrates incidental but overt attention to form in otherwise exclusively meaning-based instruction (see, e.g., Leeman et al., 1995), may benefit both comprehension and acquisition. A recent study by Rodgers (2006), for instance, provided compelling evidence that such an approach may lead to growth in both content knowledge and linguistic abilities. Rodgers' research, however, has also revealed a challenge: The students in the study demonstrated much development in knowledge of content but much less development in functional linguistic abilities. Moreover, some of the linguistic forms that were targeted by the instructors (e.g., prepositions) showed no improvement at all. It thus appears that content-based instruction, when combined with a focus on form, may still be inadequate for linguistic development.

A related, though less obvious, concern is whether or not the focus-on-form approach compromises comprehension. On this issue Rodgers' (2006) study (and for that matter, most extant studies) has shed little light, due to its methodological limitation—the study assumed a within-group design and did not include a comparison group that would only have had content-based instruction to allow for a comparison of comprehension, both in terms of quantity and quality. Indeed, in general, it is still typical of these kinds of focus-on-form studies to not measure and/or compare comprehension (cf. Han, Park, & Combs, in press; Grabe, this volume). Nonetheless, it is clear that until comprehension and linguistic abilities are both measured and compared, there will continue to be a lack of an empirical basis for arguing for one approach over another.

LITERACY-ORIENTED L1 AND L2 RESEARCH

Literacy-oriented research in both L1 and L2 reading is marked by a dichotomy. There is a clear distinction between research related to whole language instruction and skills instruction. Traditionally, whole language instruction has also been identified as a top-down approach to reading, while skills instruction has been identified as a bottom-up approach (see Anderson, N., 2008).

Proponents of whole language instruction argue that readers build meaning from the integration of textual information and background knowledge. The reader is searching for meaning and selectively reacts to print to confirm or reject the predictions that are made. Segalowitz, Poulsen, and Komoda (1991) point out that this higher level is concerned primarily with integration of textual information and includes resolving ambiguities in the text, linking words with their co-referents, integrating propositional units across sentences, generating and updating a schema or representation of the text as a whole, and integrating textual information with prior knowledge.

A major advocate of whole language reading instruction is Goodman, K. (1973, 1976). One line of early reading research carried out by Goodman (1967) was from a psycholinguistic perspective via qualitative methods. A method that he developed to examine reading is miscue analysis. By studying oral reading miscues, or unexpected responses to text, Goodman developed a theory of reading that holds that reading is a process of constructing meaning from text by using background knowledge, psychological strategies (including sampling, predicting and inferring, confirming and integrating), and linguistic cues from three systems—graphophonic, syntactic, and semantic. More recently, this research has been extended to include eye movement data (Paulson & Freeman, 2003). In these eye movement miscue analysis (EMMA) studies, subjects read and retell complete texts. By combining data from eye fixations with oral language miscues, researchers can better infer readers' use of psychological strategies, such as prediction, and their use of linguistic cues.

Not all research on whole language instruction uses qualitative methods. A good example is a report by Purcell-Gates, Duke, and Martineau (2007), which uses an experimental study design to examine the roles of explicit teaching and authentic experience in children's ability to read and write genre-specific text. In this study, the children read and wrote science informational and procedural texts. For example, after visiting a nature preserve, the children read a letter from the director of the preserve inviting them to write a brochure that would answer questions children have about plants and animals in a brochure. Then, the children worked in groups to write a brochure. As the authors note, this study addresses the debate regarding how content language forms are best learned. Some hold the belief that secondary discourses (Gee, 1992), such as the language of science, can only be implicitly learned. Others argue that specific genres should be taught explicitly. Results of the study showed no effect for explicit instruction on reading and writing growth for six of seven outcomes. However, there was a strong relationship between growth in reading and writing and task authenticity. This study supports the practice of engaging children in authentic reading and writing tasks for the development of academic language.

The alternative to the whole language approach to teaching L2 reading is a skill-based approach. Much of the current L1 and L2 reading research that drives most instructional practice is research grounded in cognitive theory. A skill-based approach to reading typically consists of lower-level reading processes. Students start with the basics of letter and sound recognition, which, in turn, allows for morpheme recognition followed by word recognition, building up to the identification of grammatical structures, sentences, and longer texts. Letters, letter clusters, words, phrases, sentences, longer texts, and meaning is the order in achieving comprehension.

An important early study that examined the variables that account for reading proficiency was Stanovich's (1986) synthesis of research. The variable or skill that Stanovich found to account for much of the difference between good and poor readers was phonemic awareness, the ability to perceive and manipulate the individual phonemes or sounds of spoken words. This study was influential in shaping current reading instructional policy with an early emphasis on teaching phonemic awareness.

In the United States, research that examined the separate skills involved in reading, such as phonemic awareness, received support from government grants administered through the National Institute of Child Health and Human Development (NICHD). In 1997 the NICHD convened a National Reading Panel (NRP) consisting primarily of cognitive scientists to conduct a meta-analysis of research in the teaching of reading. The panel elected to limit research studies to those that were experimental or quasi-experimental in design. Only these studies were considered scientific research. They examined five areas of reading research that had studies that met their criteria: phonemic awareness, phonics, fluency, vocabulary, and comprehension (Fang, 2008; Fang & Schleppegrell, 2008; National Institute of Child Health and Human Development, 2000). These have come to be known as the "fab 5" among teachers and researchers engaged in reading instruction and research.

This panel report was summarized and widely distributed to schools. The fab 5 have become the five pillars of reading instruction for both native English speakers and language learners (ELLs) in most schools in the United States. The No Child Left Behind Act of 2002 requires students to make progress in reading as measured by standardized tests based on the five areas the NRP studied.

Pressley (2006), however, argues that the whole language and skills approaches represent the extremes and that "either extreme misses the mark" (p. 11). Pressley is a great advocate of what is known as a balanced approach to the teaching of reading. This approach draws on elements of both whole language and skills approaches. His work has involved examining effective classrooms, effective schools, and effective literacy programs. He points out "the classrooms where reading and writing seem to be developing best are ones in which there is a lot of coverage of skills and a great deal of teacher support as children apply the skills they are learning to the reading of excellent literature and to writing" (p. 427).

It appears, therefore, that within the context of L1 reading research, although there are debates about whether a whole language approach or a skills approach to reading development is better, it is the combination of both that results in the most effective reading instruction.

The same issues that are part of L1 reading research exist in L2 reading (Anderson, N., 2008; Grabe & Stoller, 2002). Moreover, according to a report of the National Literacy Panel (NLP) (August & Shanahan, 2006), there is relatively little research on L2 reading, there were more studies on word-level skills than on text-level skills, and there was "little or no difference between the performance of language-minority students and their native-speaking peers on measures of word reading accuracy" (p. 61). August and Shanahan (2006) argue that the same factors that influence L1 reading—phonemic awareness, phonics, fluency, vocabulary, and comprehension—should guide L2 literacy instruction.

The NLP report includes a section with studies of sociocultural contexts and literacy development. These studies examine factors such as immigration, discourse differences between home and school, parents and families, language policies, and language status. One conclusion August and Shanahan (2006) reach is that attempts to bridge the home-school differences in interaction can "enhance students' engagement and level of participation in classroom instruction" (p. 256). Other factors seemed less important, although language policies and language status are shown to affect student self-concept and reading achievement.

The report also includes studies that examine crosslinguistic relationships in L2 reading. As August and Shanahan (2006) point out, "The majority of studies . . . have investigated cross-language relationships with reference to one of two theoretical orientations: the contrastive analysis hypothesis (Lado, 1964) and the interdependence hypothesis (Cummins, 1978, 1979)" (p. 154). The authors caution that reading is complex and that neither transfer nor interdependence alone can account for L2 reading.

Both are important, but other factors, such as differences among languages and the development of oral proficiency in an L2, also come into play.

The studies that were examined point to the importance of students' developing high levels of L1 literacy for L2 literacy achievement. For example, the studies that examined cross-language relationships in word reading suggested that aspects of word knowledge, such as cognates in related languages, transfer across languages. The NLP report also identified a significant correlation between L1 and L2 comprehension. Students with higher levels of comprehension in their L1s attained higher levels of comprehension in reading an L2 than those with low levels of L1 comprehension. Metacognitive reading strategies also appeared to transfer across languages.

Although the NLP report is heavily weighted toward experimental research and a view of reading as a set of skills whose subcomponents can be analyzed separately, it also includes a number of studies that take a more holistic view of reading and use qualitative methods. The report includes both social and cognitive factors involved in reading.

As with Pressley's research in L1 reading, Anderson, N. (2008) argues that a balanced or integrated approach to L2 reading is also appropriate. Such an approach requires a synergy of elements of a whole language approach, a skills approach, and an acquisition approach to teaching and researching.

THE ORGANIZATION OF THIS VOLUME

This volume has four chapters on research and four on instruction and concludes with an epilogue. Each chapter ends with a list of reflection questions for use in courses or for self-reflection.

Part 1 opens with an empirical study by Toshihiko Shiotsu that examines the relationship between word recognition and reading proficiency, taking as its premise that skilled deployment of lower-level processes may free up attentional resources for higher-order processes such as inferencing, which lead to better comprehension. Two hundred and nineteen Japanese EFL learners were given four test tasks that measure the latency of visual orthographic processing and lexical semantic access, passage comprehension, and sentence comprehension speed. Based on their reading ability as demonstrated on the last two tests, the participants were divided into two proficiency groups. Statistical analyses of their orthographic processing and lexical semantic access speed suggest that extensive reading activities may provide for ease of word recognition, including familiarity with orthographic regularities. Shiotsu recommends that classroom practice aimed at developing learners' word recognition fluency should entail both form and meaning recognition.

Chapter 2 addresses reading as a source of vocabulary acquisition. Drawing on three identified benefits of extensive reading—comprehensible input, modified input, and focus-on-form—as its theoretical basis, Marlise Horst's research addressed two questions: (1) To what extent do learners learn and retain meaning of previously unknown words as a result of participating in a program of extensive reading? and (2) Do learners recognize frequently met words more quickly than comparable words that have been met less frequently? Forty-seven adult, intermediate ESL learners with various L1 backgrounds served as subjects. While all of them were invited to participate in a five-week, after-school extensive reading program that provided a mini-library of graded readers for students to freely choose from, 29 of them read one book or more; the rest of the students did not read anything. Overall, the results indicate that the five-week reading program allowed the readers to develop knowledge of infrequent words as well as fluency in making form-meaning connections, particularly for words that made frequent appearances in the books they had selected to read.

Chapter 3 explores the differential vocabulary gains of students from reading. Diana Pulido reviews research on reader-based factors and their impact on reading and vocabulary growth. The existing research has robustly shown that three learner-related factors best predict vocabulary learning via reading: background knowledge, passage sight vocabulary, and general L2 reading proficiency. Thus, the more learners possess with regard to these, the more words they are able to acquire through reading (i.e., text comprehension). Simply put, the rich get richer—to use Stanovich's concept of what is known as the Matthew effect.

Chapter 4 reviews SLA research on three types of text modification: simplification, enhancement, and glossing. A long-held belief among many researchers and practitioners is that textual modification facilitates comprehension, and for some, this facilitates acquisition. Ronald Leow's review challenges this assumption. With regard to text simplification, research has offered mixed evidence on its effect on comprehension, but little evidence that it promotes intake, the initial process of language acquisition. Likewise, empirical findings concerning textual enhancement are inconsistent (cf. Han, Park, & Combs, 2008). On the other hand, research has quite consistently shown that glossing facilitates comprehension and incidental vocabulary learning. Based on the extant research, Leow offers a number of pedagogical suggestions, stressing the need to promote noticing and awareness through multiple opportunities for learners to repeatedly encounter linguistic forms in context.

In Part 2 on instruction-related issues, Chapter 5 highlights reading as a universal process. David Freeman and Yvonne Freeman make two recommendations for teachers. First, instruction should strive to capitalize on learners' L1 reading proficiency. In the event that such proficiency is absent, it should be built by "teaching reading in a student's primary language" (p. 103). Second, a socio-psycholinguistic approach should be used that strengthens the universal process. By way of illustration, Freeman and Freeman describe two classroom scenarios to contrast the socio-psycholinguistic approach, which is holistic in nature, with the skills approach that emphasizes discrete and decontextualized decoding skills.

Chapter 6 by Neil Anderson presents the research basis for ACTIVE, a pedagogical approach he proposed for L2 reading instruction that focuses on comprehension. This approach has six components: Activate prior knowledge, Cultivate vocabulary, Think about comprehension, Increase reading rate, Verify reading strategies, and Evaluate progress. For each of the components of the framework, Anderson briefly reviews its research basis and offers practical suggestions. For activating prior knowledge, he suggests three pre-reading strategies: creating and having students fill out an anticipation guide, discussing text type and structure, and using titles of the reading passages to elicit predictions. For cultivating vocabulary, he suggests using both direct and indirect strategies to deal respectively with vocabulary items prior to and during reading, including teaching word structure analysis skills. With regard to thinking about comprehension, Anderson suggests getting students to formulate their own questions, asking students to summarize what they have read, and asking students to question the author. For increasing reading rate, he recommends "rate buildup" reading, repeated reading, class-paced reading, and self-paced reading. To verify reading strategies, he suggests asking students to produce verbal reports and think-aloud protocols. To assess progress, he recommends the use of reading logs, reading rate graphs, reading rate records, and records of repeated reading.

Chapter 7 by Tom Cobb discusses the role of computers in L2 reading instruction, with specific reference to vocabulary building. He first presents a computer-based analysis of the learning task and difficulty confronting L2 readers, concluding that learning to read in an L2 is different from learning to read in the L1, particularly in terms of (a) the rate of vocabulary acquisition, (b) the coverage of the vocabulary acquired, and (c) lexical access. Cobb then introduces web-based programs that may help to overcome these deficiencies. These programs may (a) offer large amounts and varieties of reading to help close or prevent gaps in high-coverage lexical zones; (b) help choose reading texts to maximize learners' skill development, vocabulary growth, and pleasure; (c) help create dedicated word frequency lists for particular reading objectives; (d) help speed up the acquisition of new words; (e) help generate contextualized word frequency to enrich word knowledge; and (f) facilitate transfer of word knowledge to novel contexts.

Chapter 8 addresses the issue of how to balance comprehension and acquisition in instruction. Drawing on L2 acquisition research, ZhaoHong Han and Amy D'Angelo argue that a comprehension-exclusive approach to reading instruction may lead to skewed development in the L2 such that learners may be able to comprehend texts but still be weak in linguistic competence. They subsequently propose a pedagogical approach, dubbed the "dual approach," to allow reciprocity between comprehension-based (semantic) processing and language-based (syntactic) processing. The instruction begins by teaching reading for comprehension, including teaching skills for achieving comprehension and for increasing efficiency. Once basic comprehension is in place, the instructor then draws learners' attention to certain linguistic forms and helps learners detect form-meaning mapping relations in context, using strategies such as input enhancement (Sharwood Smith, 1993), processing instruction (VanPatten, 1996), and narrow reading (Krashen, 1981).

Bill Grabe provides an epilogue synthesizing how the chapters meet a growing need for understanding L2 reading ability and reading instruction. Grabe emphasizes the importance of the connection between theory and practice, a central theme in this volume. He then outlines ten components that help educators understand how reading comprehension functions (letter-sound correspondences, lexical access, a large vocabulary, morphological information, syntactic processing, forming meaning units, connecting main ideas to build a text model of reading, building a situation model of the text, directing attention and executive control, and processing concepts). He also identifies eight common themes across multiple chapters in the book (the L2 reader, the component skills for reading, a large recognition vocabulary, extensive reading, fluency and automaticity of processing, strategic instruction and the importance of strategic reading, the role of background knowledge, and finally, instructional applications). Grabe concludes by highlighting three issues that deserve further attention to increase our understanding of L2 reading, and these are (a) the roles of fluency development, motivation, and content and language integrated instruction, (b) the need for additional experimental and qualitative research, and (c) the relationship between reading comprehension and second language acquisition.

SHARED UNDERSTANDINGS

This volume provides a window into the diversity of conceptions on L2 reading and instruction. Some researchers view reading as isomorphic with comprehension itself an end, while others deem reading (and comprehension) a means to an end. Nevertheless, it is clear that regardless of their epistemological differences, researchers do have some shared understandings. They all believe that comprehension should be the primary goal of reading instruction; that vocabulary is essential to text comprehension; that vocabulary is best acquired through frequent encounters with words in multiple contexts; that skilled word recognition frees up mental resources for performing higher-order comprehension processes such as predicting and inferring, confirming and/or disconfirming predictions, and integrating new information with previous ideas; and that extensive reading develops efficiency in lexical and orthographic processing.

However, this volume exposes a wide array of issues for future research to resolve. One set of issues concerns whether there is a tradeoff between speed reading and comprehension, whether there is a tradeoff between speed and input processing, and whether speed reading should be promoted across the board given that the goal of communicative language teaching is to develop learners who can utilize a variety of skills for a variety of communicative purposes. A second set of issues relates to the teaching of word recognition skills. For example, should they be taught in context (e.g., during reading) or in isolation (e.g., before reading)? A third concerns the role of text modification, in particular, text simplification. According to Leow's review, simplified texts aid, in some cases, in comprehension, but not acquisition. Given this, should texts be simplified for L2 readers? A fourth set of issues relates to whether a whole language approach is good for both comprehension and acquisition. Does it encourage use of nonlinguistic means more than linguistic means in achieving comprehension? Does it lead to early stabilization of interlanguage? An equally contentious set of issues revolves around the role of the L1 in learning to read in an L2. Does L1 reading proficiency facilitate or hinder L2 reading proficiency? Should transfer be encouraged from the L1 to the L2? Does an emphasis on universal processes overlook language-specific reading processes? Can learners without literacy in the L1 learn to read in an L2 directly? What are the consequences of L1 transfer for L2 comprehension and acquisition? These issues, we hope, will constitute a point of departure for future collaboration between researchers of different orientations, in particular, of the three described (i.e., whole language, skills, and acquisition).

With a recognition of the dual potential of L2 reading comes the need to re-conceptualize L2 reading instruction: Rather than stressing one at the expense of the other, instruction should aim to develop learners' reading proficiency as well as their linguistic competency. In this light, the traditional boundaries separating a literacy-oriented paradigm from an acquisition-oriented paradigm are no longer tenable; rather, researchers from both camps must come together to create a common empirical basis for instruction.

This volume is a preliminary attempt to cross the research boundaries. Its goal is to garner existing insights but, more important, to foreshadow issues for future research on the dual dimension of L2 reading. It is our hope that this initial attempt will arouse interest in L2 reading researchers and instructors in following up on the many ideas, insights, and issues discussed in the book by subjecting them to all kinds of empirical investigations (experimental, quasi-experimental, and observational) (cf. Grabe, this volume). On a more global level, we would like to call on empirical research to clarify, in precise terms, the relationship between comprehension and grammar and the relationship between comprehension and vocabulary. The existing literature has been fuzzy and is therefore not quite helpful on these issues. The existing studies are mostly *post facto*, using test results for correlational analysis. Although the field may, as a consequence, be content with the notion of "reciprocal causality," a clear understanding of the relationships can be crucial for any instructional attempt to fulfill the dual potential of L2 reading. For one thing, an understanding of the extent to which grammar contributes to comprehension (or vice versa) may aid in decision-making on how to counterbalance comprehension and grammar in order for both to develop robustly in L2 learners.

PART 1

Research

Reading Ability and Components of Word Recognition Speed: The Case of L1-Japanese EFL Learners

Toshihiko Shiotsu, Kurume University, Japan

Reading is a complex cognitive activity that requires an integration of information from the text and knowledge in our minds, and successful reading comprehension depends on skilled processing of the visually presented text. Reading comprehension is thought to be supported by both the so-called "lower-level" (e.g., word recognition) and the "higher-level" processes (e.g., integrating the textual information within and across the sentences). It is also thought to draw on our cognitive resources that are limited at any given moment, and achieving automaticity (i.e., effortless, fast, and stable processing) in such lower-level processes as word recognition should lead to the desired condition of more mental resources becoming available for higher-level processes. Conversely, if recognition of many words in the text is non-automatic and requires controlled processing (i.e., effortful, slow, and unstable), it may leave little mental resource for the higher-level processes to draw on and can seriously affect the overall reading performance. Such must be the case whether one is reading in an L1 or L2 (McLaughlin, Rossman, & McLeod, 1983). The L1 reading research has produced evidence for a fundamental role that word recognition skills play in reading comprehension (Stanovich, 1991), and L2 research should pay serious attention to this significant aspect of reading.

However, simply applying the findings from L1 word recognition research to the case of L2 readers is often insufficient and even inadequate, since the nature of L2 reading development is often quite different from that of L1. For instance, many L2 learners start to read in their target language before achieving the kind of grammatical maturity and the level of oral vocabulary the L1 readers attain before they begin to read. Thus, while initial difficulties in L1 reading development can often be attributed to the lack of knowledge in grapheme-to-phoneme correspondence or that of phonological awareness (Goswami & Bryant, 1990), L2 reading difficulties may also arise from the lack of oral vocabulary against which to match the visually identified sequence of graphemes. In the case of L1 readers, lexical-semantic access efficiency may automatically follow from successful decoding of visual input. However, the same cannot be assumed in L2 word recognition.

Also, L2 readers have diverse experiences and abilities in reading in their own L1, and their L1 writing systems vary in relative similarity to that of their target language (Cook & Bassetti, 2005). This distance between the L1 and L2 writing systems may interact with the learner's experience and ability in L1 reading (Koda, 2005). To illustrate, beginning ESL learners proficient in an L1 that uses a Roman script are expected to be relatively more advantaged than other beginners of ESL whose past reading experiences were restricted to a non-Roman or non-alphabetic L1 writing system. In short, L2 word recognition research must address its own agenda and attempt to discover regularities observed within or across different learner groups.

Identifying L2 word recognition patterns or regularities associated with learners from particular writing system backgrounds has pedagogical values since such findings can cumulatively lead to theories or models that will help predict potential sources of difficulty for a particular group of learners or possibly even contribute to organizing a unique reading syllabus for them. However, as Koda (2005) argues, "word recognition, despite its significance, has received scant attention in L2 research" (p. 37), and there is an urgent need for research expansion in this area.

This chapter reports on a study conducted to investigate the word recognition speed of English as a Foreign Language (EFL) learners from a non-alphabetic writing system background. It first reviews the previous research with some focus on their methodological features relevant to the study.

PREVIOUS RESEARCH ON L2 WORD RECOGNITION SPEED

Word knowledge is multifaceted—that is, the learner must acquire various types of knowledge about the target lexical item including its phonological and orthographic forms, its meanings, its morphological structure, its syntactic behavior, and its association and collocation with other words (Meara, 1996; Nation, 2001). Learning the word's form is essential for developing other types of knowledge about the word, and learning the word's orthographic form and its meaning is crucial for developing reading skills. Although the learner might "know" the forms and meanings of words, speed of access or level of automaticity in recognizing them can be underdeveloped. It is thus important to develop efficient word recognition skills.

Word recognition involves such sub-processes as: (1) visual recognition of letter features, (2) letter identification, (3) the generation of grapheme-phoneme correspondences, (4) utilization of orthographic redundancies such as regularities in letter sequences, and (5) the association of words to their semantic representations (Segalowitz, Paulsen, & Komoda, 1991). The desired state should be one in which as many of these sub-processes are automatized and require as little attentional resources as possible. Processing accuracy is necessary but accuracy alone cannot constitute skilled processing, unless accompanied by reasonable speed. Therefore, researchers have attempted to obtain information on the reader's processing speed by means of speeded tasks or measures of recognition latency (e.g., Segalowitz, Segalowitz, & Wood, 1998) together with response accuracy.

Investigations of bilinguals' word recognition speed have shown that their processing speed was much slower in the L2 than in the L1 even when Roman-script languages like French and English (Favreau & Segalowitz, 1982) or Irish and English (Macnamara, 1970) formed the language pair. Such findings would seem to predict that learners of an alphabetic L2 from a non-Roman or a non-alphabetic L1 orthographic background are further disadvantaged. Some crosslinguistic studies have explored the effects of disparate L1 orthographic backgrounds on the word recognition speed of an alphabetic L2.

For example, Brown and Haynes (1985) subjected groups of ESL learners from L1 Japanese (non-alphabetic), Arabic (alphabetic, non-Roman), and Spanish (Roman script) backgrounds to a battery of instruments including sets of speeded same-different decision tasks to compare their efficiencies in the visual discrimination of Roman letter strings, including real English words (*pressing*), regularly spelled non-words, called *pseudo-words* (*prossing*), and irregularly spelled non-words (*prngesis*). The non-words were thought to require word-internal analysis, while the real words could be recognized as an unanalyzed whole if they existed as such in the learners' long-term memory. When compared against the learners' pseudo-word processing latency, the irregularly spelled non-words served to assess the effect of the learners' familiarity with the common letter sequencing patterns or orthographic regularities observed in the English language.

Contrary to what one might expect, the results showed that the L1 Japanese group performed the best and the L1 Spanish group the worst in all of the three stimulus categories in both response accuracy and latency. The latency differences among the three stimulus types were also the smallest for the Japanese group. When each language group was divided into higher and lower ESL proficiency sub-groups, the more proficient sub-groups consistently did better than the less proficient ones, but they were affected more adversely by the lack of orthographic regularity when processing the irregularly spelled non-words. According to Brown and Haynes (1985), this "corresponds well with studies of L1 reading, in which increased sensitivity to spelling regularity is associated with better reading" (p. 29), though the reasons for the crosslinguistic performance differences in the unexpected direction remain unclear.

Of interest are the results from a separate measure of spelling-to-sound translation efficiency Brown and Haynes (1985) included in their instrument battery. This was an oral reading task requiring the learners to pronounce, as quickly and accurately as possible, lists of letter strings, half comprising real English words and the other half pseudo-words. The time spent on each list was recorded, and again the response time gap between the real words and pseudo-words was consulted. The results of this portion of their study revealed that the Japanese groups were slower than the other groups, and they were more adversely affected by the shift from the real words to the pseudo-words. Therefore, the results from this task contradicted those from the same-different decision task, although they were more in line with the prediction that the non-alphabetic L1 background of the Japanese group would negatively affect performance. The diverging results from the two tasks may reflect a dissociation of the underlying abilities between visual discrimination of alphabetic letter sequences and fluently pronouncing such sequences.

Latency in pronouncing the target letter strings was also examined in a crosslinguistic study by Akamatsu (1999), who employed case alternation (e.g., "cAsE") as a tool for comparing the learners from alphabetic (Persian) and non-alphabetic (Japanese and Chinese) L1 orthographic backgrounds in relation to their sensitivity to alphabetic orthography. Akamatsu contended that the visual disruption of word-shape cues caused by the case alternation should not affect the processing of intra-word letter sequences among the learners efficient in alphabetic processing and that a deterioration in performance would signal inefficiencies in alphabetic processing. Akamatsu recorded the response latencies of the ESL learners and a control group of English native speakers as they read aloud each of the monosyllabic real words appearing singly on the computer screen and varying in case (normal lowercase vs. alternated), general frequency of appearance (high vs. low), and regularity of spelling (regular vs. exception).

The comparison across the four groups indicated that the native speakers outperformed the ESL groups in every combination of the stimulus conditions and they were not significantly affected by the case alternation (e.g., "time" vs. "tImE"), reduced frequency ("tImE" vs. "fAtE"), or relatively irregular spelling ("fAtE" vs. "dEbT"). In contrast, all three ESL groups were slowed down by case alternation and reduced frequency, and the Japanese and Chinese groups were also affected by the relatively irregular spelling. When only the three ESL groups were compared, the Persians were less affected than the other groups by case alternation, which Akamatsu argues was an indication of the more experienced alphabetic processing of the L1 Persian group. Therefore, different studies requiring learners to read aloud the stimuli converged on the relative robustness of the learners with an alphabetic L1 orthography against a lack of familiar word shape.

Another study by Akamatsu (2003) involving the same combination of L1 groups (Japanese, Chinese, and Persian) in silent reading for comprehension of normal and case-alternated English passages also indicated that the non-alphabetic groups' passage reading time was more adversely affected by case alternation than was the Persian L1 group's, although their comprehension was not any more affected than was the Persian group's. It is notable that for this study Akamatsu established that the three L1 groups were comparable in terms of their academic reading proficiency. This is a significant point but one that was not clarified in Brown and Haynes (1985) or Akamatsu (1999). As the learners' L2 reading experiences and reading proficiency may interact with their L1 background, a crosslinguistic comparison should at least provide information on the comparability of the L1 groups in their proficiency in the target language.[1] Nevertheless, provided that the learners' L2 proficiency had no impact on their results, Akamatsu's two studies and the part of Brown and Haynes's results on the letter string naming task support the notion that learners of an alphabetic L2 from non-alphabetic L1 orthographic backgrounds are more prone to inefficient intra-word processing than are those with an alphabetic L1.

Other crosslinguistic studies addressing the roles of the readers' L1 orthographic background have established a positive correlation between the L2 reading proficiency and experiences of the participants (Muljani, Koda, & Moates, 1998; Wade-Woolley, 1999; Wang, Koda, & Perfetti, 2003; Wang & Koda, 2005). Muljani et al. (1998) had L1-Indonesian (alphabetic) and L1-Chinese (non-alphabetic) ESL learners perform a timed lexical decision task together with a native-speaker control group. In this task, the participants were timed as they made decisions on whether a given letter string forms an existing English word or not. The researchers varied the stimulus words in terms of frequency (high vs. low; e.g., *dance* vs. *dense*) and congruence with the Indonesian syllabic pattern of having no more than one consonant each in the syllable onset and coda (congruent vs. incongruent; *kidnap* vs. *smuggle*) and used them in a random sequence with a corresponding set of non-words (e.g., *danse, denze, kiznap, smugkle*). The response time data revealed that with respect to all stimulus types, the control group outperformed the ESL groups, within which the L1-Indonesian sub-group did better than the L1-Chinese sub-group. Additionally, although the control group showed no frequency or congruence effect, the ESL groups were adversely affected by reduced frequency and a lack of congruence, indicating the effects of both L2 word processing experiences and transfer of L1 syllable processing in L2 word recognition.

Two studies by Wang and colleagues (Wang, Koda, & Perfetti, 2003; Wang & Koda, 2005) compared the intra-word processing performances of L1-Korean (alphabetic) and L1-Chinese (non-alphabetic) ESL learners. The researchers employed a speeded semantic category judgment task, in which the learners responded on whether or not each target word displayed singly on a computer screen (e.g., *feet*) was an exemplar of a semantic category displayed immediately before (e.g., *a body part*). The groups' response accuracies and latencies on homophone foils (*feat*) and spelling controls (*fees*) were examined to compare the effects of phonological interference.

---

[1] If the L1 groups compared should differ in their L2 proficiency, then differential word recognition performances can not only be attributed to L1 differences but also to the L2 proficiency.

Also, the researchers created category-exemplar pairs that would result in either similarly spelled foils (*a body part–feat*) or less similarly spelled ones (*a flower–rows*) to test the effects of spelling similarity. The Korean group made more errors on homonyms than on controls regardless of spelling similarity, while the Chinese group did so under similarly spelled conditions only. Moreover, the Koreans outperformed the Chinese in accuracy on the similarly spelled items and in decision latency on all item types. The two groups were also tested on their ability to manipulate intra-word phonological structure through a phoneme deletion task, whose results suggested the Korean group's general advantage in phonological skills. Wang et al. argue that the Korean group's alphabetic L1 literacy leads to their reliance on phonological processing, and the Chinese group's non-alphabetic and logographic L1 literacy leads to their tendency to rely less on phonology and more on spelling information. An earlier study by Holm and Dodd (1996) compared ESL groups with alphabetic and non-alphabetic L1 experiences, noting that the latter had a much poorer level of phonological awareness, which is consistent with Wang et al.'s interpretation of their results.

Wang and Koda (2005) compared L1-Korean and L1-Chinese groups in response accuracy and latency with respect to naming real English words and pseudo-words. The Korean group outperformed the Chinese in accuracy but not in response latency, possibly indicating that an alphabetic L1 contributes to the accuracy of processing alphabetic L2 words but not to the speed with which they are processed. However, as the researchers themselves point out, the interpretation of the response time results from both Wang et al. (2003) and Wang and Koda requires caution, as the analyses were based on reduced sets of responses due to varying degrees of response inaccuracy. Wang and Koda also found the effects of word frequency and spelling-to-sound regularity regardless of the group, which supports the effects of L2 reading experience.

Comparisons of ESL groups from alphabetic and non-alphabetic L1 backgrounds were also conducted by Wade-Woolley (1999) and Sasaki (2005). Wade-Woolley found that her L1-Japanese group (non-alphabetic) was faster and more accurate than her L1-Russian group (alphabetic) on tasks requiring an awareness of legitimate orthographic patterns, whereas the L1-Russian group did better on the phoneme deletion task. Wade-Woolley suggests that the Japanese group's L1 reading experience with kanji logography may be the basis for their greater sensitivity to visual information expressed by orthographic patterns, while the relative dissimilarity of the Japanese phonology to that of English was associated with their poorer performance in phoneme deletion.

Sasaki (2005) reported that her L1 Japanese group (non-alphabetic) was much less efficient at English word recognition than her L1 Italian group (alphabetic) based on a task involving timed decision on whether or not the target word was the same as the one shown on a previous screen. The Japanese group was much more affected by homophone foils, especially when they were spelled similarly to the targets, whereas the Italians performed at a similar level to the L1-English control group in accuracy and even outperformed them in speed. It is difficult to judge from Sasaki's descriptions whether there was truly no effect of ESL reading proficiency, but her interpretation that a combination of phonological similarity and spelling similarity affected the non-alphabetic group's performance is consistent with the results from an earlier report by Wang et al. (2003).

Though not crosslinguistic in nature, a study by Akamatsu (2005) compared more proficient and less proficient English readers with Japanese L1 literacy in the naming accuracies and latencies of normal lowercase and case-alternated real English words (cf. Akamatsu, 1999). Akamatsu reported that even the more proficient readers were slower and less accurate in naming the case-alternated words compared to the normal case words although they did better on both case types than their less proficient peers. He interpreted this result as supporting the hypothesis that "the nature of L1 orthography affects L2 word-recognition processes so deeply that L2 reading proficiency could not influence L1 orthographic effects on the efficiency of processing the constituent letters in an English word" (p. 253).

Most of the studies reviewed so far have produced results supporting L1 orthography effects on L2 word recognition (Akamatsu, 1999, 2003, 2005; Muljani, Koda, & Moates, 1998; Sasaki, 2005; Wade-Woolley, 1999; Wang et al., 2003; Wang & Koda, 2005). The findings appear to imply that some L1 groups may be more adversely affected due to a larger "distance" between their L1 and L2 writing systems. Crosslinguistic research is worth expanding so that a finer-grained model of the L1 background effects on L2 word recognition can be constructed and potential difficulties of particular L1 groups can be predicted. However, such research alone is not sufficient.

As seen in most of the aforementioned studies (Akamatsu, 2003; Muljani et al., 1998; Wade-Woolley, 1999; Wang et al., 2003; Wang & Koda, 2005), crosslinguistic comparisons of L2 word recognition must, first of all, establish the comparability of the contrasted L1 groups in terms of their L2 proficiency in order to avoid the possibility of L2 proficiency interacting with the L1 background or even becoming the main factor. Despite the significant L1 effects observed in the L2 word recognition processes, the comparability of the different L1 groups in their L2 reading proficiency seems to suggest that the qualitatively different nature of L2 word recognition did not lead to differing levels of performance on measures of reading comprehension in the L2. Although a major goal of L2 reading pedagogy is to facilitate improvement in reading proficiency, the relationship between word recognition efficiency and reading proficiency nevertheless deserves attention. To date, only a small number of studies (Haynes & Carr, 1990; Nassaji & Geva, 1999; van Gelderen et al., 2004) have attempted to explain the individual differences in L2 reading proficiency in terms of word recognition efficiency, and are reviewed below.

Nassaji and Geva (1999) examined the effects of phonological and orthographic processing skills on reading ability with a group of L1-Farsi ESL learners. Their measures of phonological processing efficiency and orthographic processing efficiency were both speeded paper tests. The phonology measure consisted of non-word pairs and required the learners to decide whether each pair consisted of two homonyms or not (e.g., *flemb-flem*). The orthography measure also consisted of non-word pairs, and the participants were to choose which of the two items in each pair was orthographically more "acceptable" (e.g., *gnub*) than the other (e.g., *gmub*). On both measures, the accuracy and speed formed a composite efficiency variable. According to the researchers, the orthographic processing efficiency variable made significant and unique contributions to the prediction of the learners' reading comprehension and rate.

A study by van Gelderen et al. (2004) of EFL readers in the Netherlands adopted a computer-based lexical decision task as a measure of word recognition speed. This measure was found to correlate only moderately with the reading comprehension ability measure. Furthermore, it was noted that in predicting EFL reading comprehension performance, the effects of word recognition speed were smaller than those of meta-cognitive knowledge about reading and vocabulary knowledge.

Haynes and Carr (1990) examined the extent to which Taiwanese EFL learners' orthographic processing efficiencies and other language skills account for their text reading abilities. They reported that listening comprehension predicted passage reading comprehension the best, while lexical-semantic access efficiency and grammar knowledge were the best predictors of passage reading speed. Orthographic processing efficiency and L1 reading ability accounted for smaller portions of text reading variances.

Although Haynes and Carr's paper-based assessment of recognition speed is expected to be less precise compared to today's computer-based approaches, it introduced useful design features that, unfortunately, have received little attention. In addition to the same-different decision tasks similar to Brown and Haynes's (1985), they included speeded number matching (i.e., deciding whether the two numbers in a pair are the same or different) and synonym vs. antonym (i.e., deciding whether the two words in a pair are synonymous or antonymous to each other). Through number matching, they were able to isolate the aspect of the speeded decision tasks that is unrelated to alphabetic processing and to statistically parcel out this variance. Also, by employing the synonym-antonym decision that required lexical-semantic access, they were able to compare the contributions of component processes involving lexical-semantic access and those without. These features of the study are worth replicating with more precise, computer-based methodology in order to validate the original results.

THE STUDY

Research on the relationship between L2 text reading abilities and word recognition skills is scarce, which contrasts sharply with the growing body of research on the effects of L1 literacy background on L2 word recognition (Akamatsu, 1999, 2003, 2005; Brown & Haynes, 1985; Muljani et al., 1998; Sasaki, 2005; Wade-Woolley, 1999; Wang et al., 2003; Wang & Koda, 2005). More work should be worthwhile that relates text-level reading performance to word recognition efficiency. Among the various aspects of word recognition, orthographic processing efficiency was a significant predictor of text reading, according to Nassaji and Geva (1999) and Haynes and Carr (1990). Also, Haynes and Carr showed that lexical semantic access efficiency can be a good predictor of text reading ability.

The present study attempted to address visual orthographic processing efficiency and lexical semantic processing efficiency by adapting the task format from Haynes and Carr (1990) for computer delivery and measurement. The study sought to answer the following questions:

1. Do the more skilled Japanese EFL readers and the less skilled ones differ in their visual recognition speed of Roman letter strings?

2. If so, is the difference related to their familiarity with the intra-word orthographic regularity commonly observed in English words?

3. Does removing orthographic regularity from the target letter sequences affect the recognition speed of more skilled readers and less skilled readers equally or differently?

4. Do the more skilled readers and the less skilled readers differ in their speed of lexical semantic access in visual word recognition?

5. Does requiring semantic processing affect the recognition speed of more skilled readers and less skilled readers equally or differently?

METHOD

Participants

The present study is based on a subset of data from a total of 219 L1-Japanese EFL students at five different universities in western Japan. They represented ten different academic disciplines and a wide range of motivation and proficiency levels, and the male-female ratio was 116 to 103. More than 96 percent of them fell within the traditional age range for Japanese undergraduate and master's level students of between 18 and 23, and their mean age was 19.96. They had received similar length of formal EFL instruction with a mean of 8.50 years (six years of English at secondary school and a few more years at university). The remaining small number of students who had experience staying in an English-speaking country for a combined total of more than 10 months did not demonstrate any unusual patterns of response, nor did those who were older than 23. Therefore, no one was excluded from the data analysis.

Materials and Tasks

Components of Word Recognition Speed

Following Haynes and Carr (1990; see also Brown, Carr, & Chaderjian, 1987), the present study adopted sets of speeded same-or-different and synonym-or-antonym decision tasks to compare visual orthographic and lexical semantic processing efficiencies (Table 1.1). Whereas Haynes and Carr employed the paper-and-pencil mode of testing, the present study delivered the test on computer. Each participant saw a pair of items on the screen and responded by pressing a designated key to indicate whether the two items were matched (same/synonymous) or unmatched (different/antonymous).

TABLE 1.1
Sample Stimuli for Recognition Speed Measures

	Visual Orthographic Process			Visual and Lexical Semantic Process		Non-Alphabetic Process	
	Real Word Pairs	Non-Word Pairs			Synonym or Antonym		Number Pairs
		Pseudo-Word Pairs	Irregular Letter Strings				
Sample Matched (Same) Pair	fact fact	dace dace	cfat cfat	Sample Synonym Pair	road street	Sample Matched (Same) Pair	190 190
Sample Unmatched (Different) Pair	fact face	dact dace	cfat cfae	Sample Antonym Pair	clean dirty	Sample Unmatched (Different) Pair	190 198
No. of items	8	8	8	No. of items	18	No. of items	18

Their response accuracy and latency were recorded for each pair of items. Further procedural details are discussed in the Procedure section.

Visual Orthographic Processing

The visual orthographic processing speed was assessed via a set of same-or-different decision tasks presenting pairs of four-letter, monosyllabic, high-frequency[2] words (real words), or non-words, which further consisted of those that conformed to the English orthographic regularities (pseudo-words) and those that did not (irregular letter strings). Pseudo-words served to assess the speed with which the learners processed the novel but orthographically English-like sequences of letters. As mentioned earlier, Haynes and Carr's (1990) native-speaker control group processed pseudo-words as fast as they did real words, although they were much slower in processing the irregular letter strings. However, the same pattern was not observed for their EFL learners despite their high level of proficiency. The difference

---

[2]The real words, taken from Haynes and Carr (1990), were high-frequency words with a mean frequency of 670 occurrences/million according to Kucera and Francis (1967).

between processing time for pseudo-words and irregular letter strings provides an indication of the extent to which individuals benefited from the orthographically familiar sequencing of letters (orthography effect). It may be recalled that only the more proficient subgroup in Brown and Haynes's (1985) study showed a significant orthography effect. Additionally, by comparing the real word matching and pseudo-word matching latencies, it was possible to examine the extent to which the learner was affected by the lack of complete spelling of an existing word and of meaning (lexicality effect).

Lexical Semantic Access

The speed of visually identifying common English words and accessing their lexical semantic meanings was assessed through a synonym-or-antonym decision task, utilizing pairs of high-frequency real words, half mutually synonymous and half antonymous. Since the purpose of the study was not to see whether the participants knew the meanings of the words but how fast they accessed the meanings of known words, care was taken, through preliminary testing, to select word pairs that produced few incorrect responses but created a sufficient variance in response time.

Number Matching

There is a danger that the above-mentioned measures of processing efficiency were partially influenced by individuals' ability to perform efficiently on any speeded same-or-different decision tasks on computer, which is irrelevant to the orthographic or lexical semantic processing. To address this possible task effect, the present study followed Haynes and Carr's (1990) strategy of having a separate same-or-different decision task with three-digit Arabic numerals. This was used to assess the participants' efficiency in performing the same-or-different decision task on the same computer, with the stimuli being familiar to them but non-alphabetic. The variable was used as a covariate to statistically parcel out the variance in performance unrelated to alphabetic processing.

Reading Ability

There were two measures of English reading proficiency: one concerned with passage comprehension and the other with sentence comprehension speed.

Passage Comprehension

After careful trialing with similar student samples, four passages with a total of 20 multiple choice comprehension questions (Lee & Schallert, 1997; Yang & Weir, 1998) were used to assess the participants' passage comprehension. The passages ranged in length from 79 to 261 words, and their Flesch-Kincaid Grade Level Scores were between 8 and 15. All questions targeted the ability to integrate information across multiple sentences in a given passage.

Sentence Comprehension Speed

As the second measure of reading proficiency, the students' speed of comprehending English sentences was assessed on a separate set of materials. Isolated sentences, rather than passages, were chosen as the unit of analysis. The items were selected from a computer-based test of sentence reading speed previously used with Japanese EFL students (Shizuka, 2000, 2004). Each item was followed by a multiple choice comprehension question in the participants' L1 to encourage real processing of the sentence semantics rather than mere key pressing without understanding the content. Since the purpose of this task was not to record individual differences in how much the participants understood but how quickly or slowly they read the sentences while comprehending them, Shizuka's original 40 items were trialed with a separate population, resulting in ten items of the highest response accuracy for use in the present study.

All of the computer-based speed measures were administered on a laptop computer (Apple's PowerBook 5300c, equipped with a 10.4 inch TFT display) with the software PsyScope (Cohen, MacWhinney, Flatt, & Provost, 1993). The stimulus items were programmed to appear in black letters/numbers in the center of the display screen over a white background and the response time was measured at 17-millisecond accuracy. The order of items was randomized within each test.

Procedure

The participants received instructions in Japanese at the beginning of each test. The paper-based passage comprehension measure was group-administered, while the computer-based speed measures were administered individually by appointment. Efforts were made to schedule the two types of testing within the shortest time frame possible, and there was no case of an interval longer than two weeks. A questionnaire on the participants' biography and English language training/use was also administered within the same time frame.

The four speed tests were administered in one session, in the order of Number Matching, Visual Orthographic Matching, Synonym-Antonym Decision, and Sentence Comprehension. Each test was preceded by oral instructions given by a trained proctor, a screen-by-screen online tutorial, and practice items.

The first three types of speed tests all required binary decisions of same-or-different (or synonym-or-antonym) and followed the same procedure. That is, each trial started with the participant's self-paced key press, which caused a fixation point marker (three asterisks) to appear in the center of the screen for 300 milliseconds, after which the target item pair, lined up vertically, appeared and remained in the center until the participant pressed one of the two keys indicating either "same" or "different" (synonym or antonym in the case of synonym-antonym decision). The duration of the display of the target was timed and recorded by the computer.

For the sentence reading speed items, the initial participant-paced key press also led a fixation point marker to appear at the center for 300 milliseconds, followed by the target sentence in full. A subsequent pressing of the same key caused the answer choices to replace the target sentence, and the participant was to choose the best answer by pressing the corresponding key. The computer timed and recorded the duration for which the target sentence was shown. Under no circumstances was feedback given online to any participants on the accuracy of their responses.

Analysis

The participants who performed above average on both of the Passage Comprehension and Sentence Reading Speed measures were placed in the higher-level group, whereas those performing below average on both were put in the lower-level group. A series of analyses of covariance (ANCOVAs) were performed with each of the four latency measures of (1) real word matching, (2) pseudo-word matching, (3) irregular string matching, or (4) synonym-antonym decision as the dependent variable, the number matching latency as the covariate, and the subgroup membership as the between-group factor. Also subjected to separate ANCOVAs were (5) the lexicality effect (the gap between real word and pseudo-word matching latencies), (6) the orthography effect (the gap between pseudo-word and irregular string matching latencies), and (7) the meaning effect (the gap between synonym-antonym decision and real word matching latencies).

Results

Descriptive Statistics

The initial analysis of the full sample of 219 participants produced the accuracy and response time results on the reading proficiency and the recognition measures summarized in Tables 1.2 and 1.3.

Since the sentence reading task aimed to create variance in response time on sentences that the participants understood, its reliability is calculated from the response time on the ten items rather than from the accuracy. However, the comprehension scores on the sentence reading items were far from perfect (5.42/10), and there were considerable individual differences in this aspect of speeded sentence reading (SD = 2.2). The mean response time based only on accurate responses was 527.98 as shown in brackets in Table 1.2, and the correlation between the response time means from all ten items and from only accurate responses was 0.95. Though this is a very high correlation, the overlap between the two variables is 90 percent, which is far from perfect. Therefore, for further analyses, sentence reading time was calculated from the accurate responses only rather than from all responses.

The results revealed that the speeded recognition tasks commonly had greater than 90 percent accuracy with small individual differences. The real word and pseudo-word matching accuracy means were very close to that of

TABLE 1.2
Descriptives: Reading Proficiency Measures (n = 219)

	k	Accuracy		Response Time		Reliability
		Mean	SD	Mean	SD	
Passage Reading	20	11.16	4.00	-	-	.75
Sentence Reading	10	5.42	2.20	534.87 (527.98)	200.62 (194.11)	.92

Note: Response time unit is milliseconds per syllable.

TABLE 1.3
Descriptives: Recognition Speed Measures (n = 219)

	k	Accuracy		Response Time		
		Mean	SD	Mean	SD	Reliability
Real Word	8	0.96	0.07	813.90	175.82	.79
Pseudo-Word	8	0.95	0.08	831.37	182.63	.80
Irregular String	8	0.91	0.10	928.43	208.37	.78
Synonym-Antonym	18	0.91	0.09	1753.28	474.90	.90
Number	18	0.95	0.05	731.66	146.66	.90

Note: The accuracy score is based on dichotomous scoring (1 or 0). Response time unit is milliseconds per item.

number matching. Since the participants were familiar with the numbers as codes, recognition errors of this ratio might not be due to unfamiliarity with the target stimuli but might be a result of prioritizing speed over accuracy. Irregular strings and synonym-antonym tasks had somewhat lower accuracy means, likely due to increased challenge. The correlation between the response time mean calculated from all items and that from only accurate response items was 0.99 for each of the five stimulus categories. Therefore, further analyses of the recognition latencies are based on means computed from all items rather than from the correct ones only, and so are the reliability coefficients in Table 1.3. The high reliability and substantive dispersion on number matching latency seems to suggest its usefulness for minimizing the task effect.

Group Comparisons

Of the full sample of 219 participants, 81 were assigned to the higher-level group and 58 to the lower level. Controlling for the individual differences in the number matching latency, the response time means of the two groups were compared in the seven dependent variables of (1) real word matching, (2) pseudo-word matching, (3) irregular string matching, (4) synonym-antonym decision, (5) the lexicality effect (the gap between real word and pseudo-word matching latencies), (6) the orthography effect (the gap between pseudo-word and irregular string matching latencies), and (7) the meaning effect (the gap between synonym-antonym decision and real word matching latencies).

Table 1.4 summarizes the group means and the results of the ANCOVAs. The first four are the comparisons of the means in response time, with the smaller values indicating greater performance. While the values on all four latency measures appear to favor the higher-level group, statistically significant between-group differences ($p < .05$) were found only for (2) pseudo-word matching and (4) synonym-antonym decision. As Figure 1.1 graphically displays, the largest inter-group difference was in synonym-antonym decision latency.

The three "effect" variables uniformly resulted in significant inter-group differences but not in the same direction. As previously noted, (5) lexicality effect represents the degree to which the learners were negatively affected by the lack of intact word form. On this variable, the lower-

TABLE 1.4
Response Time Means and ANCOVA Results

Measure	Higher		Lower	F	p
1. Real word matching	806.33 (14.42)	=	828.96 (17.07)	1.018	.32
2. Pseudo-word matching	803.55 (15.30)	<	879.70 (18.10)	10.246	.00**
3. Irregular letter string matching	925.77 (17.82)	=	948.11 (21.09)	.650	.42
4. Synonym-antonym decision	1505.50 (42.36)	<	2066.04 (50.12)	72.429	.00**
5. Lexicality effect	-2.79 (18.32)	<	50.74 (16.35)	6.203	.01*
6. Orthography effect	122.22 (14.42)	>	68.41 (17.06)	5.763	.02*
7. Meaning effect	699.17 (45.03)	<	1237.09 (53.28)	59.018	.00

Notes:
df = (1, 136) for each analysis. SDs are in brackets.
*$p < .05$, **$p < .01$
Measure 5 is the result of subtracting Measure 1 from 2.
Measure 6 is the result of subtracting Measure 2 from 3.
Measure 7 is the result of subtracting Measure 1 from 4.

FIGURE 1.1

Group Comparisons by Stimulus Type

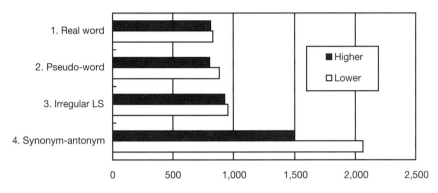

FIGURE 1.2

Group Comparisons by Effect Type

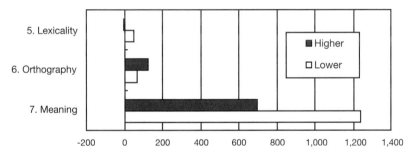

proficiency group had a larger mean than the higher-proficiency group. The analysis also revealed, however, that there was a significantly larger (6) orthography effect for the higher-proficiency group than the lower-proficiency group. Finally, the lower-proficiency group was under a larger (7) meaning effect than the higher-proficiency group. As shown in Figure 1.2, the inter-group difference in the meaning effect is considerably large, compared with those in the other two effects (i.e., lexicality and orthography).

Discussion and Conclusion

As the non-significant difference in real word matching latency shows, the two groups performed at a similar level when the stimulus items consisted of existing, high-frequency English words. However, there was a significant difference between the two groups in pseudo-word matching latency. That is, the more skilled readers were faster than the less skilled ones in processing unknown words whose internal orthographic structures were like those of many common English words. Also, the latency means on the irregular letter strings demonstrated that the two groups were not significantly different, and were therefore comparable in processing unknown words containing unusual letter sequences.

Thus, the two groups differed in the speed of visually processing Roman letter sequences, but only when the target stimuli were novel words whose internal spelling sequence adhered to the orthographic rules of English word formation. The lack of inter-group difference in real word matching indicates that the less skilled readers were not particularly slower at recognizing the visual forms of existing words included in this study. The size of the lexicality effect indicates the extent to which the use of pseudo-words (as opposed to real words) affected the recognition speed, and the results showed the more skilled readers were virtually unaffected whereas the less skilled ones were affected. The effect for the less skilled group was significantly larger than for the more skilled. It is worth noting that in Haynes and Carr (1990), the native speaker control group was not affected while their highly proficient Taiwanese learners of EFL were.

The extent to which individual participants relied on orthographic regularities in the recognition tasks was assessed by calculating the size of the orthography effect, which is the difference in latencies between pseudo-word matching and irregular string matching. While both groups were affected, the effect for the more skilled group was significantly larger than for the less skilled. The orthographically irregular features of the irregular letter strings slowed down the more skilled readers much more than they did the less skilled. However, this does not necessarily mean that the less skilled readers were more robust against such irregular features. Rather, the less skilled readers did not benefit from the orthographically regular features of the pseudo-words as much as the more skilled readers did. From this inter-group difference, it can be inferred that the more skilled readers relied more on orthographic regularities than the less skilled ones did, probably because they were more familiar with such regularities. The result here is consistent with earlier findings from Brown and Haynes's (1985) proficient L2 readers and Haynes and Carr's (1990) L1 readers and strengthens the view that the significance of sensitivity to spelling regularities holds for both L1 and L2 readers of English.

The discussion so far has focused on visual orthographic recognition without semantic processing, and we now turn to the remaining important questions on individual differences in accessing the meaning in word recognition. From the statistically significant inter-group difference in synonym-antonym decision latency, the more skilled readers appear to have the ability to access word meanings much more quickly than the less skilled readers could. The added requirement of processing the meanings of the target words clearly affected both groups of readers. Even the more skilled readers required an average of 0.7 seconds more (an additional 90 percent) to complete these meaning-based tasks than in the simple real word matching, which required no semantic processing. However, as evident from the significant inter-group difference and from the graphic comparison of the response time (Figure 1.2), it was the less skilled readers that were more severely slowed down. In fact, they spent an average of 1.2 seconds more (an additional 150 percent) when the task required semantic judgment than when it did not. However, this gap and the ratio are necessarily approximate, since the word length of the synonym-antonym items was non-uniform, unlike the real word matching items. Nevertheless, the magnitude of the effect of involving meaning in the speeded recognition tasks is far more salient when compared with the relatively smaller effects of lexicality or orthography previously discussed.

To recapitulate the main results from the present study, faster processing of meaning characterizes word recognition by the more skilled readers, and the less skilled readers are slower in accessing meaning but not necessarily slower in visual identification of existing word forms. The more skilled readers were also able to process orthographically regular sequences of unknown words as fast as they did known words, while the less skilled readers were not. This is likely due to differences in their familiarity with the acceptable spelling sequences or syllabic structures of the English words. The more skilled readers exhibited a pattern of performance on the pseudowords similar to that observed for the native speakers in Haynes and Carr's (1990) study. Despite the collective finding from extant crosslinguistic studies (Akamatsu, 1999, 2003, 2005; Muljani et al., 1998; Sasaki, 2005; Wade-Woolley, 1999; Wang et al., 2003; Wang & Koda, 2005) that L1 orthographic structure is an influential factor in how L2 words are recognized even among highly proficient L2 readers, the more skilled readers in the present study may have developed an L2-specific processing ability clearly distinguishable from the less skilled readers' and closer to that of the L1 readers of English.

Research on the relationship between reading proficiency and word recognition is worth expanding, and one way to start it is by considering the limitations of the present study. One of the limitations was the lack of baseline data from L1 readers against which to compare the L2 learners' word recognition speed. Another area of the present study that can be improved is the operationalization of the more skilled and less skilled readers. In the present study, the constructs were quite subjective and arbitrary; future research should employ standardized test scores or proficiency ratings to define more skilled versus less skilled readers. Such information would help place learners into different proficiency levels that can be referenced across studies. Last but not least, generalizability of the results from the present study is also limited to the L1-Japanese EFL learners at the university level, so additional studies involving different learner populations would be informative.

PEDAGOGICAL IMPLICATIONS

Accurate and automatic word recognition is achieved as a result of massive exposure to words in the target language and, for that purpose, the learners should be encouraged to read as much as possible. Extensive reading provides learners with the necessary opportunities for processing words in the text while attending to their semantic contents. In light of what the present study has found, the ability to quickly access words' meanings should be considered vital. In that respect, efforts should be made to ensure that learners engage in processing the lexical as well as the contextual meanings of the extensive reading materials so as to develop the learners' lexical access speed.

A familiarity with the intra-word orthographic regularities was a characteristic that differentiated the more and less proficient readers in the present study, and it may be an important asset in language learning. At least at the level of visual discrimination of letter sequences, the more skilled readers in the present study processed unknown pseudowords almost as well as they did real words. When learners face unknown words in an L2, in a way it is like facing those pseudo-words. Learning the word's form is essential for developing other types of knowledge about the word, and orthographic processing is required in learning its written form. Thus, sophisticated orthographic knowledge may positively contribute to word learning, whereas underdeveloped orthographic knowledge may hinder it. Again, learners should be exposed to the printed words through extensive reading activities, which can engage them in implicit learning of orthographic regularities.

To supplement efforts to develop reading fluency through extensive reading, recommendations have been made on how to devise exercises specifically for improving word recognition speed (Grabe & Stoller, 2002; Morrow, 1980). One of the most widely recommended exercises is one in which the learner searches for the target word from among distractors as quickly as possible (Crawford, 2005; Folse, 2007; see also Paran, 1996 for other variations of this exercise). According to Crawford, the majority of word recognition exercises in textbooks and articles related to L2 word reading resemble the one illustrated in Figure 1.3.

However, the results of this study suggest that the less skilled readers are not necessarily slower than the more skilled at processing the visual forms of real words, but they were much slower at accessing the meanings of such words. If this finding also holds for learners at large, the type of automaticity exercise illustrated on page 38 appears to fall short of providing substantive help to less skilled learners, who need more practice in quickly identifying the meanings of the words as opposed to their forms. As is, this type of exercise requires no semantic processing for the completion of the task. Exercises specifically designed for word recognition fluency should instead include the element of lexical semantic processing. A task requiring the learners to find a match on the basis of semantic criteria under time pressure may serve that purpose, whether delivered on computer or on paper.

FIGURE 1.3
Example of Word Recognition Exercise

1. approximated	accommodation	acknowledged	administration	approximated	automatically
2. consistent	challenge	concurrent	confirmed	constraint	consistent
3. financial	financial	flexibility	formula	founded	functional
4. legal	labor	license	layer	legal	lecture
5. sector	section	sector	select	similar	solely
6. assessment	anticipated	appreciation	amendment	assessment	assistance
7. commission	components	commenced	commission	commitment	constitution
8. percent	percent	parallel	passive	primary	priority
9. policy	policy	passive	posed	primary	pursue
10. evidence	enhance	equation	evidence	excluded	exposure
11. error	ethic	exceed	erode	error	equip
12. alternative	assessment	amendment	analogous	ambiguous	alternative
13. implies	ignored	implies	implicit	indicate	induced
14. code	cycle	credit	code	create	confirm
15. theory	target	theory	thesis	topics	trendy
16. authority	arbitrary	assembly	assigned	available	authority
17. contact	convert	convince	converse	contact	contrast
18. source	solely	sought	source	sphere	status
19. security	security	specific	stability	statistics	survive
20. focus	focus	format	founded	function	funds
21. income	implicit	income	indicate	induced	integral
22. credit	create	chart	cited	civil	credit
23. required	retained	required	revealed	rejected	removed
24. entities	estates	exports	extracts	ensures	entities
25. expert	ethical	exhibit	expert	export	extract

From *Rapid Reading Practices: Developing Word Automaticity in Reading* by Keith S. Folse, University of Michigan, 2007.

Reflection Questions

Reflection Questions

1. How can word recognition in L2 be different from that in L1?

2. What are some components of word recognition skills for L2 reading?

3. How were the two groups of learners in this study different in terms of word recognition speed? What characterized the more skilled and the less skilled readers in this study?

4. What might help the less skilled readers improve their word recognition speed?

CHAPTER 2

Developing Definitional Vocabulary Knowledge and Lexical Access Speed through Extensive Reading

Marlise Horst,
Concordia University, Montreal, Canada

D
o teachers of second language learners see communicative classroom activities and independent reading as unrelated types of instruction? If so, this would hardly be surprising. As Grabe (2005a) pointed out, theory and research in the areas of SLA and literacy development have followed distinctly different paths with little evidence of cross-influence over the years (Han, Anderson, & Freeman, this volume). More specifically, mainstream SLA research has devoted a great deal of attention to the acquisition of L2 syntax, often with performance on authentic oral tasks as the preferred indicator of attainment. Less attention has been paid to the acquisition of aspects of skilled L2 reading such as a large, rapidly accessed sight vocabulary (Grabe & Stoller, 2002). Therefore, language teachers who have been educated in the mainstream tradition may well see L2 grammar development through spoken interaction as the central focus of communicative language teaching. How extensive reading fits into the SLA-informed communicative paradigm is likely to be much less clear.

This chapter argues that extensive reading has an important place in the L2 curriculum because key aspects of linguistic competence cannot readily be acquired without it. The chapter attempts to show that extensive reading fits more comfortably in the mainstream tradition of SLA-informed communicative language teaching than might usually be assumed. This involves drawing a number of parallels between extensive reading and meaning-focused oral interaction. In describing extensive reading as a learning activity, the emphasis is on the development of L2 lexis, but it is clear that extensive reading also plays an important role in other aspects of language development like grammar (see Day & Bamford, 1998 and Waring, 2001 for overviews of this research). The chapter presents findings from two recent corpus-based investigations that explore specific word learning benefits than can be ascribed to extensive reading.

Grabe and Stoller (2002) define extensive reading as "reading in which learners read large quantities of material that are within their linguistic competence" (p. 259). In Day and Bamford's (1998) extended definition, the communicative aspects of extensive reading are highlighted: learners read materials they have selected themselves for purposes related to "pleasure, information, and general understanding" (p. 8). The emphasis on pleasure may prompt the unfortunate perception that extensive reading is a peripheral extra, not quite on a par with real classroom instruction. It is true that extensive reading often serves as a supplement to regular classes, especially in EFL settings where learners may have limited exposure to English outside of class (e.g. Bell, T., 2001; Mason & Krashen, 1997). However, extensive reading need not play an adjunct role. In an interesting study by Lightbown, learners in a rural French-speaking region in the Canadian province of New Brunswick read age- and level-appropriate materials during class (and also listened to recordings) instead of being taught by ESL teachers—simply because there was a shortage of trained personnel. The learners' language development was assessed using a variety of measures including tests of oral proficiency. Somewhat surprisingly, the research showed that the performance of these learners equaled or bettered that of comparable learners in regular ESL classes (Lightbown, 1992).[1]

Though they provide convincing evidence of the powers of extensive reading for L2 language development, Lightbown's findings are hardly

---

[1]Delayed post-testing six years later revealed that learners who had participated in the extensive reading and listening program for two or three years continued to perform as well as the comparison group on most measures. However, they scored lower than the comparison groups on measures of written ability. These results are detailed in Lightbown, Halter, White, & Horst (2002).

an argument for replacing classroom teachers with collections of simplified reading materials. However, there are reasons why extensive reading
deserves a more central role in the language curriculum than it is often given.
Vocabulary acquisition research indicates that extensive reading contributes
to learner development in crucial ways. First, exposure to large amounts of
written text is an important component in the communicative curriculum
because of its potential for driving vocabulary acquisition. Comparisons of
large corpora of English texts consistently show that written texts are richer
in lexis than spoken ones; according to analyses reported by Nation (2001),
a typical English conversation proves to contain very few words that are
likely to be unfamiliar to language learners beyond the most basic stages.
There is also evidence that the spoken language learners are exposed to in
communicative classrooms contains very few words not found on lists of the
most frequent English word families (Meara, Lightbown & Halter, 1997).
Thus, learners hoping to move beyond basic oral communication skills (e.g.,
to read academic texts or to function professionally in English) must read
written texts in order to expand their lexicons. Direct classroom instruction
can do a great deal to help such learners increase their vocabulary knowledge, but this is constrained by limitations on the numbers of words that can
be readily treated during class in the time frame of most language courses.
By contrast, extensive reading provides ongoing opportunities for learners
to meet many new words they would otherwise be unlikely to encounter,
with the syllabus bounded only by the amounts of reading they can manage
to accomplish.

In addition to providing crucial opportunities to meet new words,
extensive reading is seen as crucial to the development of abilities that
underlie successful reading comprehension. In their overview of the reading process, Grabe and Stoller (2002) draw on L1 research to describe the
lower-level processes that support reading comprehension (see also Shiotsu,
this volume). Of these, lexical semantic access (the ability to recognize the
meaning of a word automatically) is seen as "most fundamental" (p. 20);
automatic access to word meanings is required for rapid syntactic parsing
and proposition formation—two other basic processes in constructing the
meaning of a text. If these processes are slow, demands on mental resources
are increased and reading becomes less efficient. For instance, if L2 readers
are not able to make rapid form-meaning associations, mental resources
normally used for holding idea units in memory and constructing the overall
meaning of the text must be used to work out the meanings of the problem words instead. Pausing frequently to attend to words may result in a
breakdown of comprehension (Grabe & Stoller, 2002). Although little L2
research has addressed how such automatic sight vocabulary is obtained, it

is logical to assume that just as in the case of skilled L1 reading, many hours of exposure to print are required (Day & Bamford, 1998). Snellings, van Gelderen, and de Glopper (2002) found that lexical access speed improved when students worked on computerized training exercises that required them to make simple decisions about target L2 words (e.g., whether an item was used appropriately in a sentence). But few language learners will have access to this kind of special training; clearly, opportunities to read L2 texts at length are far more readily available. In sum, research shows that extensive reading is crucial to two important aspects of proficiency development: expanding learners' vocabulary size beyond that which is required for basic oral communication and acquiring the large automatic sight vocabulary that is needed for skilled reading.

Before reporting on two experiments—one that investigated acquisition of new word meanings through extensive reading, and another that explored changes in lexical access speed—these questions are considered: What, if any, are the parallels between learning through communicative speaking tasks and learning in extensive reading contexts? To what extent do the two activities resemble each other? This discussion will allow use of a conceptual framework likely to be familiar to many language teachers to outline some recent insights into learning L2 vocabulary through reading and the conditions that are needed to support it. Highlighting similarities between the two learning activities may also help bridge the gap outlined at the beginning of the chapter. In this exploration, three core principles of instructed SLA in the communicative paradigm are considered: (1) the importance of input that is comprehensible yet also challenging, (2) the usefulness of interactionally modified input, and (3) the benefits of brief attention to formal aspects of language during meaning-focused exchanges (focus on form). Other principles might have been explored, but these were selected because the connections to recent vocabulary acquisition research seemed especially clear.

EXTENSIVE READING AS A COMMUNICATIVE LEARNING ACTIVITY

Comprehensible Input

A long-recognized condition for learning new structures in communicative speaking tasks is exposure to language input that the learner can readily comprehend (Long, 1983). Here the connection to learning through extensive reading is straightforward. Although comprehensible input is often used in reference to the speech learners are exposed to in classrooms, for Krashen, who originated the term, it has long also meant exposure to comprehensible written language (1989, 1993, 2003). For learners of English, one important source of comprehensible text comes in the form of graded ESL/EFL readers; these are book-length narratives written specially for learners using simplified language grammar and vocabulary. Quality publishers such as Cambridge, Oxford, Penguin/Pearson, and others have published hundreds of these texts designed to meet the needs of learners of varying proficiency levels, ages, and literary tastes. As can be seen in the excerpt taken from the opening pages of the unsimplified literary classic *Anne of Green Gables* (available at www.gutenberg.org), a text written for a native speaker readership confronts learners of English with many potentially difficult words such as *dint, prop,* and *warp.* By contrast, the second excerpt, which is taken from a version that has been simplified for learners of English (Montgomery, 2002), features more common vocabulary and can be assumed to be fairly easy for intermediate-level learners to process.

Original version

There are plenty of people in Avonlea and out of it, who can attend closely to their neighbor's business by dint of neglecting their own; but Mrs. Rachel Lynde was one of those capable creatures who can manage their own concerns and those of other folks into the bargain. She was a notable housewife; her work was always done and well done; she "ran" the Sewing Circle, helped run the Sunday-school, and was the strongest prop of the Church Aid Society and Foreign Missions Auxiliary. Yet with all this Mrs. Rachel found abundant time to sit for hours at her kitchen window, knitting "cotton warp" quilts.

Simplified version

One fine spring afternoon in Avonlea, Mrs. Rachel Lynde sat by her kitchen window. She often sat there because she could see the Avonlea road very well from there. A man with a horse and buggy came up the road. It was Mrs. Lynde's neighbor, Matthew Cuthbert.

"Where's Matthew going?" thought Mrs. Lynde in surprise. "It's half past three in the afternoon and he has a lot of work on his farm. Where's he going and why is he going there?" Matthew Cuthbert lived with his sister, Marilla, in Green Gables, a large old house near Mrs. Lynde's home. Later, Mrs. Lynde walked to Green Gables. Marilla Cuthbert was busy in the kitchen. She was a tall, thin woman with gray hair.

But is the simplified version so easy to comprehend that it fails to offer the level of challenge needed to promote new learning? The classic definition of input that is conducive to the acquisition of new language specifies that it should contain structures that are a little beyond the learner's present level of ability. That is, for the learner whose current competence is at level i, input that is conducive to learning is slightly higher, at level $i + 1$ (Krashen, 1982, 1985). A well-known problem with this definition is that it is difficult to operationalize (e.g., McLaughlin, 1987). In the absence of a clear way of specifying precisely what language that offers this manageable amount of challenge looks like, teachers have been encouraged to simply depend on their intuitions to rough-tune classroom talk to suit the level of their learners.

However, research has specified the nature of input that supports the acquisition of new vocabulary knowledge in more concrete terms. Investigations of reading comprehension and known word densities (see Nation, 2001, for an overview) consistently show that if learners know the meanings of 95 percent or more of the words they meet in a text, they are likely to be able to comprehend it. In other words, with 95 percent of the lexis known, learners have a sufficient basis for inferring the meanings of the remaining unfamiliar words and understanding the message of the text (as indicated by answering comprehension questions correctly). Research by Hu and Nation (2000) indicates that this balance of text support and new-word challenge is available to ESL/EFL learners if graded readers are chosen appropriately. Online tools that determine percentages of frequent and infrequent words (available at www.lextutor.ca via the *VocabProfile* link) can help identify texts that provide the appropriate amount of challenge for learners at a particular level of proficiency. For instance, the *VocabProfile* output for the excerpt from the simplified version of *Anne of Green Gables* indicates that 97 percent of the words are on West's (West, M., 1953) list of the 2,000 most frequent English word families. Thus, an ESL/EFL reader who knows these common words is in a good position to work out the meaning of the more unusual words in the text such as *buggy*. This information about the minimum known-word density that supports successful inferencing takes much of the guesswork out of matching learners and texts for optimal word learning opportunities. To identify texts that will provide a useful mixture of comprehensibility and challenge, teachers can use online profiling tools such as *VocabProfile* to evaluate reading materials and administer frequency-based measures such as Schmitt's (2000) Vocabulary Levels Test to assess learners' vocabulary size (see also Cobb, this volume).

Modified Input

Does reading a simplified text such as the Pearson ESL version of *Anne of Green Gables* also offer opportunities for the kind of interaction that has been advocated by SLA theorists (e.g., Long, 1983, 1996) as playing a crucial role in making spoken input comprehensible? In the case of an ESL learner alone with his or her graded reader, it is clear that any dialogue that occurs is an internal one. But even though there is no spoken interaction, some of the benefits of modified (i.e., more comprehensible) input[2] are available by definition when a learner opts to read a simplified text such as a graded reader. In addition, it is not unreasonable to suppose that as learners encounter new words repeatedly in a variety of contexts in their reading, they engage in mental dialogue that may resemble the negotiation of oral input. One of the most robust findings in investigations of acquiring vocabulary incidentally through L2 reading is evidence that words met often while reading are more likely to be learned than words met once or twice (e.g., Horst, Cobb, & Meara, 1998; Saragi, Nation, & Meister, 1978). This research has not converged on a single number of exposures that guarantees a word learning event (because readers, words, contexts, and ways of measuring growth vary greatly), but eight to ten reading encounters with new items have been consistently associated with high levels of retention (Nation, 2001; see also Cobb, this volume).

To illustrate how repeated contextual encounters might prompt internal dialogue, consider the case of a learner who reported at the outset of a reading experiment (Horst, 2005a) that she did not know the meaning of the word *moor*. The learner subsequently read the simplified version of *Wuthering Heights* (West, C., Hedge, & Bronte, 2000) in which *moor* occurs twenty times. The first ten instances are shown in the concordance lines below. It seems plausible that initial encounters prompted questions about the possible meaning of *moor* with subsequent encounters providing elaboration and opportunities to confirm hypotheses. Eventually, this particular L2 reader was able to provide the acceptable definition of a *moor* as "the open place where green grass grows" and to write the semantically acceptable sentence, *There is a moor nearby that mountain.* But since her responses do not refer to *heather* or *Britain* (associations that come to mind

---

[2]See Leow's chapter in this volume for an alternate view on the benefits of modified input.

for many native speakers of English), the learner's dialogue with *moor* may be considered to be ongoing.

1. the north wind, which blows over the <u>moors</u> every day of the year. Fo
2. will teach you not to walk over the <u>moors</u> in bad weather: he answer
3. them. They often ran away on to the <u>moors</u> in the morning and stayed
4. let me feel a breath of air from the <u>moors</u>, just one breath!' I open
5. irl again, wild and free, out on the <u>moors</u> with Heathcliff! Open the
6. ere she can breathe the air from the <u>moors</u>. Her husband's grave is n
7. the floor, fighting. I came over the <u>moors</u> through the snow to the G
8. ionally went for lonely walks on the <u>moors</u>, and regularly visited hi
9. he hills in the distance, beyond the <u>moors</u>, and wanted to ride her p
10. tened now. She could be lost on the <u>moors</u>! She could have tried to

Focus on Form

A third core concept is form-focused instruction, defined as "instruction that draws attention to the forms and structures of the language within the context of communicative interaction" (Lightbown & Spada, 2006, p. 199). Focus-on-form episodes typically occur in response to an error in the speech of a learner who is intent on communicating a meaningful message. The teacher briefly draws the learner's attention to the error, often by restating the problem word or phrase in its correct form (Lyster & Ranta, 1997). In the reading context, learners' erroneous hypotheses about the meanings of words may go undetected, even after repeated exposure to a word in context. By way of example, consider the case of a learner who at the outset of a reading study (Horst, 2005b) reported that she did not know the meaning of the word *van*. After completing the simplified readers *How I Met Myself* (Hill & Prowse, 2001) and *Staying Together* (Wilson & Prowse, 2001), in which she met the word a total of five times, she was asked to give a definition of *van* and to use it in a sentence. Responses on this post-test and on a delayed measure administered seventeen weeks later are shown on page 48. As can be seen in the second set of responses where she gives two definitions, the learner has clearly discovered the correct meaning but has not yet rejected her earlier incorrect hypothesis.

Post-test Responses
    Definition: *van* = the back of a big car
    Example: We put a lot of thinks in the <u>van</u> when we go in holidays.

Delayed Post-test Responses (17 weeks later)
    Definition: *van* = 1. A big car; 2. The back of the car
    Example 1: This week-end I am going to travel to Quebec City in my brother's <u>van.</u>
    Example 2: Put all these big things in the back of the <u>van</u>.

This learner would clearly be well served by consulting a dictionary. When readers do this, the conditions for learning through focus on form resemble those on offer in speaking activities in communicative classrooms: That is, the learner is involved in a meaning-focused interaction (with a text), but his or her attention is diverted to attend to feedback from an authoritative source (a dictionary). In a dictionary consultation, focus on form is usually both reader-initiated and delivered at the moment of need—factors deemed likely to heighten its impact (Williams, 2001). Research by Hulstijn, Hollander, and Greidanus (1996) and others confirms the learning effects of consulting dictionaries; in their study learners looked up only a few words but rates for retention of accurate meanings were higher for these words than for those that were glossed in the margin of the experimental text or not looked up at all.

Proponents of focus on form emphasize that ideally, feedback episodes should be brief and selective so as to not interrupt the flow of meaningful interaction in ways that might limit opportunities for practice or discourage learners (Lyster & Ranta, 1997). The implication for the extensive reading context is that dictionary look-ups should also be infrequent so as to not interrupt the flow of narrative in ways that limit opportunities to develop reading fluency. In a two-year study of extensive reading at a Montreal community center, my assistants and I collected data on the dictionary look-up behaviors of adult intermediate-level ESL learners. Each time a participant returned a book to the collection of graded readers made available for the research, he or she was asked to indicate the numbers of times a dictionary had been consulted on a simple survey form. Participants responded using the scale shown in the first column of Table 2.1. The findings are based on 357 completed titles; if a participant reported not having completed a book, the response was excluded from the analysis. The results suggest that the

TABLE 2.1
Dictionary Look-Ups While Reading Graded Readers (Self-Report)

How often did you look up words in a dictionary?	Responses (357 total)	Responses in %
Never	93	26.05
1–5 times	111	31.09
6–10 times	71	19.89
11–20 times	42	11.76
> 20 times	40	11.20

readers were indeed engaged in comprehension-focused reading with pauses for only the most necessary dictionary consultations. The most frequent response, representing about one-third of the total, was in the 1–5 consultations category (31 percent). An additional 20 percent of the readers reported consulting a dictionary only 6–10 times.

LEARNING VOCABULARY THROUGH EXTENSIVE READING: TWO EXPERIMENTS

What are the learning benefits of extensive reading in the communicative context outlined that features access to large amounts of comprehensible input, opportunities to infer meanings over the course of multiple contextual encounters, and infrequent but informative form-focused episodes? In mainstream SLA research, studies of the effects of meaning-focused language instruction that includes focus-on-form typically explore the acquisition of grammatical accuracy. For instance, studies have examined the acquisition of English question forms (Spada & Lightbown, 1993), gender of articles in French (Harley, 1998), English past tense and conditional verbs (Doughty & Varela, 1998), and English modals (Samuda, 2001), to mention just a few. Vocabulary acquisition researchers who have explored the learning effects of L2 reading have also focused on accuracy gains—that is, the extent to which learners acquire correct definitional knowledge of previously unknown words. This research consistently shows that learners make gains in accuracy, but findings in terms of numbers of new words for which learners are able to identify correct meanings or provide accurate translations are small—often on the order of just two or three words per reading event (see Horst, 2005a and Waring & Takaki, 2003 for overviews). Conditions in these experiments have not always been conducive to acquiring new definitional knowledge, and this may have led to an underestimation of the growth that was possible (Horst, 2005a). Therefore, an important goal of the study reported was to determine whether definitional accuracy gains are more substantial in a highly supportive extensive reading setting. Thus, instead of reading passages chosen by researchers, participants in the study selected and read book-length texts that interested them. Also, since they are likely to have selected materials they could read without difficulty, chances of encountering new words in contexts that supported successful inferencing were probably greater than in studies where texts were clearly difficult for the learners to process (e.g., Pitts, White, & Krashen, 1989). Participants in the study also had opportunities to read at much greater length than in studies where learners read short texts (e.g., Day, Omura, & Hiramatsu, 1991). In addition, individualized tests of definitional knowledge were developed to ensure that eventual gains could be registered as fully as possible.[3]

In addition to increases in numbers of words learners can define correctly (or recognize), extensive L2 reading is also expected to lead to increases in learners' speed in making form-meaning connections. Reasons to assume this and the importance of vocabulary knowledge that is both large and automatically accessed were previously outlined in the discussion of fluent reading comprehension. In 1993 and again in 1997, Meara observed that although psychologists frequently use tests of lexical access speed in explorations of the bilingual lexicon, lexical access is a relatively unexplored dimension in investigations of L2 vocabulary acquisition and pedagogy. This continues to be largely the case. An exception is the study of a single learner by Segalowitz, Watson, and Segalowitz (1995) in which the learner showed increased lexical access speed for words that occurred in a passage that he studied repeatedly. Two more recent Dutch studies showed that learners who completed word recognition training exercises exhibited speed increases (Snellings et al., 2002; van Gelderen et al., 2004). Previous research has not explored the effects of L2 reading on lexical access speed in an authentic extensive reading context. In the experiment reported, speed of lexical access was investigated using a reaction-time (RT) mea-

---

[3]Factors such as opportunities to meet words repeatedly in the materials or the use of dictionaries were not explored in this experiment.

sure of responses to words drawn from a corpus of graded readers. The main goal of this part of the investigation was to determine whether the proposed methodology for detecting differences in lexical access speed was feasible.

The research questions were:

1. To what extent do learners learn and retain meanings of previously unknown words as a result of participating in a program of extensive reading?

2. Do learners recognize frequently met words more quickly than comparable words that have been met less frequently?

METHOD

The questions were explored in a quasi-experimental study of adult ESL learners who participated in an extensive reading program for six weeks. Gains in definitional knowledge were determined by comparing performance on measures of word knowledge at the start of the session to performance on measures administered at the end of the session and again seventeen weeks later. Comparisons were also made to performance in a control group. The methodology for assessing lexical access speed involved comparing mean reaction times for words that were likely candidates for undergoing increases to means for words that were less likely to exhibit change.

PARTICIPANTS

The participants in the experiment were 47 adult immigrant ESL learners at a community center in Montreal. There were a variety of first languages in the group including Arabic, Chinese (Mandarin), Czech, Farsi, French, Hungarian, Korean, and Russian. All attended regular integrated skills ESL classes that met twice weekly; the extensive reading materials were made available to students who had placed in the intermediate proficiency range on an in-house placement test. Five students, all participants in the larger investigation, participated in the pilot study that explored changes in lexical access speed.

MATERIALS

Graded Readers

The mini-library of graded readers collected for the research consisted of a set of 60 titles from series published by Cambridge, Oxford, and Penguin/ Pearson. There were at least two exemplars of each title in the collection for a total of roughly 130 books. Most were either new or classic fiction in the romance, suspense, and mystery genres. Levels of simplification ranged from 1,000 to 3,800 headwords. Each week of the experimental period, participants had the opportunity to check out books during a break in their regular ESL classes. Students were expected to read independently at home; no class time was spent on reading the books or on related activities. By the end of the five weeks allotted for reading (one week of the six-week session was taken up by testing), 29 participants reported having completed one book or more. Eighteen students did not read any books at all. Performance on measures of word knowledge in the group of eighteen non-readers served as a basis for comparison to performance in the group of readers (i.e., students who had completed one book or more). Among the readers, the mean number of books completed was about three (mean = 2.61; SD = 1.31). One very prolific reader who read sixteen books was not included in this calculation.

MEASURES

Definitional Knowledge

The 60 graded readers in the collection were electronically scanned so that target words for testing could be identified in a systematic manner. Cobb's *VocabProfile*, an online version of Laufer and Nation's (1995) lexical frequency profiling software, was used to identify off-list words in this corpus of scanned readers. Off-list words are defined as words not found on lists of the 2,000 most frequent English word families (M. West, 1953) or on the Academic Word List, a list of word families that occur frequently in university texts (Coxhead, 2000). Off-list words were considered suitable targets for definitional learning through extensive reading since they were less likely to be already known to participants than words on the lists of more frequent word families. To arrive at a sense of the extent to which participants already knew meanings of off-list words that occur in graded readers at the outset of the program, a pre-reading checklist measure that required participants to report their knowledge of 300 words was prepared. The words were selected at random from the off-list output from each of eleven graded readers that ranged in numbers of headwords from 1,000 to 3,000. Participants were asked to indicate their ability to recognize the meanings of listed items by circling one of three rating options: Yes (I am sure I know the meaning of the word), NS (I have an idea about the meaning of this word but I am not sure), and No (I do not know what this word means). A segment of this pre-reading instrument with off-list items from the simplified version of *Anne of Green Gables* is shown in Figure 2.1 (Items 51–58).

Tests using an identical 300-word checklist format were administered at the end of the program. However, these were individualized to reflect the titles that each participant had selected to read. Thus, in the case of a participant who read *Wuthering Heights, Staying Together,* and *How I Met Myself,* the participant's individualized post-test consisted of off-list items that occurred in these three books. Non-readers were post-tested using the same 300-item instrument that had been used as a pre-test at the outset of the program. Participants did not expect to be tested at the end of the program; thus, any learning that occurred can be termed incidental rather than intentional.

A second post-reading measure that required participants to demonstrate definitional word knowledge was administered as a check on the checklist self-ratings. This individualized instrument targeted a participant's

---

FIGURE 2.1
Sample Items from Checklist Measure

51. croup	YES NS NO
52. gables	YES NS NO
53. gray	YES NS NO
54. orchard	YES NS NO
55. orphan	YES NS NO
56. slate	YES NS NO
57. bored	YES NS NO
58. boss	YES NS NO

knowledge of five words that met two criteria: First, all five items had all been rated No (I do not know what this word means) by the participant at the outset of the study, and second, the items were known to have featured in books that the participant selected to read. For instance, if a learner indicated that he did not know the meaning of *gables, orchard,* and *orphan* on the pre-reading measure but later chose to read *Anne of Green Gables* (a book in which the items are known to occur), the items qualified for inclusion on the reader's individualized demonstration test. This test required participants to provide a definition of a target word and, if possible, an example sentence. The format was inspired by Wesche and Paribakht's (1996) Vocabulary Knowledge Scale. A sample item is shown in Figure 2.2.

Lexical Access Speed

For the tests of recognition speed, target words were selected with two criteria in mind: Words that recurred often were needed in order to allow scope for the effects of frequent encounters to operate, but it was also important that the words were not so well known that no further speed-up in recognition could occur. In this pilot study, it was assumed that words from West's (1953) list of the 1,001–2,000 most frequent English families (e.g.,

---

FIGURE 2.2
Sample Item from Knowledge Demonstration Test

What do you know about these words?

       orphan

1. I know what this word means ___ YES ___ NO

2. It means _____
       (Give the meaning in English, French, or your language.)

3. I can use the word in a sentence _____
       (Write the sentence.)

fasten, repeat, stretch) would meet these criteria. It was also assumed that words chosen from this single frequency category would be roughly equal in terms of the extent to which they were already familiar to the learners. The *VocabProfile* program was used to identify words from this frequency band in three books that a particular participant had completed. Two groups of targets were selected for each of these individualized tests: one group consisted of 45 items encountered fifteen times or more in the three books, and the other consisted of 45 items encountered five times or less. Words in the two conditions were matched for length (4–10 letters); their frequencies in the BNC corpus were also checked to ascertain that words in the two conditions were comparable. In addition, 45 non-word distractor items were taken from tests by Meara and Buxton (1987) and matched for length to the real words. Sample items are shown in Table 2.2. The items were entered into the RT-Test Builder available at *Lexical Tutor* (www.lextutor.ca); individualized tests based on three books were created for six participants and saved on a laptop computer. The software randomized the items; test takers requested to see a test item by pressing a key. Their task was to identify whether the string that appeared was a real English word by pressing the appropriate key (1 if the word is real and 3 if it is not). Participants' reaction times and accuracy rates were recorded by the software.

PROCEDURES

To answer the first question about definitional word knowledge gains achieved through extensive reading, we compared pre- and post-treatment means for numbers of Yes (I know what this word means) responses on

---

TABLE 2.2
Sample Items from Lexical Decision Test

Frequent Words (Encountered ≥ 15 times)	Infrequent Words (Encountered ≤ 5 times)	Non-Words
afraid	plenty	*gurely*
politeness	restaurant	*proctalize*
message	warning	*wallage*
sorry	nurse	*rudge*

the 300-item self-report measures in both reader and non-reader groups. A repeated-measures ANOVA was used to test within- and across-group differences for statistical significance. Gains were also determined by comparing performance on the five-item demonstration test in reader and non-reader groups. This test asked students to produce a definition or translation of words that had been rated No at the outset of the experiment, and if possible, to use the words in a sentence. Definitions (or translations) were considered either right or wrong. Each correct definition was given a score of one point, while incorrect or absent definitions were given a score of zero. Thus, "It means a rank of aristocracy" for the target word *duke* was judged to be correct and awarded one point, while the definition of *airfare* as "an object that make fresh air" received a score of zero. An example of a sentence that was judged correct is *The owner of all the fields is the duke of Nottingham*. Semantically incorrect or uninformative sentences such as *I met a burglar at that street* received a score of zero. The sentence judgments were based on semantic appropriateness only; spelling and grammar mistakes were not taken into account. Overall inter-rater reliability was high, with agreement in 92 percent of cases.

Measuring retention of new word knowledge acquired through extensive reading using a delayed post-test was not part of the original design of the experiment. But when it proved possible to contact ten of the 29 participants in the reader group seventeen weeks after the end of the reading program, we decided to test these learners again. Each participant first took the same individualized checklist and five-word demonstration tests administered at the end of the program again; a research assistant also asked each participant about the reading program and ongoing efforts to learn English. To assess levels of retention, performance on the delayed post-tests was compared to performance at the end of the reading program seventeen weeks earlier.

To determine whether items met often (fifteen times or more) in the extensive reading materials were recognized more quickly than comparable items that had been met less often (five times or less), we compared mean reaction times for words in the two conditions for each of six participants from the group of readers who had completed three books. Participants completed the individualized measures about a week after finishing the third book. RTs that were more than two standard deviations from the mean in each condition were excluded from the data. A *t*-test for independent samples was used to determine whether the difference in a participant's means for words in the two conditions was statistically significant.

RESULTS

An initial answer to the first research question about amounts of new word knowledge acquired through extensive reading is evident in Table 2.3. The mean percentage of Yes responses (I know what this word means) on the pre-reading baseline measure indicates that participants in the readers group already knew the meanings of 68.63 percent of the 300 off-list items (SD = 12.32) at the outset of the experiment. But at the end of the reading program, this percentage was substantially higher, amounting to 82.40 (SD = 11.75). In other words, about two-thirds of the tested words were familiar to these participants at the outset of the experiment, leaving a knowledge gap of about one-third (100 − 68.63 = 31.37 percent). By the end of the study, the gap of 31.37 percent had been reduced to 17.7 percent, almost half its original size (100 − 82.40 = 17.7 percent). Thus the figures suggest that readers gained new definitional knowledge of roughly one of every two unfamiliar off-list words they met in their reading.

Means in the last row of Table 2.3 show that the non-readers scored lower than the readers on the pre-test but that they too made gains over the five weeks. However, the mean gain of 7.31 percent among non-readers amounts to roughly half of the 13.77 percent gain achieved in the reading group. A repeated measures ANOVA indicated significant differences between groups [$F(1, 45) = 6.53$, $p < .05$] and over time [$F(1, 45) = 69.58$, $p < .05$]. The interaction between group and time was significant [$F(1, 45) = 5.36$, $p < .05$]. In other words, even though the two groups are not strictly comparable given their different starting points, the difference between endpoints can be ascribed (at least in part) to participation in the reading program.

A possible explanation for these gains is that participants in both conditions simply overrated their end-of-course knowledge. However, results of

TABLE 2.3
Off-List Words Rated Yes (in Percent): Readers vs. Non-Readers

	Pre-Test %	Post-Test %	Difference
Readers (n = 29)	68.63 (12.32)	82.40 (11.75)	13.77 (9.32)
Non-Readers (n = 18)	62.44 (14.15)	69.75 (14.69)	7.31 (9.70)

the demonstration test suggest that this was not the case. As mentioned, the demonstration test required participants in the reading group to produce definitions (or translations) of five words they had rated No (I do not know the meaning of this word) at the outset of the experiment but had subsequently encountered in their reading, and also to supply sentence examples using these words, if possible. Non-readers performed the same task with five off-list words they had rated No on the pre-reading measure. The definitions and sentences were evaluated by two native speakers of English as outlined above. Definitions deemed accurate by both raters were awarded a score of one point; no half-points were awarded. Mean scores in both groups are shown in the first row of Table 2.4. The results of an analysis using a stricter criterion of one point for each correct definition that was also accompanied by a correct sentence appear in the second row. On both measures, readers outperformed non-readers. Means indicate that readers were able to provide correct definitions of about two (mean = 1.76) of five words that were previously unknown to them, while non-readers could do this for only one (mean = .94) of the five. Analyses using t-tests for independent samples showed that the means for numbers of correct definitions differed significantly in the two groups [$t(46)$ = 1.93, $p <. 05$], but mean performance at the definition-plus-sentence criterion did not differ significantly.

These results appear to substantiate the rate of new word pick-up that was identified in the analysis of the checklist self-ratings (though results must be interpreted with caution given the small numbers of participants and test items). That is, in the readers group, the mean number of previously unknown words that were defined accurately amounted to 1.76 words in five, or 35 percent ($1.76 \div 5 = .35$). This amounts to a mean pick-up rate of about one new word in three when the criterion is accurate recognition of word meaning.

TABLE 2.4
Performance on 5-Word Demonstration Test: Readers vs. Non-Readers

	Readers (n = 29)	Non-Readers (n = 18)	p Values
Correct definitions	1.76 (1.53)	.94 (1.09)	$p < .05$
Correct definitions with correct sentences	1.30 (1.47)	.65 (.93)	ns

Retention Results

The question of the extent to which participants retained new word knowledge gained in the extensive reading program over time was addressed by analyzing the performance of ten participants from the readers group seventeen weeks after the end of the extensive reading program. The same individualized checklist and demonstration instruments used at the end of the reading program served as the delayed measures; participants in the control group were not tested again. At the end of the program, the mean percentage of items the ten readers rated Yes (I know the meaning of this word) on the 300-word ratings instrument was 86.53 (SD = 7.92). Seventeen weeks later, the mean amounted to the virtually identical figure of 86.40 percent (SD = 7.71), suggesting that there was no decline in knowledge of the words over time. This was confirmed statistically by an ANOVA of the pre-, post-, and delayed post-test scores, which indicated that there were significant differences in the data [$F(2, 29) = 16.57$, $p < .0001$)]. Post hoc comparisons showed that means for the immediate and delayed post-test were both significantly higher than the pre-reading mean of 73.46 percent (SD = 14.23), but there was no significant difference between immediate and delayed post-test means. Performance on the demonstration measure supported this finding. Of the 50 words that were rated No (I don't know the meaning) in the group at the outset of the study, twenty had been defined correctly at the end of the reading program. Rather surprisingly, this figure rose to 25 after the seventeen-week interval. Closer examination of the results revealed a mixed picture with some of these learners experiencing substantial gains while others experienced losses. Information gathered in the interviews suggested that the main explanation for gains was continued exposure to English. Learners who reported that they worked and socialized in French (the official language of Quebec) tended to experience attrition, while gains were more pronounced among learners who reported continuing to study and read English.

Lexical Access Speed Results

The results of the reaction time comparisons between words met frequently in participants' extensive reading and comparable words met less often are shown in Figure 2.3. For five of the six participants, mean RTs for words encountered fifteen times or more were lower (i.e., faster) than the means

FIGURE 2.3

Comparisons of Mean RTs for Frequently and Infrequently Encountered Words
(6 Participants)

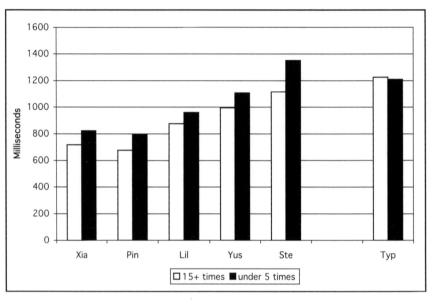

for words encountered five times or less; *t*-tests for independent samples showed that the differences were statistically significant. Means for one participant (see bars at right of Figure 2.3) did not differ significantly. Thus, the findings of the pilot study suggest that even a relatively small program of extensive reading (three graded readers) can result in measurable fluency differences—on a fairly consistent basis. In addition, the corpus-based experimental methodology was shown to be feasible; it proved possible to find comparable targets at the 1,001–2,000 level in two frequency conditions (fifteen or more occurrences vs. five occurrences or fewer) in the graded readers—in sufficient numbers to be able to create the individualized RT measures.

DISCUSSION

This experiment provides evidence of development of two types of lexical competence in L2 learners who participated in a program of extensive reading. On the individualized self-report measure of words met in books they selected to read (measure of definitional knowledge), participants rated more words Yes (I know the meaning) than they had on a baseline measure at the outset of the experiment. These gains were confirmed on a second measure of definitional knowledge that required participants to demonstrate their understanding of previously unknown words. Means indicated that the participants were able to provide accurate definitions of about one-third of the unfamiliar words they had encountered while reading. Performance on delayed post-tests showed that this knowledge was retained; retention and growth appeared to depend on continued exposure to English. There were also indications that lexical access speed increased. Means on a measure of lexical access speed showed that words that occurred frequently in the graded readers tended to be recognized more rapidly than comparable words that occurred less frequently.

The gains in definitional knowledge outlined in this study stand in marked contrast to findings of earlier studies that have typically found low rates of growth. How can the more substantial gains detailed here be accounted for? One likely explanation is the support for learning in the ecologically valid context of the study that allowed learners to select books that they found comprehensible and interesting. The opportunity to read large amounts of text and meet words repeatedly in a variety of contexts was probably also important. The finding that word knowledge was retained (and in some cases expanded) is also striking. By contrast, in a carefully controlled study by Waring and Takaki (2003) that tested learners three months after reading a simplified story, incidentally acquired definitional knowledge was shown to have virtually disappeared. Perhaps the use of non-words (i.e., items that could not be encountered again outside of the reading context) as learning targets explain the results. The study reported in this chapter found that continued exposure to L2 input was crucial to retention, much as White, Spada, Lightbown, & Ranta (1991) found in their study of the acquisition of question forms.

So overall, the outlook for acquiring new definitional word knowledge is more positive than other studies have given reason to expect, at least for the intermediate-level ESL learners in this study who had ready access to simplified reading materials. However, several caveats are in order: First, many learners, especially those in resource-poor settings, may not have easy access to a large and varied collection of level-appropriate reading materials. Second, even when such materials are available, students may choose not to take advantage of them. In this study where materials were available and participation was encouraged, eighteen of the 47 students opted not to read any books at all and sixteen read only one or two. It is also important to point out that reading a single graded reader is not enough to result in sizeable amounts of new definitional word knowledge. By way of illustration, suppose that a graded reader contains 100 off-list words (a plausible number according to the analyses), and an L2 learner already knows a large proportion of them (e.g., two-thirds, as was found in the study). In this case, even at the high rate identified in this experiment (one new word in two or three), the number of new words learned amounts to about a dozen. Although it is likely that a few other words not in the off-list category are likely to be learned as well, the picture is clear: Much larger amounts of regular reading are required to promote and support vocabulary development.

The finding that words encountered frequently in graded texts were recognized more quickly than those encountered infrequently represents a first step in the direction of exploring the effects of extensive L2 reading on lexical access speed. The effect reported here seems a promising confirmation of what might be expected: meeting words often appears to make them more rapidly recognizable. However, this preliminary finding must be treated with a great deal of caution due to several shortcomings of the experimental methodology. First, although the RT-Builder software identified error rates (which ranged from 6.67 to 20 percent among the six participants), it did not identify which of the real words were mistakenly identified as non-words; therefore reaction times for these erroneous responses could not be eliminated from the comparisons. This problem has been rectified in the current version of the software. It is also possible that target words in the two conditions were not really comparable. Both sets came from the 1,001–2,000 most frequent range on West's (M. West, 1953) lists, but Snellings et al. (2002) point out that print-based frequencies may not be accurate reflections of language learners' familiarity with target items. Thus, words in the frequent condition in our study may have been more familiar to the participants at the outset of the experiment than words in the infrequent condition. In a future project, it may be useful to select targets on the basis of their frequency in a corpus that is more representative of input that participants have been exposed to (e.g., a corpus of course texts) or to administer a measure of prior knowledge of targets. Future experiments will clearly also benefit from the inclusion of a pre-reading baseline RT measure against which post-treatment performance can be compared.

This chapter has argued that extensive reading plays a key role in moving learners beyond the basic levels of proficiency required for basic communication so that they are well positioned to achieve personal and professional goals. I have also attempted to show experimentally that the benefits are real—in terms of increases in definitional knowledge of infrequent words and in terms of making form-meaning connections more rapidly. The exploration of the conditions of extensive reading and resemblances to conventional communicative learning activities had the none-too-hidden agenda of showcasing teacher-friendly computer tools that can aid the learning of L2 vocabulary through reading. Thus, the discussion of comprehensible input demonstrated how a lexical frequency profiling tool such as *VocabProfile* can help teachers and learners choose texts with densities of potentially difficult, infrequent words that are low enough for learners of a particular proficiency level to be able to read them and infer the meanings of the unfamiliar items (see also Cobb, this volume). The discussion of the internal dialog that may take place as words are encountered repeatedly in a variety of contexts showed how a concordancer can gather many uses of a particular word in a text instantly and present them in a convenient format for readers to examine; a comparison study by Cobb, Greaves, and Horst (2001a, 2001b) outlines the vocabulary gains achieved through extensive reading with concordance support. The discussion of focus on form did not showcase online ESL dictionaries; suffice it to say that these are widely available. Increasingly, the written text that many L2 learners read is on computer; this means that tools such as profilers, concordancers, and dictionaries that can make any text a rich resource for vocabulary learning are increasingly important.

ACKNOWLEDGMENTS

This research was supported by a grant from the Social Sciences and Humanities Council of Canada. I would also like to acknowledge the assistance of graduate students in the Applied Linguistics program in the Department of Education at Concordia University in Montreal: Elizabeth Bulhoes, Angela Kleanthous, and Michèle Plomer. I am also grateful to Petronella Beran, Wahiba Ibrahim, and students at the Tyndale St-George Community Centre.

Reflection Questions
Reflection Questions

1. Horst argues that extensive reading parallels the experience of learning a second language in a communicative classroom. What do the two kinds of instruction have in common? Do you see any problems with this analogy? What does a communicative classroom offer that is not available to learners in a reading-only program?

2. Does Horst's idea of internal dialogue about new words match your experience? To what extent are you aware of testing hypotheses as you encounter unfamiliar words in your first language reading? In your second?

3. In the extensive reading program Horst investigated, more than one-third of the ESL students opted not to read the graded materials. Did this surprise you? Why do you think this happened?

4. Horst's experiment shows that reading a graded reader results in a rather small amount of new word learning—on the order of a dozen words. What ideas for increasing the vocabulary learning potential of extensive reading does she mention? What other strategies might be useful?

CHAPTER 3

Vocabulary Processing and Acquisition through Reading: Evidence for the Rich Getting Richer

Diana Pulido, Michigan State University

W hy is the rate of L2 vocabulary acquisition through reading lower for some learners than for others? To answer this, it is necessary to address individual differences in L2 reading and vocabulary development through reading. What do these two processes entail? This chapter considers L2 learner involvement when processing new lexical items during reading in the presence or absence of strategic reading tasks. The lexical items under consideration in this chapter are open class, or content words, such as nouns and verbs. It argues that the nature of learner involvement and processing is robustly related to reader-based factors known to influence L2 reading and general lexical input processing mechanisms—namely, background knowledge, passage sight vocabulary, and general L2 reading proficiency. Thus, it connects the skills and knowledge sources involved in learning to read in an L2 with vocabulary learning outcomes that accrue as a result of engaging in reading activities in an L2. It commences with an overview of research on reading and input processing requirements to establish form-meaning connections for new lexical items during reading. It highlights the importance of the aforementioned reader-based factors during L2 reading and lexical input processing vis-à-vis conclusions from recent research. It concludes with implications of the research for language learning and teaching and makes pedagogical recommendations for promoting vocabulary learning through reading.

A QUICK OVERVIEW

L2 reading is a complex cognitive process where the reader, using previous knowledge, interacts with information in the text to construct and integrate meaning (e.g., Bernhardt, 1991; Carrell, Devine, & Eskey, 1988; Grabe & Stoller, 2002; Koda, 2005; Swaffar, Arens, & Byrnes, 1991). During reading there is simultaneous cognitive processing involving pattern recognition, letter identification, lexical access, concept activation, syntactic analysis, propositional encoding, sentence comprehension, inter-sentence integration, activation of prior knowledge, information storage, and comprehension monitoring. Furthermore, the processes involved in reading are not only interactive, but also compensatory. When a component of processing is deficient, it can be compensated for, with variable success, by other components of processing such as background knowledge (Stanovich, 1980; Walczyk, 2000). The processes described are also crucial in L2 vocabulary development through reading.

L2 vocabulary development through reading is also complex and incremental, occurring through text processing and comprehension as well as other explicit processes (e.g., N. Ellis, 1994). The degree to which there are memory traces, or intake, of lexical items processed during reading is largely determined by the level of comprehended input. Recent research within an incidental learning paradigm[1] illustrated a robust role of passage comprehension on vocabulary gains, where weaker readers demonstrated lower levels of passage comprehension, worse recognition memory for passage target words (TWs), and overall lower vocabulary gains, compared to stronger readers (Pulido, 2004a). These results were attributed to weak

---

[1] The term *incidental* refers to vocabulary learning that occurs as a byproduct of engaging in another task, such as reading, where the focus is not on learning vocabulary in preparation for an upcoming vocabulary test but rather on reading for comprehension. *Incidental* does not refer to "unconscious," "without attention," or "subliminal" but rather to the task and research paradigm orienting instructions. See Hulstijn (2001, 2003) for further descriptions of incidental and intentional learning research paradigms.

language and processing skills that hindered the ability to engage in higher-level processing required for assigning meaning and storing information about the new word and context, processes crucial to lexical intake and gain. In other words, the readers of the group who comprehended more (i.e., encountered more comprehensible input) also achieved greater levels of lexical intake and gains through reading.

Form-meaning mapping of new vocabulary commences when readers first notice that words are unfamiliar. Without assistance, they must infer meaning using context cues, and linguistic and extra-linguistic knowledge (Faerch, Haastrup, & Phillipson, 1984). There are numerous sub-processes that serve to activate various types of knowledge when creating a new L2 lexical entry. For example, readers can use the activated semantic information about meaning relations and pragmatic information about conventional or contrastive uses of words and expressions to assign meaning to unfamiliar words. Readers can also use morphological information (e.g., roots and affixes) to obtain clues about word class, word meaning components, grammatical function, and semantic roles. During sentence processing, readers can use syntactic information (e.g., word order and argument structure) in combination with knowledge about event probabilities to identify semantic information and roles of new lexical items. For example, in the sentence *The dog ate the bone,* guesses about the meaning of the word *ate* may be constrained by using knowledge of English word order (subject-verb-object) to identify *dog* as the subject and *bone* as the object and by applying such knowledge to then identify *ate* as the verb and combining that with knowledge about what dogs typically do with bones (e.g., eat, chew, play with, carry, etc.). When a word is not known, new form-meaning mapping can occur through these bootstrapping processes (de Bot, Paribakht, & Wesche, 1997), in combination with cues in the local or global context (Chern, 1993; Nagy, 1997; Sternberg, 1987). The syntactic, semantic, and pragmatic knowledge that is activated, held in working memory,[2] and utilized online during text processing thus constrains textual and lexical interpretations. Adult L2 learners may use whatever information available to the extent that their proficiency and background knowledge enable them to use such information. Additionally, readers must attend to the connections between new

---

[2]Grabe and Stoller (2002) in their book *Teaching and Researching Reading* define *working memory* as an "active component of memory processes in cognition. It is limited in capacity, retains active information for a relatively short period of time and integrates information and processes to construct comprehension. It is not a separate part of brain functioning but is a network of currently active information and related processes being used at a given moment" (p. 268).

forms and their meanings and integrate this new linguistic information into their developing language system. This involves some unspecified degree of elaborative rehearsal—associating the form-meaning connections with previous knowledge (Baddeley, 1998). If there are too many constraints on processing (Just & Carpenter, 1992; McLaughlin, 1987), characteristic of lower-proficiency learners, or if unfamiliar words are not deemed important enough to warrant deeper processing (Craik & Tulving, 1975), then these words may be processed more superficially, resulting in weaker memory traces and a lesser likelihood of being retrieved from memory (see also N. Ellis, 1994, 2001; Gass, 1999; Hulstijn, 2001, 2003; Laufer & Hulstijn, 2001; Robinson, P., 2003; Schmidt, 2001).

Laufer and Hulstjn (2001) proposed the Involvement Load theory to explain the variable nature of incidental vocabulary learning and retention.[3] They suggested that retention of new words depends upon levels of *need*, *search*, and *evaluation* imposed by reading tasks. *Need* concerns the need to comply with the task. *Search* entails making attempts to determine the meaning of an unknown word, and *evaluation* involves making a decision about the semantic and grammatical fit of the word within the context. The theory predicts that the greater the cognitive involvement in a given task, the better the retention. Thus, to establish form-meaning connections for new words through reading, new words must be noticed and sufficient attention allocated. The quality of processing during reading and on any tasks to facilitate lexical processing and integration should also be affected by the interaction between reader-based factors, such as L2 sight vocabulary knowledge, L2 reading ability, and background knowledge, factors that are described in more detail below. Evidence for the rich getting richer in L2 vocabulary development through reading is provided. It is illustrated that, in general, there are superior levels of vocabulary processing, gains, and retention for learners of a group who possess superior levels of passage sight vocabulary knowledge, background knowledge, and L2 reading ability.[4]

---

[3]The reader is reminded that *incidental* is not meant to refer to "unconscious" or "subliminal" learning, as explained on page 66. The explanation provided by Laufer and Hulstijn (2001) proposes explicit cognitive involvement in learning and retaining new word meanings during various tasks, even when learners are not forewarned about a test on the new words that is administered after such tasks.

[4]Stanovich (1986, 2000) describes the phenomenon of and evidence for the 'rich getting richer' in L1 literacy, in particular, reciprocally strong relationships between vocabulary knowledge, print and language exposure, and reading ability. N. Ellis (1994) has also described this phenomenon for L2 vocabulary acquisition. In general the 'rich getting richer' phenomenon has been investigated in a variety of educational and psychological camps interested in individual differences in cognitive abilities and knowledge and performance outcomes in complex cognitive skills.

Background Knowledge

What is background knowledge? Background knowledge refers to knowledge about the world like situations, events, places, and things (for further description, see Graesser, Singer, & Trabasso, 1994). Such knowledge can be gained through previous experience. Background knowledge contributes to the efficiency of attentional allocation to input during reading, enabling richer textual interpretations and superior memory (e.g., Graesser et al., 1994; Kintsch, 1998; Nassaji, 2002; Robinson, P., 2003; Rumelhart, 1980; Schank & Abelson, 1977). Research has demonstrated positive effects of background knowledge on L2 text comprehension (e.g., Barry & Lazarte, 1998; Carrell, 1987; Chen & Donin, 1997; Hudson, 1982; Pulido, 2004a). As the reader processes the textual input, the meaning that is generated then "becomes integrated into the reader's global knowledge, forming a coherent mental representation of what the text is about"(Nassaji, 2002, p. 453). The information that is generated and is stored in working memory acts as a "signal in an associative manner to all the information stored in long-term memory" (p. 455). Thus, background knowledge becomes activated in response to this signaling mechanism and can influence the construction of meaning. The role of background knowledge in lexical development through reading is also determined by the *quality* of the textbase that is constructed during reading, which is affected by reading and text processing efficiency, and working memory. That is to say, the activation of background knowledge in relation to text comprehension plays a role in lexical development that occurs through text processing. It must also be kept in mind that all of the elements described above function in tandem in generating initial form-meaning connections for new words.

Background knowledge also affects lexical input processing. First, research within a lexical inferencing and introspection paradigm, where learners are instructed to make guesses about new words, observed that ESL and EFL learners of all levels used background knowledge to guess word meanings (Chern, 1993; Haastrup, 1989; Nassaji, 2003; Parry, 1997). However, some studies with intermediate learners of German (Rott, 2000) and ESL (de Bot et al., 1997; Paribakht & Wesche,1999) reported less use of background knowledge relative to other knowledge sources (e.g., grammar). In a unique, cross-sectional study Lee and Wolf (1997) reported native Spanish speakers using background knowledge the most, followed by the advanced, intermediate, and then beginning learners of Spanish.

When background knowledge was systematically studied, Adams (1982) found that statements describing the topic facilitated lexical inferencing for beginning learners of French when reading paragraphs about everyday activities. Studies addressing guessing in discrete sentence contexts varying in degree of semantic richness reported greater success and ease in inferencing within the semantically rich sentences, which provided clues to meaning (e.g., Li, 1988, with Chinese advanced English learners; and Mondria & Wit-de Boer, 1991, with Dutch intermediate French learners). Li also reported superior retention of the words in the semantically rich sentences. However, Mondria and Wit-de Boer (1991) assessed retention after a verification task to confirm or correct the guesses made in semantically rich contexts and reported low retention on an L2–L1 translation task, and weak and negative relationships between inferencing and retention. Similarly, Mondria (2003), with intermediate learners of Dutch, also found low retention of correctly inferred words after a verification task and high correct retention of incorrectly inferred words. The latter two studies concluded that due to the strong association of context and meaning, and assumed ease in guessing, learners likely did not pay sufficient attention to the word form and its meaning during the learning tasks because they thought they knew the word. Within extended discourse contexts some readers may also regard passages depicting familiar topics, as well as any accompanying learning tasks, as easy, such that they may have less of a need to pay attention to the connection between the new word form and its meaning because the context may be readily understood. Given the potential negative role of topic familiarity in lexical input processing, I conducted several studies to address this issue in narrative reading tasks, where I operationalized background knowledge as *topic familiarity*. The results are presented below.

Pulido (2000, 2003) assessed the role of topic familiarity on incidental vocabulary gains and retention with a cross-section of university learners of Spanish ($n = 99$). All participants read four brief narratives (from 164–174 words each), two depicting more familiar scenarios (grocery shopping, going to the doctor) and two depicting less familiar scenarios (buying a home, publishing an article). Degree of familiarity was confirmed by results from a Likert-scale topic familiarity questionnaire. The passages were similar in length, average sentence length, and number of semantic ideas. Embedded in each passage were eight nonsense target words (TWs) representing concepts central to each scenario.[5] The use of nonsense words in vocabulary input processing research is common to study initial form-meaning mapping

---

[5]The nonsense words maintained orthographic and morphological rules of Spanish. Examples of some of the TW concepts that were replaced with nonsense words were *conveyer belt, aisles, prescription, mortgage, agent, cover letter,* and *proofs.*

processes because it ensures no prior knowledge on the part of the participants. To measure short-term and delayed effects of topic familiarity on receptive gain and retention of meaning, participants took two tests: translation production (L2–L1), followed by multiple choice translation recognition (L2–L1) two days and four weeks after the reading, respectively. The results revealed a short-term consistent positive effect of topic familiarity on the easier, translation recognition test administered two days after reading. However, these effects were not maintained 28 days later, due to forgetting. On the more difficult, translation production test there were no differences in gains or retention attributed to topic familiarity due to extremely low scores on both occasions. The lack of any long-term effects of topic familiarity was attributed to a variety of factors, including the nature of the task (i.e., an incidental orienting task that did not forewarn learners of the vocabulary test that was subsequently administered), the time lag between the reading tasks and vocabulary retention tests (i.e., two and 28 days), and the very limited exposure to the TWs (i.e., they appeared only once in each story).

In another incidental learning study, with 23 intermediate Spanish learners (Pulido, 2004b), I examined the effects of cultural background knowledge on immediate vocabulary gain of five nonsense words when participants read two brief narratives (231–259 words), one depicting a culturally familiar version of one scenario and the other depicting a culturally unfamiliar version of another scenario (e.g., registering for university classes and grocery shopping in the U.S. vs. in Paraguay). On an open-ended measure to tap various levels of vocabulary knowledge (i.e., an adapted version of the Vocabulary Knowledge Scale–VKS, Paribakht & Wesche, 1993), scores were greater after reading within the culturally familiar versions of the scenarios. The scores reflected only self-reported episodic memory for the new lexical items (i.e., memory of having seen the TWs within the stories), but little more. Such low scores may be an artifact of the instrument or experimental conditions, where learners briefly saw the TWs once in a sentence during an online sentence-by-sentence reading task.

With a cross section of 35 adult university learners of Spanish (beginning through advanced), Pulido (2005) investigated Mondria's (2003) and Mondria and Wit-de Boer's (1991) conclusions within extended discourse contexts. The impact of topic familiarity (Likert-scale questionnaire) on lexical inferencing (i.e., initial meaning assignment), attentional allocation during an online verification task, intake, strategies in verifying, and receptive retention of meaning were examined. All participants read two brief stories (from 164–174 words each), one depicting a more familiar scenario (grocery shopping) and one depicting a less familiar scenario (publishing an article). Embedded in each passage were eight highlighted nonsense TWs representing concepts central to each scenario (see Pulido, 2007). Participants guessed the meanings of the boldfaced, underlined TWs by writing the L1 translation or definition. They then rated the degree of difficulty in guessing, using a six-point Likert scale. After reading both stories, participants completed an online verification task in which they saw the TW sentence from the story accompanied by the L1 translation in the right-hand margin. They were instructed to confirm or correct their guesses and to understand the sentence before continuing to the next sentence. Their study times were measured. After completing each set of TW sentences, the participants completed a word recognition memory, Yes-No verification test to tap intake, or memory traces, for the recently processed TWs. The ability to recognize new lexical forms is also considered to be a crucial stage in the development of new lexical entries. If learners were better at recognition memory for certain words relative to others, this might provide evidence for differential levels of attention and/or use of processing strategies on the previous tasks. Participants saw a series of words on the computer, one at a time, and indicated if each word had appeared in the particular story or TW sentences by pressing one of two computer keys. This task required participants to discriminate between words from the stories (including the TWs) and distractors, and measured degree of accuracy and speed in recognition. Participants then repeated the online verification task for the TWs from the second story, followed by the corresponding intake recognition memory test. Afterward, they listed the strategies they used during the online verification task. This was followed by two translation tests: L2-L1 translation production, followed by translation recognition.

There were complex patterns of results in that topic familiarity interacted with reader-based proficiency variables on various measures, suggesting threshold effects. For example, topic familiarity only had positive effects on guessing for the more proficient readers of the group, an instance of the rich getting richer. For the weaker readers, there was no observed facilitation in lexical guessing within the more familiar story scenario. Similar findings were observed for difficulty in guessing: only the more proficient readers regarded the TWs from the more familiar story as significantly easier to guess. However, all learners of the group were faster to complete the online verification task for the TWs from the more familiar story, in spite of initial difficulty by weaker learners in guessing the TWs from that story. After the online verification task there were no differences in recognition memory for the TWs from the different topic familiarity conditions. The verification task was beneficial in promoting the forging of an initial memory trace for information related to all TWs. However, in spite of an error-free verification task, there were differences in ability to demonstrate receptive retention of meaning. On the more difficult, translation production test, more TW meanings were remembered from the more familiar scenario by all learners. Thus, in addition to forging initial memory traces for these words, learners were able to store and retrieve information about meaning. This was superior to what was demonstrated for the TWs from the less familiar scenario. However, on the easier, multiple-choice recognition test, the stronger readers demonstrated comparable TW retention from both scenarios. From an analysis of the changes in scores between the guessing and retention phases for the stronger readers, there were positive gains for the TWs from the less familiar condition and some forgetting of the TWs from the more familiar condition. On the other hand, the weaker readers benefited from the more familiar topic, remembering significantly more TWs from this condition, in spite of initial difficulty and lack of success during the guessing phase.

Participants reported using strategies during the online verification task that lend support to the results above. First, 83 percent of the learners reported moderate ease in processing the TW sentences from the more familiar story, compared to only 29 percent who made similar reports for the less familiar story. In addition, 63 percent of the participants used processing strategies that may have been conducive to building or strengthening form-meaning connections and that involve noticing, retrieving, and generating (for more detail see Nation, 2001). For example, previous research has reported positive effects of using a wide range of strategies, some of which may involve selectively attending to the new word, retrieving the new word and information about it from previous encounters, and engaging in elaboration and semantic encoding, or creating semantic associations and networks and making conscious connections to previous knowledge (e.g., N. Ellis, 1995; Gu & Johnson, 1996; Lawson & Hogben, 1996; Nation, 2001; Schmitt, 1997). Participants in the study reported the following: "focus on the shape of the word"; "made a mental note of the correct translation and went back to fit it in and compare it with the overall context"; "try to read it slowly"; and "link the translation to the meaning of the story and sentence." However, 31 percent (two graduate, five advanced, one high-intermediate, three intermediate) reported more superficial processing strategies such as, "I was mostly looking at the definitions of underlined words because I had understood the majority of the rest of the stories"; "if I was correct I didn't think about it too long because I knew I had understood it"; "when they were the same I dismissed the sentence"; and "I was trying to remember the events taking place in the story more than the vocab." In terms of the overall relationship between lexical inferencing and retention and possible effects of topic familiarity, these results are similar to Mondria's (2003) and Mondria and Wit-de Boer's (1991), namely, weak and negative relationships for the more familiar and easier condition, compared to the less familiar, more difficult condition.

These combined results illustrate a generally strong short-term role of background knowledge in lexical input processing when reading for comprehension. However, when completing strategic tasks, such as lexical inferencing and verification of meaning, only the stronger readers appeared to capitalize at first on their background knowledge in inferencing, evidence for the rich getting richer, but may subsequently have regarded learning tasks as easy in familiar conditions and might not have experienced the need to engage in the requisite processing to sustain such initial benefits, although they were highly capable. Weaker readers appeared to compensate somewhat for weaker skills, likely with the help of topic familiarity and with additional opportunities for further processing via strategic tasks.

L2 READING PROFICIENCY

Reading is a complex cognitive skill, entailing the simultaneous use of various knowledge sources and processing skills. Readers need efficient strategies for acquiring information from texts. Strong readers have such strategies and can efficiently carry out the various processes involved in reading. For example, strong readers demonstrate automaticity[6] in lower-level processing, that is identifying letters and visual patterns of words and accessing their meanings. Such automaticity frees up attentional resources to enable the construction and integration of ideas from context, and the use of information from long-term memory (i.e., background knowledge). Having efficient processing skills results in a greater likelihood of successful inferencing to resolve the meaning of unfamiliar words. In contrast, weak readers experience difficulty in both local and global comprehension.[7] In other

---

[6]Grabe and Stoller (2002) define *automaticity* as the "ability to carry out a skill accurately and rapidly, without being able to reflect on the processes involved, and without being able to suppress the skill" (p. 257).

[7]Local comprehension refers to establishing a coherent representation at the sentence level. This involves computing the relationships among words and phrases in a sentence by generating semantic propositions, or idea units, from words, as well as engaging in syntactic parsing, or connecting the words in a sentence. Global comprehension refers to connecting the sentences within a paragraph, generating inferences via the use of knowledge stored in long-term memory, and integrating the information that is constructed across paragraphs within larger discourse contexts in order to form a coherent representation of the passage as a whole.

words, they experience problems in accessing word meaning, understanding sentences, connecting sentences within a paragraph, and computing and integrating ideas within and across paragraphs, and across the overall discourse context. This breakdown in comprehension frequently translates into a short-circuit of the lexical inferencing and integration process, minimizing the chances for vocabulary development through reading, (e.g., Bernhardt, 1991; Grabe & Stoller, 2002; Just & Carpenter, 1992; Kintsch, 1998; Koda, 2005; Laufer, 1997; Segalowitz, 1986; Stanovich, 1986, 2000). Although there is ample theoretical support that L2 reading proficiency should contribute substantially to L2 lexical input processing and acquisition, there are few empirical studies addressing the nature of this relationship.

Chern (1993) reported that ESL learners with superior L2 reading proficiency (based on TOEFL scores) were more successful at lexical inferencing. However, more recent studies did not observe any statistically significant effects of L2 reading proficiency on lexical inferencing and retention (Bengeleil & Paribakht, 2004), or on retention only (Fraser, 1999) when the CanTEST and TOEFL®, respectively, were used and L2 reading proficiency was treated as a between-group variable (i.e., learners were divided into two groups based upon scores on the L2 reading proficiency measures). The lack of significant findings might be due to methodological reasons, such as small sample sizes, the presence of focused instruction on lexical processing strategies (Fraser, 1999), which might have mitigated any differences in reading ability among the eight participants in the study, as well as the lack of sufficient variation in reading ability (e.g., Bengeleil & Paribakht, 2004; Fraser, 1999). For example, in the Fraser study, although learners were grouped into high and low reading ability based on the reading proficiency test scores, they were recruited from the same, intermediate, level and, based upon the statistical reporting that was offered, may not have really differed in L2 reading ability to an extent that would have affected outcomes in lexical inferencing and retention. In addition, the participants in the studies might not have processed the TWs for internalization, but simply to access their meanings.

Pulido (2000, 2003) investigated the role of L2 reading proficiency in vocabulary learning via a standardized test of reading comprehension, the Spanish version of the *Adult Basic Learning Examination* (*ABLE*) (Karlsen & Gardner, 1990). This is a timed 48-item multiple choice test containing readings of a functional (e.g., letters, ads) and educational (e.g., expositions) nature and measures a participant's literal and inferential comprehension ability, involving extraction of local and global information from the readings as well as ability to infer what is not explicitly stated at a local and global level. A wide range of reading ability was observed. Results revealed robust effects on both measures of gain and at both time intervals. The variable of L2 reading proficiency was also more robust than that of passage sight vocabulary (i.e., knowledge of the vocabulary contained within the texts, described in more detail in the following section), and revealed that with increases in general L2 reading ability there were accompanying increases in incidental vocabulary gain and retention. That L2 reading proficiency was a more robust predictor of gains than passage sight vocabulary was likely so because the former assessed skill in decoding, parsing, and integrating sentences, connecting information across discourse, accessing information in long-term memory, and storing information, which are processes more relevant to those involved in learning and remembering new vocabulary through reading. On the other hand, the latter assessed only previous vocabulary learning (likely through direct translation), lexical access, and translation.

Pulido (2005) also considered the role of L2 reading proficiency (via the ABLE exam) on the following stages in lexical input processing: lexical inferencing, attentional allocation during the online verification task, intake, strategies used during the online verification task, and retention of meaning. Results revealed a significant interaction by way of inconsistencies in the role of reading proficiency on lexical inferencing, difficulty in inferencing, and immediate retention. As previously discussed, a threshold effect was observed in these three areas. These findings lend some support to interactive models of reading emphasizing the combined role of various knowledge sources and skills, namely, those that serve to build a strong textbase and those that serve to activate information from long-term memory, which can be used to facilitate and constrain processing of new words. Weaker readers are less efficient in carrying out these processes, especially on difficult tasks for which they lack familiarity. Stronger readers have more attentional resources to dedicate to efficient processing and storage of information about new and difficult words, and to the retrieval of such information, but only if the test provides some cues (e.g., translation recognition). These findings also corroborate Pulido (2000, 2003), suggesting that when the going gets tough (e.g., in more difficult and less familiar reading conditions) second language reading and lexical input processing skills become especially relevant to vocabulary learning outcomes.

L2 PASSAGE SIGHT VOCABULARY

Laufer (1997) suggested that for L2 readers the "threshold for reading comprehension is, to a large extent, lexical" (p. 21; see also Koda, 1989; Laufer,

1992; Laufer & Sim, 1985; Ulijn & Strother, 1990). Likewise, research reports a lexical threshold (general vocabulary knowledge) for learning vocabulary through reading (Cobb, this volume; Haynes & Baker, 1993; Horst, Cobb, & Meara, 1998; Nassaji, 2004). Yet, crucial to reading and lexical input processing is knowledge of vocabulary specifically associated with the passages, or *passage sight vocabulary*. The more knowledge that readers have of the vocabulary specific to a given passage (i.e., the higher the text coverage), the more comprehensible the input becomes. And, with sufficient passage sight vocabulary and efficient decoding skills, readers can then allocate attentional resources to constructing and integrating ideas from context, and accessing and using information from long-term memory, processes that are involved in comprehension. That is, when readers know most of the vocabulary contained within a passage, the input becomes more comprehensible. This, in turn, results in a greater likelihood of successful lexical inferencing and further lexical growth. Without such knowledge and efficiency, readers are apt to experience a short-circuit of the lexical inferencing and integration process, a failure to understand the relationships among ideas in the text, and fewer chances for vocabulary development (e.g., Cobb, this volume; Grabe & Stoller, 2002; Koda, 2005; Laufer, 1997). Put simply, knowing little vocabulary in the context results in failed or inefficient lexical access, and inaccurate local and global comprehension. This, in turn, translates into having very little context to support inferencing processes that are necessary to build coherence during reading, processes that include making guesses about the meanings of new words. Thus, inability or problems in lexical guessing during reading are expected to hamper further lexical development that could potentially occur through the cognitive processes engaged during reading, resulting in a domino effect.

Several studies on lexical inferencing also observed more successful guessing when readers knew vocabulary in the passage (e.g., Haynes & Baker, 1993; Lee & Wolf, 1997; Parry, 1997; Rott, 2000). Weaker learners experienced more difficulty in integrating multiple textual cues and background knowledge than stronger learners, who appeared to know more words in the context. These results were determined by anecdotal observations, rather than quantitative measurements of passage sight vocabulary.

There is scant empirical evidence illustrating the precise relationship between vocabulary knowledge specific to a given text and lexical development associated with processing that text. In my studies passage sight vocabulary was measured by an L2-L1 translation test of the words in the passage for which participants had reported prior familiarity. Pulido (2004b) did not obtain a robust role of passage sight vocabulary, attributed to the restriction in range of ability of the learners and sample size in the study (all intermediate level) and the small amount of passage sight vocabulary tested (e.g., only 22–23 percent of the passage vocabulary). Pulido (2000, 2003) studied the role of passage sight vocabulary. Approximately 42–48 percent of the unique word tokens were tested. High-frequency function words and cognates were excluded because they were assumed to be very familiar to the learners. Results revealed a significant role of passage sight vocabulary (moderate and positive correlations) on both measures two and 28 days after reading. Moreover, on the difficult production measure, passage sight vocabulary had stronger effects than background knowledge.

In Pulido (2005, 2007), when learners were assigned to the strategic tasks of lexical inferencing, difficulty rating, recognition memory, and TW verification, results revealed robust effects for passage sight vocabulary, where a substantially larger proportion of words was tested (77–81 percent). As L2 passage sight vocabulary increased, so did success in lexical inferencing (for both familiarity conditions), TW recognition memory, and receptive retention on both measures. In addition, the learners with more sight vocabulary also reported greater ease in guessing the TWs from the more familiar story. These combined findings concerning the investigation of passage sight vocabulary underscore the importance of knowledge of vocabulary specific to passages, which is one of many knowledge sources critical to reading and lexical input processing. That passage sight vocabulary was more relevant to retention from the less familiar passage (Pulido, 2005, 2007) suggests that more lexical input processing difficulties arise when learners lack familiarity with both the topic and the vocabulary contained within text.

In summary, the results of the research reported above illustrate a generally strong, but sometimes variable, short-term role of topic familiarity in lexical input processing. When reading and simultaneously completing strategic tasks, such as lexical inferencing in context, topic familiarity appears to facilitate processing for only the stronger readers of the group, those with substantially more text coverage and who are more efficient in simultaneously carrying out the lower- and higher-level processes involved in reading. Yet, if strong readers regard subsequent processing tasks, for example, verification of meaning, as easy or too familiar, perhaps due to the high degree of familiarity with the topic, any initial benefits derived from familiar contexts may be short-lived. Weaker learners, through various tasks providing multiple encounters and attention to the new words, however, benefit, and may even compensate for other deficiencies in processing by using background knowledge. Still, the rich tend to get richer, that is, L2 passage sight vocabulary and L2 reading ability play a significant role in lexical input processing, such that learners with greater text coverage and better reading skills also experience greater levels of vocabulary development during reading.

PEDAGOGICAL IMPLICATIONS

L2 learners frequently encounter completely new words that are amenable to learning via association with previously known concepts. Form-meaning mapping of this nature is typical of initial stages of L2 lexical development, especially through reading. The results from the studies reported above point to several important implications for L2 teachers.

Since guesses about new word meanings and short-term gains were greater when learners read passages that depicted very familiar topics, it might be beneficial for language practitioners to familiarize learners ahead of time with the specific topics in reading passages to promote vocabulary learning. Teachers should ascertain whether or not learners have the requisite background knowledge and engage in pre-reading activities to activate such knowledge or to present it for the first time (e.g., Anderson, N., 1999; Grabe & Stoller, 2002; Lee & VanPatten, 2003; Swaffar, Arens, & Byrnes, 1991). Such activities are often contained in pre-reading sections of language textbooks. If they are not, or if additional background knowledge activation tasks are warranted, then text activities could be augmented with others to include: (a) brainstorming about the topic and related concepts via graphic organizers to illustrate the connections between ideas and key concepts; (b) pre-teaching the relevant information; or (c) assigning advance organizer quizzes or questionnaires, accompanied by feedback, to direct learners' attention to relevant content. In addition, since more familiar and easy contexts may be more conducive to initial form-meaning mapping for new vocabulary, initial presentation of vocabulary in such contexts might provide a cognitive foothold for later vocabulary learning opportunities and for new words that might be considered more difficult to learn, due to their presence within less familiar or more difficult contexts.

Strategic tasks that also draw learners' attention to new vocabulary and that encourage additional processing, such as guessing and subsequently verifying meaning through gloss consultation, can be beneficial for promoting vocabulary learning through reading. In the absence of such tasks (e.g., Pulido 2000, 2003, 2004b), there was on average only 3 percent correct retention on the open-ended translation measure from both familiarity conditions. However, after strategic inferencing and verification tasks (Pulido,

2005, 2007), there was on average 48 percent retention, and a much wider gap in retention between the more and the less familiar conditions (53 percent and 43 percent, respectively). Although a direct comparison is not possible, it appears as if directing learners' attention to guessing meaning may be more conducive to vocabulary retention compared to simple exposure to new vocabulary while reading L2 input, where learners may not necessarily allocate sufficient attention and engage in subsequent processing to the extent required for internalization. Moreover, since weaker learners experience difficulty and little success in lexical inferencing, providing a verification task to confirm or correct guesses for new words may provide additional benefits beyond a mere reading-inferring task, especially if learners are familiar with the topic (e.g., Fraser, 1999; Mondria, 2003; Schouten-van Parreren, 1989). Verification tasks can be assigned in the form of dictionary look-up, CALL hyperlink or marginal gloss look-up, or even cooperative learning tasks to read and verify meaning in small groups and with instructor guidance so that learners engage in sufficient processing.

Additionally, teachers should bear in mind that weaker learners may not learn as many new words nor as quickly as stronger, more advanced learners. Vocabulary learning is an incremental process. With limited exposure to new vocabulary, gains might be limited to association of new words with particular contexts, which is still considered to be an initial step in acquisition. However, there may be little or no knowledge accrual of the exact meanings of those words. The finding that stronger readers, as determined by scores on the standardized reading test, were also more successful at lexical input processing suggests that it may be beneficial to teach reading strategies to promote comprehension. For example, teachers can design activities that focus on both lower- and higher-level processing, such as previewing titles, headings, and illustrations for ideas in the text; scanning for specific information; reading the passage one section at a time and completing comprehension questions; selecting key words and local and global context cues; identifying main ideas; and writing summaries in the native language, if the students' and teacher's native languages are the same, or in the target language for more proficient learners if production skills are sufficiently developed. In addition, students can identify how the different ideas contained in the text relate to each other and contribute to the global meaning through the use of teacher and student-generated graphic organizers that reveal relationships among ideas, words, new and old content, and patterns of organization within texts (e.g., see Grabe & Stoller, 2002). Students can also be encouraged to reread to monitor and confirm ideas, as well as to reread for new ideas (e.g., Anderson, N.,

1993a, 1993b, 1999; Bernhardt, 1991; Day, 1993; Lee & VanPatten, 2003; Swaffar et al., 1991). Reading contexts present learners of all levels with opportunities for vocabulary growth; therefore, instructors may also consider increasing opportunities for reading through extensive, free and voluntary, and graded reading activities (e.g., Elley, 1991; Grabe & Stoller, 2002).

Given the parallel findings with respect to the impact of passage vocabulary knowledge, instructors may also wish to engage in the following: (a) match texts to learners based upon their vocabulary knowledge; (b) dedicate time and resources to promoting frequency-based vocabulary and reading instruction, through the use of computer-aided resources (see Cobb, this volume; Horst, this volume); (c) incorporate graded readers and opportunities for learners to meet the same words in a variety of contexts in order to promote more efficient lexical access (see also Shiotsu, this volume); and (d) use texts or create materials that contain textual glosses, with particular emphasis on key words in the readings (see Cobb, this volume, for computer-aided pedagogical recommendations; also see Nation, 2001). At the same time, instructors should be aware of the other factors related to performance, such as the varied availability of context cues to support guessing, and variations in L1 and L2 reading skills, background knowledge, and metacognitive ability (e.g., the ability to detect gaps in knowledge and comprehension, and to monitor one's learning). Thus, linguistic knowledge alone, such as knowledge of the lexical items contained within the passage (which includes meaning as well as syntactic, morphological, and orthographic/phonological components), is necessary, but not sufficient in and of itself to promote vocabulary gains.

Finally, teachers should be aware that one form of assessment compared to another might provide greater opportunities for learners to demonstrate vocabulary gains through reading. Transfer-appropriate processing (TAP) effects on memory (Morris, Bransford, & Franks, 1977) suggest that memory improves when there is more similarity between the task at the time of study and at the time of testing. The inference verification task depicted the TWs in the original sentences along with their L1 translations, which was more similar to the translation recognition task (compared to the production task), which contained retrieval cues (i.e., L1 translation options) that could have better facilitated access to memory traces about the new words.

In sum, the outcomes from the L2 reading and vocabulary research that has been reported in this chapter lend support to Stanovich's (1986) conclusion for native language literacy: that the rich do get richer.

Reflection Questions

Reflection Questions

1. Given that there are differences in reading ability among learners and that comprehension outcomes are related to vocabulary gains, what instructional techniques can be provided during reading to promote comprehension?

2. What other types of background knowledge can you think of that might facilitate reading comprehension and vocabulary learning from texts aside from knowledge about everyday situations?

3. Besides requiring learners to verify the meanings of words that are guessed during reading, what other follow-up activities can be assigned to promote the strengthening of form-meaning connections for new words that are guessed and verified during reading?

4. How can you increase students' understanding of certain words in passages before and during reading so that they will have more available context to support guessing new words when they are reading?

CHAPTER 4

Modifying the L2 Reading Text for Improved Comprehension and Acquisition: Does It Work?

Ronald P. Leow, Georgetown University

Textual modification—that is, modifying written second/foreign language (L2) input—is quite a common practice in many pedagogical settings. There are three major strands of research on the effects of textual modification in SLA: simplified written input, textual input enhancement, and glossing. Studies purporting to address the benefits of textual modifications over unmodified input have generally viewed such modifications as a pedagogical intervention on the part of the researcher/teacher to either reduce the processing demands of the L2 reader by making the input more comprehensible or making targeted items in the L2 input more salient in an effort to draw readers' attention to these targeted items. In other words, studies in all three research strands of textual modification share the same underlying hypothesis—that textual modification promotes implicitly readers' attention to targeted items (vocabulary, forms or structures) in the input (text) and that learners exposed to modified input should substantially perform better in understanding the content, paying more attention to and processing targeted grammatical items in the modified input when compared to learners not exposed to such pedagogical modifications. This chapter will (1) briefly review current theoretical approaches to the roles of attention and awareness in L2 learning, (2) briefly describe the theoretical underpinnings of each strand of textual modification research in the SLA literature, (3) provide a concise and critical review of current studies addressing L2 textual modifications, (4) address a major limitation of previous studies and report on studies addressing this limitation, and (5) conclude with suggestions for teachers to consider in their role of language facilitators in the classroom setting.

THEORETICAL MODELS OF ATTENTION AND AWARENESS IN SLA

Given that attention and awareness potentially play important roles in modified input in the L2 classroom setting, it is useful to discuss briefly three current major theoretical approaches (e.g., Robinson, P., 1995; Schmidt, 1990, 1993, 1995, 2001; Tomlin & Villa, 1994) to the roles of attention and awareness in L2 learning.

Tomlin and Villa's Functional Model of Input Processing in SLA

Drawing on the work of Posner (1992) in cognitive science, Tomlin and Villa (1994) propose a functionally based, fine-grained analysis of attention. In their model of input processing in SLA, attention has three components with neurological correlates: (1) alertness (an overall readiness to deal with incoming stimuli), (2) orientation (the direction of attentional resources to a certain type of stimuli), and (3) detection (the cognitive registration of stimuli). Tomlin and Villa postulate that it is detection alone that is necessary for further processing of input and subsequent learning to take place. The other two components—alertness and orientation—can enhance the chances that detection will occur, but neither is necessary. One crucial aspect of Tomlin and Villa's claims is that, in their model, detection does *not* imply awareness. Awareness is defined as "a particular state of mind in which an individual has undergone a specific subjective experience of some cognitive content or external stimulus" (Tomlin & Villa, 1994, p. 193).

Awareness, according to Allport (1988), is demonstrated through (a) some resulting behavioral or cognitive change, (b) a report of the experience, or (c) metalinguistic description of an underlying rule. Recently, Tomlin and Villa's model has been questioned (Schmidt, 2001; Simard & Wong, 2001; Truscott, 1998) with respect to its generalizability to the SLA field and for being too general to be of use.

Schmidt's Noticing Hypothesis

Schmidt's (1990, 1993, 1995, 2001) noticing hypothesis contrasts sharply with Tomlin and Villa's (1994) view that awareness is not necessary for learning, in that without awareness, input can be processed only in short-term memory and, therefore, cannot be deeply processed for learning to occur. According to Schmidt's noticing hypothesis, attention controls access to awareness and is responsible for noticing, which he says is "the necessary and sufficient condition for the conversion of input into intake"[1] (Schmidt, 1993, p. 209). He views attention as being isomorphic with awareness and rejects the idea of learning without awareness. In addition, Schmidt posits that, in addition to awareness at the level of noticing, which leads to mere intake, there is another higher level of awareness, which he refers to as awareness at the level of understanding. Schmidt proposes that this level of awareness leads to deeper learning marked by restructuring and system learning since it is characterized by learners' ability to analyze, compare, and test hypotheses of L2 data.

Robinson's Model of the Relationship between Attention and Memory

A third model of attention proposed in SLA is that of P. Robinson (1995). Robinson's model reconciles Tomlin and Villa's (1994) notion of detection, which does not involve awareness, and Schmidt's (1990 and elsewhere) notion of noticing, which involves awareness. In Robinson's model, detec-

---

[1]Intake is defined as "that part of the input that has been attended to by second language learners while processing the input. Intake represents stored linguistic data that may be used for immediate recognition and does not necessarily imply language acquisition" (Leow, 1993, p. 334).

tion is posited to be one early stage in the process, sequentially prior to noticing. Noticing, in Robinson's model, is "detection plus rehearsal in short-term memory, prior to encoding in long-term memory" (P. Robinson, 1995, p. 296). Robinson, then, supports Schmidt's hypothesis that noticing does involve awareness and that it is crucial for learning to take place. At the same time, Robinson does not reject Tomlin and Villa's notion of detection but simply relegates it to an earlier stage in the learning process, thereby giving Schmidt's noticing hypothesis a more prominent role in input processing.

Awareness and Learning

As can be seen from the different theoretical models of attention, the facilitative role of attention in L2 development[2] is generally accepted, but the role of awareness is not without debate. Specifically, Schmidt's noticing hypothesis and Robinson's model of the relationship between attention and memory posit a crucial role for awareness, whereas Tomlin and Villa's functional model of input processing does not. What is not controversial, then, is that attentional resources may be allocated to a specific linguistic item in the input, but whether learner awareness is required for the grammatical information to be processed by the learner is open to debate. Several researchers have supported a dissociation between learning and awareness (e.g., Carr & Curran, 1994; Curran & Keele, 1994; Hardcastle, 1993; Tomlin & Villa, 1994; Velmans, 1991) while others have rejected this dissociation (Robinson, P., 1995; Schmidt, 1990 and elsewhere).

Empirical Studies on the Role of Awareness in L2 Development

A number of empirical SLA studies have provided support for the role of awareness and the differential effects of higher levels of awareness in SLA. Overall, these studies appear to provide support for the facilitative effects of awareness on foreign language behavior and learning. More specifically,

---

[2]L2 development is typically measured via several tests that include oral or written production (e.g., picture-cued, sentence completion, sentence combination, narration, fill-in-the-blank) and grammaticality judgment tests.

the main findings indicate that (a) awareness at the level of noticing and understanding contributed substantially to a significant increase in learners' ability to take in the targeted form or structure (Leow, 1997a, 2000, 2001a; Rosa & Leow, 2004a; Rosa & O'Neill, 1999) and produce in writing the targeted form or structure (Leow, 1997a, 2001a; Rosa & Leow, 2004a), including novel exemplars (Rosa & Leow, 2004a); (b) awareness at the level of understanding led to significantly more intake when compared to awareness at the level of noticing (Leow, 1997a, 2001a; Rosa & Leow, 2004a; Rosa & O'Neill, 1999); (c) there is a correlation between awareness at the level of understanding and usage of hypothesis testing / rule formation (Leow, 1997a, 2000, 2001a; Rosa & Leow, 2004a; Rosa & O'Neill, 1999); (d) there is a correlation between level of awareness and formal instruction and directions to search for a rule (Rosa & O'Neill, 1999); and (e) there is a correlation between awareness at the level of understanding and learning conditions providing an explicit pre-task (with grammatical explanation) as well as implicit or explicit concurrent feedback (Rosa & Leow, 2004a).

SIMPLIFIED WRITTEN INPUT: THEORETICAL UNDERPINNINGS

An early theoretical postulation for the importance of simplified input was the view that simplified input makes the input more comprehensible to L2 learners (e.g., Hatch, 1983; Kelch, 1985; Long, 1983, 1985). It was argued that the comprehensibility of the input would indirectly affect language acquisition by providing more linguistic information to the learner's developing linguistic system. For example, according to Krashen (1982, 1985) and Long (1983, 1985), exposure to simplified input would allow learners to pay attention to form and structures that may not be a part of their internal system due to a reduction of complicated input that may overload their processing capacity.

This initial theoretical premise fits neatly within cognitive theory, in which humans are viewed as limited capacity processors who suffer from cognitive overload when they are forced to simultaneously process different bits of information that draw from the same cognitive resource pool (e.g., McLaughlin, 1987; Wickens, 1989). According to this theory, L2 learning is considered to be the acquisition of a complex skill that begins as a controlled process, which is capacity-limited and under strict control of the learner, and gradually becomes an automatic process through routinization, which requires less cognitive effort. While the role of attention is without controversy in this strand of research, the role of awareness has not been explicitly addressed.

SIMPLIFIED WRITTEN INPUT: EMPIRICAL STUDIES

The simplification of written input employed in experimental designs typically included modifications for vocabulary (e.g., high-frequency vocabulary; fewer idioms; fewer pronoun forms of all kinds; high use of names for *one*, *they*, and *we*; marked definitions; lexical information in definitions), syntax (e.g., short, propositional syntax, repetition, reinstatement), and length of text. Early studies of simplified written input have addressed its effects on reading comprehension (e.g., Blau, 1982; Davies, 1984; Doddis, 1985; Young, 1999) while more current studies have begun to address also its effects on the input-to-intake phenomenon in order to arrive at a clearer understanding of the relationship between the nature of the input L2 readers are exposed to and how such input is processed (e.g., Leow, 1993; Wong, 2003).

The lengths of simplified texts ranged from 147 words (compared to 236 in the original) to 517 words (compared to 530 in the original), and the topics and genres were varied. For intake, targeted forms in the input included Spanish present perfect and present subjunctive (Leow, 1993) and French past participle agreement (Wong, 2003). Time provided to L2 readers to read the experimental texts ranged from ten minutes to read a text of 517 words (simplified) or 530 (unsimplified) (Wong, 2003) to instructions to read at their own pace texts of 222 words (simplified) or 233 (unsimplified) (Leow, 1993).

The research designs employed to measure the effects of simplified written input on comprehension and L2 development were the following: for comprehension, exposure to either a simplified or unsimplified text followed by a comprehension task; for intake, the classic pre-test—exposure—post-test design with no study including a delayed post-test to measure for retention of intake of targeted items in the input. Post-tests employed to measure comprehension included written recalls (Wong, 2003; Young, 1999), cloze tests (Davies, 1984), and multiple choice questions (Blau, 1982; Young, 1999), while for intake, a multiple choice recognition task (Leow, 1993) and an error correction task (Wong, 2003) were used.

For comprehension, while a significant benefit was found for simplified written input in some studies (Davis, 1984; Wong, 2003), this benefit was not reported in other studies (Blau, 1982; Doddis, 1985; Young, 1999). No significant benefit was also reported in the two studies that addressed the relationship between simplified written input and intake (Leow, 1993; Wong, 2003).[3]

In sum, while there is inconclusive evidence for the role and effects of simplification on L2 comprehension, it appears that simplifying written input does not promote statistically superior intake of targeted linguistic forms in the input when compared to a control group exposed to unsimplified written input. There are several plausible explanations to account for these findings, which include (1) "the open-ended approach to what constitutes simplification" (Leow, 1997b, p. 294), (2) text type, (3) level of language experience, (4) length of experimental text, (5) number of items in the experimental texts, (6) amount of time allowed to read the text, (7) type of assessment task, and so on. However, these findings need to be viewed with caution, given that there is no reported empirical evidence that supports or refutes the premise that simplifying L2 input does indeed permit L2 readers to pay substantially more attention to targeted forms in the input when compared to L2 readers exposed to unsimplified input. From a methodological perspective, there is clearly a need to employ more robust research designs to establish that simplified input did indeed allow L2 readers to direct more of their attention to the targeted items in the input when compared to L2 readers exposed only to unsimplified input.

TEXTUAL INPUT ENHANCEMENT: THEORETICAL UNDERPINNING

Textual input enhancement (also known as written input enhancement, enhanced written input, or visual input enhancement) is one methodological manifestation of the term "input enhancement" first coined by Sharwood Smith (1991, 1993; see also Han & D'Angelo, this volume) to override his previous term "language consciousness-raising" (Sharwood Smith,

---

[3]Two studies (Greenslade, 2000; Leow, 1995) also reported similar findings in the aural mode, that is, aural simplification did not lead to statistically superior performance on either comprehension (Greenslade, 2000) or intake (Greenslade, 2000; Leow, 1995) when compared to an unsimplified group.

1981)—that is, the guidance teachers provide for promoting L2 learners' self discovery or consciousness of the formal features of the L2. According to Sharwood Smith, input enhancement can be defined from two perspectives, namely, an external perspective and an internal perspective. An external perspective views input enhancement as any pedagogical attempt (usually by a teacher) to make more salient specific features of L2 input in an effort to draw learners' attention to such enhanced features. An internal perspective views the L2 input as being enhanced by the learners' internal mechanism that makes salient specific features in the input, for example, paying attention to words at the beginning of a sentence. The major theoretical underpinning of either perspective is, without doubt, that learners need to pay attention to specific items in the input before such information can be taken in with the potential of being processed further into the learners' language system. Of less certainty is the role learner awareness plays in input enhancement, although Sharwood Smith (1991, 1993) appears to view awareness as playing a reduced role in input enhancement.

TEXTUAL INPUT ENHANCEMENT: EMPIRICAL STUDIES

Textual input enhancement involved types of typographical cues to enhance the saliency of targeted linguistic forms (usually one or two types) in the input. In this strand of research, many studies have visually modified or enhanced written input via the use of bolding, capitalizing, underlining, italicizing, different fonts and sizes, and so on (e.g., Alanen, 1995; Bowles, 2003; Izumi, 2002; Jourdenais, 1998; Jourdenais, Ota, Stauffer, Boyson, & Doughty, 1995; Leow, 1997c; Leow, Egi, Nuevo, & Tsai, 2003; Overstreet, 1998; Shook, 1994, 1999; White, J., 1998). These studies typically compared the performance of a group exposed to modified, enhanced input with that of an unenhanced group.[4]

Quite a large range of linguistic items has also been empirically investigated in studies of textual input enhancement. These include Span-

---

[4]Studies that have subsumed the variable enhancement (metalinguistic or visual) within some type of instruction, be it focus on form (e.g., Doughty & Varela, 1998; Leeman et al., 1995; Park, 2004) or processing instruction (e.g., VanPatten & Cadierno, 1993; Cheng, 2002; Morgan-Short & Wood Bowden, in press), are not included in this review, given that they have not methodologically teased out the independent variable of enhancement in their research designs.

ish imperatives (e.g., Bowles, 2003; Leow, 1997c, 2001b), imperfect and preterit forms (e.g., Jourdenais, 1998; Jourdenais et al., 1995; Overstreet, 1998), present perfect forms (e.g., Leow et al., 2003; Shook, 1994, 1999), relative pronouns (e.g., Shook, 1994, 1999), Finnish locative suffixes (e.g., Alanen, 1995), English possessive determiners (e.g., White, J., 1998), relative clauses (Izumi, 2002), and French past participle agreement (Wong, 2003). Different levels of language experience have also been explored, ranging from beginner learners (e.g., Alanen, 1995) of an L2 to intermediate levels (e.g., Bowles, 2003). Amount of exposure is also differential, ranging from less than an hour (e.g., Leow, 1997c) to over several days (e.g., White, J., 1998).

The typical research design comprised a pretest—exposure—post-test with very few studies including a delayed post-test in the design (e.g., Leow, 2001b, Leow et al., 2003). Post-tests typically were designed to measure learners' intake (e.g., recognition and error correction tasks), written production (e.g., picture-cued, sentence completion, sentence combination, narration, fill-in-the-blank), grammaticality judgment, and comprehension.

Several studies (e.g., Leow, 1997c) have reported significant gains for textual input enhancement from pre-test to post-test. However, when compared to a control group (unenhanced) on the post-tests, some studies have reported significant benefits for textual input enhancement on L2 intake and linguistic development (e.g., Jourdenais et al., 1995; Shook, 1994), while other studies appear to indicate no benefit on either comprehension (e.g., Leow, 1997c, 2001b; Shook, 1999; Wong, 2003), intake (e.g., Leow, 1997c, 2001b; Leow et al., 2003; Bowles, 2003), or L2 development (Alanen, 1995; Izumi, 2002; Jourdenais, 1999; Leow, 1997c, 2001b; Overstreet, 1998; White, J., 1998; Wong, 2003). Like the research on simplified written input, many of these studies have failed to operationalize and measure the process of attention before addressing the effect of textual input enhancement on L2 comprehension and L2 development.

In sum, it appears that enhancing written input does not promote statistically superior comprehension of text content, nor intake and written production of targeted linguistic forms in the input, when compared to a control group exposed to unenhanced input. Studies that have employed concurrent data elicitation procedures (e.g., think-aloud protocols[5]) will be

---

[5]See Leow and Morgan-Short (2004) and Bowles and Leow (2005) for empirical support for the use of think-aloud protocols as one kind of concurrent data elicitation procedure. In these studies, comparing a think-aloud and a non–think aloud group revealed no significant effect for the issue of reactivity—that is, the potential detrimental impact of thinking aloud while performing a task.

discussed in an effort to explicate the findings and gain a clearer under-standing of the processes involved while L2 readers read an enhanced L2 text.

GLOSSES: THEORETICAL UNDERPINNING

It is relatively difficult to find a clear theoretical underpinning of many stud-ies investigating the effects of glossing on L2 comprehension and vocabulary learning. Underpinnings appear to include a range of factors responsible for the so-called success of glossing. On the one hand, factors that are pro-vided to account for the positive effects of glosses include the use of glosses to limit dictionary consultation that may interrupt the L2 reading process (see, however, Horst, this volume) and the premise that marginal glosses are easier to use than a dictionary. On the other hand, brief references are made to several theoretical underpinnings that include consciousness-raising and input enhancement (Sharwood Smith, 1981, 1991, 1993) and the notion of form-to-meaning connection (e.g., Terrell, 1991). To date, only one study (Bowles, 2003) has been conducted within an attentional framework (for the noticing hypothesis, Schmidt, 1990, and elsewhere, see p. 85). In addi-tion, the study has also operationalized and measured the process of atten-tion before statistically submitting the data to address the effect of glossing on L2 learners' comprehension, intake, and production of targeted items in the modified input.

GLOSSES: EMPIRICAL STUDIES

Glosses are relatively similar to textual input enhancement but typically focus on a range of different items (e.g., verbs, nouns, etc.) in the input to facilitate primarily comprehension. They include the use of numerical superscripts attached to glossed items that are usually accompanied by an L1 or L2 gloss (either a direct L1 translation or an L2 elaboration) usually found to the right side of the text or below the text. In addition, computer-based studies (e.g., Al-Seghayer, 2001; Chun & Plass, 1996; Gettys, Imhof, & Kautz, 2001; Kost, Foss, & Lenzini, 1999; Nagata, 1999; Lomicka, 1998) also included additional experimental groups exposed not only to glosses but also glosses accompanied by images, references, pronuncia-tion, etc.

Texts, both authentic and non-authentic, were selected by researchers, and specific vocabulary items in the text were glossed in an effort to facilitate L2 learners' comprehension of the text content. Selection of glossed items appeared to be done from a researcher's perspective based on his/her perception that these words would be incomprehensible to the L2 readers. In addition, it was premised in some studies that accessing the glosses would somehow promote incidental learning or deeper processing of the glossed items (e.g., Nagata, 1999).

The typical research design employed to address the effects of glossing on comprehension usually included a post-exposure comprehension task while studies addressing vocabulary learning typically employed a pre-test—exposure—post-test with a few studies including a delayed post-test to measure retention of targeted items (e.g., Bowles, 2003). Only studies that have addressed a direct comparison between a glossed condition and an unglossed condition will be discussed.

In general, the studies indicate that for some studies glosses facilitated comprehension (e.g., Bowles, 2003; Davis, 1989; Jacobs, Dufon, & Hong, 1994), while for others (e.g., Johnson, P., 1982) providing glosses in a text may be detrimental to readers' global comprehension or glosses do not improve comprehension (de Ridder, 2002). While de Ridder (2002) reported no significant benefit found for glosses on vocabulary learning, other studies have reported such positive benefits for vocabulary learning (e.g., Bowles, 2003; Hulstijn, Hollander, & Greidanus, 1996; Lyman-Hager, Davis, Burnett, & Chennault, 1993; Watanabe, 1997) in that learners exposed to glossed texts demonstrated superior incidental vocabulary learning when compared to students who read an unglossed text. In addition, Jacobs, Dufon, and Hong (1994) reported that language proficiency may play a role in the effectiveness of glosses.

In sum, unlike the strands of simplified written input and textual input enhancement, current research comparing a glossed versus unglossed condition appears to support the notion that glosses overall promote L2 comprehension and vocabulary learning when compared to L2 readers exposed to unglossed texts. However, these findings need to be viewed with some caution given the paucity of empirical research on the effects of glosses when compared to the absence of such glosses and several internal validity limitations of the current literature, including the inadequate operationalization and measurement of attention/noticing of glossed items in the input. In addition, there is also a need to explore in more detail potential differences in text type, language proficiency level, and measures of comprehension used.

METHODOLOGICAL ISSUES: INTERNAL VALIDITY

As reported, the premise that textual modifications would draw L2 readers' attention to targeted items in the modified input did not appear to be supported by the findings of a majority of studies that purported to have addressed the effects of textual modification on L2 comprehension, intake, and L2 development. While these findings appear to be somewhat contradictory, they may be due, from a methodological viewpoint, to one major internal validity limitation of many of these studies—the failure to operationalize and measure the process of attention on which the notion of textual modification is unarguably based; in other words, concurrent data that established that attention was indeed paid to the textually modified content or forms in the input before any statistical analyses were conducted to address its effect were not gathered as part of the research design (cf. Leow, 1999b for a critical overview of studies premised on the role of attention in L2 development).

Instead, many studies employed post-exposure tasks and assumed that textually modified input would draw substantially more attention to the targeted forms or structures in the input, especially when compared to learners not exposed to such modifications. Such assumptions were then used to interpret and discuss the findings of the studies. For example, by employing the classic pre-test—exposure—post-test research design with no concurrent data gathered while L2 readers were interacting with the L2 input, it is relatively easy to assume that, when compared to a control group exposed only to unmodified L2 input, readers paid attention to the textually modified content or items in the L2 input, processed the targeted items for further retention, and would perform substantially better on the post-test designed to measure comprehension, intake, or written production. However, given that no concurrent or online data were gathered while learners were exposed to the L2 input to establish that learners did indeed pay attention to the textually modified forms in the input, the findings of studies addressing the effects of textually modified input on L2 readers' comprehension, intake, and vocabulary learning need to be taken with considerable caution.

In an effort to understand better the processes L2 readers employ while exposed to modified L2 input, it may be instructive in the next section to review what studies that have employed concurrent data elicitation procedures (e.g., think-aloud protocols) have revealed in regard to *what* learners do while processing modified L2 input.

STUDIES EMPLOYING CONCURRENT DATA ELICITATION PROCEDURES

Only four studies to date (Bowles, 2003 in the textual input enhancement strand; Bowles, 2004 in the gloss strand; Leow, 2001b; Leow et al., 2003) have employed concurrent data elicitation procedures (think-aloud protocols or verbal reports) to establish learner attention to textually modified or unmodified items in the input. Three other studies (Alanen, 1995; Izumi, 2002; Lomicka, 1998) also employed some form of concurrent data elicitation procedures, for example, a conflation of think alouds and other assessment measures (Alanen, 1995), note-taking (Izumi, 2002), and metalinguistic verbal reports to categorize the data into clauses as the basic unit of analysis (Lomicka, 1998). Attentional data were typically elicited via the use of nonmetalinguistic think-aloud protocols; that is, learners were requested to think aloud without providing any metalinguistic explanation on their thoughts while interacting with the L2 input. The data elicited from the think-aloud protocols of the three studies in the textual input enhancement strand revealed that reported noticing of targeted forms in the input was statistically similar in the textually enhanced and unenhanced conditions, which may provide convincing evidence to support similar results in the majority of studies investigating the effects of textually modified input on L2 comprehension and development. In the gloss strand, Bowles (2004) revealed that readers exposed to a glossed text reported noticing targeted words significantly more than readers exposed to the same text without glosses, results that appear to support the overall positive benefits of glossing on comprehension, L2 intake and written production.

In addition, these concurrent data in both strands of research also revealed that learners did not necessarily attempt to process modified or targeted items in the input for linguistic information but simply to extract semantic information from the targeted forms. This is not surprising given that instructions provided to learners in these studies typically requested that they read or listened to the L2 input for information and, in a few cases, paid attention to the grammatical items in the input (e.g., Shook, 1994). The richness of qualitative data gathered from think-aloud protocols is clearly superior to data gathered after exposure (cf. Leow, 2000 for further elaboration of the merits of the use of both quantitative and qualitative analyses in SLA research).

TEXTUAL MODIFICATION: THE ROLE OF AWARENESS

To date, there is no study that has empirically addressed whether awareness plays a role in textual modification, be it simplified written input, textual input enhancement, or glossing, in promoting superior comprehension, intake, and L2 development. This lack of empirical investigation is not surprising in the simplified written input strand given that (a) the theoretical underpinning of this strand was only premised on the role of attention in regard to learner limited attentional capacity, (b) early studies on simplified written input only focused on comprehension while the more current studies only began to include its effects on intake and learning, and (c) the process of attention has not been methodologically operationalized or measured in these studies. In the textual input enhancement strand, the role of awareness is of theoretical interest, given the original premise of input enhancement (Sharwood Smith, 1991, 1993) that was derived from the notion of language consciousness-raising (Sharwood Smith, 1981). In the gloss strand, the underlying premise that glosses not only draw readers' attention to but also promote further processing of glossed items into intake and even subsequent written production is usually perceived as a form of implicit learning, that is, without any awareness on the part of the L2 reader. Clearly, to conduct such research, the use of concurrent data elicitation procedures such as think-aloud protocols will be required. Once again, it may be informative to review what studies that have employed such elicitation procedures have revealed in the protocols in regard to learners' awareness while processing modified L2 input.

Leow (2001b) was the first empirical SLA study on textual input enhancement to employ both concurrent (during exposure) and offline data collection procedures to establish that participants noticed (attention plus minimally a low level of awareness) targeted forms in the L2 input. These data were used in conjunction with scores from immediate and delayed recognition and production tasks to determine whether textual input enhancement had significant benefits over unenhanced input. His participants were

38 first-semester college learners of Spanish with no formal previous expo-sure to the targeted form, the Spanish formal imperative. Students were randomly assigned to either the enhanced or unenhanced group and all groups were given a packet with the corresponding text to read in addition to three identical post-exposure assessment tasks (a fill-in-the-blank writ-ten production task, a recognition task, and a comprehension task). They were requested to think aloud while reading the passage and completing the assessment tasks. The think-aloud protocols, then, provided concurrent (during exposure) information about learners' reported noticing of the tar-geted L2 form. Three weeks later, participants completed a delayed post-test comprising the immediate post-test with the exception of the comprehension task. The data were then analyzed using both quantitative and qualitative techniques (the think-aloud protocols were coded for instances of noticing, which followed Schmidt's noticing hypothesis—attention plus a low level of awareness). Leow reported that no significant benefit was found for input enhancement either for (1) amount of reported noticing, (2) comprehension, or (3) intake.

While the results of this study may lay claim to the role of awareness in textual input enhancement, of even greater interest regarding this issue were the findings reported regarding the performances of the two high performers in both textually modified/enhanced and textually unmodified/unenhanced conditions. Both of these participants were coded as demonstrating a level of meta-awareness (cf. Leow, 1997a, 2001a for a definition of different lev-els of awareness in SLA) that included conceptually driven processing usu-ally associated with the more sophisticated cognitive processes of hypothesis testing, metalinguistic description of the targeted forms, and rule formation (awareness at the level of understanding) (cf. Leow 1997a; Rosa & Leow, 2004a; Rosa & O'Neill, 1999).

Interestingly, Leow concluded that the role of level of awareness and not necessarily textual input enhancement might have been responsible for the differential results found between these two participants and the others in the study. According to Leow, "noticing in discourse, then, may not neces-sarily contribute to a more profound processing of grammatical information, that is, beyond intake, unless accompanied minimally by a level of meta-awareness" (p. 505). This statement is further supported by the findings that more than 55 percent of the participants in both textually enhanced and unenhanced conditions scored zero on the written production task while 85 percent and more scored two or less out of a total of 17 items.

Similar conclusions are reached by Bowles (2004) in the gloss strand. She postulated that first, participants are less likely to use strategies like hypothesis testing with vocabulary words (see, however, Horst, this volume) than with syntactic or morphological structures, as found in other studies (e.g. Leow, 1997a, 1998b; Rosa & Leow, 2004; Rosa & O'Neill, 1999). Second, glosses like the ones in her study provided the L2 reader with all the information that was immediately necessary (the meaning of the word), and hence, they might have been viewed as a mere aid to comprehension. Consequently, the readers were not pushed to process the word with a higher level of awareness in order to continue reading and understanding the text, thereby noticing the glossed item with only a low level of awareness. Taken together, the perceived belief that enhanced, modified input, when compared to unenhanced, unmodified input, may significantly draw learners' attention to more salient forms in the input, may need to be re-examined.

Bowles (2003) replicated Leow (2001b) at the intermediate level and, while she found similar results like the original study (that is, no significant effect of textual input enhancement), she also reported that online data further revealed that more participants in the textually enhanced group made meta-linguistic comments about targeted forms than did participants in the unenhanced group (71 percent of participants in the enhanced group vs. 38 percent of participants in the unenhanced group). She concluded that in this study, textual input enhancement promoted meta-linguistic comment more than did textually unmodified input.

Given the central role of attention in the empirical strand of textual modifications and the potential role awareness may play in this strand of research, this chapter situated textual modification within an attentional framework from both an attention and awareness perspective, and discussed some of the methodological issues associated with this strand of research in pedagogical SLA literature.

This chapter has also provided an overview of studies that have isolated the variable textual modification in an effort to address its potential effects on L2 comprehension, intake, and learning. The overall results of the three strands of research reviewed indicate that while there is not much robust empirical support for the use of modifications such as simplified written input and textual input enhancement when compared to a control condition, glosses appear to promote L2 comprehension, intake, and written production. Studies employing concurrent data elicitation procedures such as think alouds have provided data that indicate that (1) the non-significant difference in performance found in many studies may be due to a similar amount of reported noticing of the textually modified forms in the input and (2) learners exposed to textually modified input may be processing such data with a low level of awareness, which may not necessarily contribute to a more profound processing of grammatical information, that is, beyond intake.

It has also been pointed out that many of the studies on the effects of textual modification in SLA suffer from one major internal validity limitation, namely that before statistically measuring its effects, they have not established methodologically that learner attention to the textually modified items in the input was indeed paid.

PEDAGOGICAL IMPLICATIONS

Teachers need to keep in mind that it may be "the learners' existing language system that defines what in the input is taken in and not any external manipulation of the input" (Leow, 1993, p. 342; Sharwood Smith, 1991).

Teachers also need to recognize the crucial role attention (and awareness) plays in subsequent processing of the L2 input that contributes to L2 development (Leow, 2001b). Any externally manipulated input should be carefully designed to promote readers' noticing of targeted linguistic items in the text. Ideally, a higher level of awareness promoted should lead to more learning (Leow, 1999a; 2001b). For example, prior to reading an L2 text with specific linguistic forms to which the teacher would like learners to pay attention, a series of questions that include such forms can be prepared and learners requested to scan for the specific information in the L2 text. What is being promoted in this activity is requiring learners to process not only the propositional content of the L2 texts but also to pay attention to the targeted forms in the input in order to provide a contextual answer. Using the targeted form several times in the responses may then lead to some hypothesis testing that can be confirmed or rejected when feedback is provided by the teacher regarding the accuracy of the response.

Reflection Questions

Reflection Questions

1. Why do you think glosses appear to promote both superior comprehension and learning but the same does not appear to hold true for textual enhancement and simplified input on L2 development?

2. Discuss the following variables (amount of exposure to the linguistic item, text length, language level, type of linguistic form, experimental instructions) in relation to the results reported in the empirical literature on textual enhancement and simplified input. Do you think that all or some or none of these variables played a role in the results reported in the studies? Why or why not?

3. What role do you think awareness plays in textual modification? Do you think that some effort should be made to raise readers' awareness of linguistic items in the text before or during the reading process or that no effort should be made?

PART 2

Instruction

CHAPTER 5

Effective Reading Instruction for English Language Learners

David Freeman and Yvonne Freeman,
University of Texas at Brownsville

Reading is the key to academic success for all students. Proficient readers can construct meaning from a variety of texts. In general, students who read extensively also write well. By reading and writing different genres, students develop the academic language proficiency that is valued in school. The importance of developing reading proficiency is the theme throughout this book.

All teachers want to help their students develop high levels of reading proficiency. Teachers of English language learners often face a challenge in helping their L2 learners become good readers. Reading texts in English can be difficult, especially for students who have not developed age-appropriate levels of literacy in their first language. Teachers also face pressures of standardized tests. In many cases, students are expected to reach grade-level norms in reading in one year, a nearly impossible task for a student who is learning English and learning how to read (cf. Cobb, this volume).

Under these conditions, it is essential that teachers choose the best approach to teaching reading to ELLs. This chapter discusses the importance of teaching reading in a student's primary language when possible. Two views of reading are explained: a word identification view and a socio-psycholinguistic view. Each view is illustrated with a scenario from a classroom with ELLs, and each scenario is analyzed to show how it reflects the view of reading the teacher holds and the research that supports that view. The socio-psycholinguistic view of reading is the best approach for teaching all English learners to read.

TEACHING READING IN A STUDENT'S PRIMARY LANGUAGE

Most younger ELLs enter school speaking a language other than English. These students need to learn how to read and they need to learn English. Older recent arrivals with limited formal schooling often enter school in intermediate or secondary grades with little or no first language literacy. For example, Hmong students from camps in Thailand, Somalis, and children from Serbia or El Salvador may have had limited access to schooling in their native countries. These older students face many obstacles. Some have almost no idea how schools in English-speaking countries work. They have never stored their books in a locker, worked in cooperative groups, or eaten in a school cafeteria.

In addition, these students may not know how to read or their reading ability may be significantly below grade level. An eighth grader from Oaxaca, for instance, may speak Mixteco as his first language, speak some Spanish, and read in Spanish at a second-grade level. For both the younger students from homes where English is not the language of communication and older students with limited formal schooling, the best approach is to teach them to read and write in their native language at the same time that they are learning oral and written English (Rolstad, Mahoney, & Glass, 2005; Thomas & Collier, 2001). Although primary language literacy instruction is not always possible due to the lack of bilingual teachers or appropriate materials, there are a number of reasons that schools should make every effort to provide English language learners with literacy instruction in their primary language when possible.

English language learners often struggle in learning to read in English simply because they do not understand the language of instruction. However, when reading is taught in their first language, the instruction is comprehensible. Teachers who provide primary language literacy build on the language strengths students bring to school. In addition, first language instruction affirms students' social and cultural identities. It sends the clear message that the home language and culture are valuable learning resources. Parents can also support literacy instruction that is provided in the language they speak at home. They can read books to their children and discuss the books children bring home to read, thus extending students' understanding of texts. For all these reasons, students who have access to primary language literacy instruction learn to read more easily than children who are taught to read in English, a language they do not speak.

Time spent teaching a child to read in the primary language is not wasted. Once a child can read in any language, the skills transfer to reading in an additional language. Cummins (1981, 2000) provides ample evidence for the existence of a common underlying proficiency between two languages. What an individual knows in one language can be accessed through a second language given an adequate proficiency in the L2. Further, studies of dual language education programs in which children fully develop their first language proficiency (Collier, 1995; Collier & Thomas, 2004; Lindholm-Leary 2001; Thomas & Collier, 2002) provide strong evidence of increased academic success as measured by scores of norm-referenced reading tests in English. Even though students in dual language programs spend less time learning in English, they score higher on tests given in English because they are able to transfer the knowledge and skills developed through primary language study to reading in English.

Students who read in their primary language have several strengths when learning to read in English: They know that reading is a process of constructing meaning. As they read, they subconsciously use cues from the linguistic cueing systems. They also apply the same psychological strategies as when they read in their first language. They understand how different texts are organized. For example, a story will have a beginning, middle, and end while an informational text may compare and contrast or present ideas and examples. In addition, they understand features of informational texts. They know how to read charts and maps, a table of contents, and an index. All this knowledge can be applied to reading in English.

Despite the benefits of primary language literacy instruction, most ELLs receive initial literacy instruction in English. As a result, the view of reading that guides the instructional choices teachers make determines to a great extent the likelihood of their developing adequate reading proficiency in English. Scenarios from two classrooms are presented, one in which the teacher takes a word identification view of reading as she teaches her English language learners and one in which the teacher bases his methods on a socio-psycholinguistic view. A brief analysis of the approach to teaching ELLs follows.

Ms. GALLEGOS' READING LESSON

Ms. Gallegos is an experienced teacher. Some of the students in her first grade class are native English speakers while others came to school speaking only Spanish. The school where Ms. Gallegos teaches does not provide primary language literacy instruction. In fact, although Ms. Gallegos speaks Spanish, she teaches only in English, in part due to her state's English-only laws. Ms. Gallegos' school received a Reading First grant, and all the teachers have been given training in research-based methods of teaching reading. During the 90-minute reading block, she includes exercises in phonemic awareness, phonics, and fluency along with vocabulary development. Later in the year she will add some lessons that help develop comprehension. Let's look at a reading lesson as Ms. Gallegos teaches her students in early October.

She begins by calling the children to the rug in the front of the room so that she can be close to the children as they work on phonemic awareness exercises. She has a list of words she wants to work on with them. She says the first word, *sad*. As she says the word, she elongates each sound. Then she asks, "How many sounds did you hear in *sad*? One of the children answers, "Three."

"Good answer!" responds Ms. Gallegos. She then has the students repeat the three sounds. As they do this, they hold up their fingers to show each sound, *s.a.d*. The lesson continues with other words. Some of these are actually nonsense words, like *tig*. The goal of this part of the lesson is to help students develop phonemic awareness, the ability to recognize and manipulate the sounds in words. After the students have completed segmenting all the words, their teacher moves on to the next phase of her lesson.

She introduces the story for the week. This is a limited text decodable book designed to help students learn the short *a* sound. The story is about a young boy named Dan who is having a bad day and is sad. Many of the words contain the target short *a* sound. Ms. Gallegos has propped a Big Book version of the story on her easel. All the students can easily see the enlarged type. As she reads the story to the class, Ms. Gallegos emphasizes the words with short *a*, such as the name of the main character, Dan.

Next, students return to their desks to complete a worksheet that contains a list of words and nonwords. Students are directed to find all the words that have a short *a* sound and circle those words. Since her ELLs often have difficulty with exercises like this, Ms. Gallegos has them work in pairs with a native English speaker. The English speaker points to the words with short *a* sounds, and the native Spanish speaker circles them. When students finish their worksheets, they draw lines from words to pictures. This exercise is designed to help them develop their vocabulary. In addition, some of the students who need extra practice with phonics, especially the ELLs, work to complete phonics exercises using the classroom computer program.

As her students engage in these activities, Ms. Gallegos calls individual students to her desk. She gives each student a passage to read. The text contains words with sounds she has taught along with some sight words the students have practiced. Each student reads the passage aloud as rapidly and accurately as possible. Ms. Gallegos times each reading and also marks any errors. This gives her a fluency score that she posts on the student's chart. Students who improve their fluency scores are very proud of their progress, and all of Ms. Gallegos' students work hard to read faster and more accurately. The teacher checks four or five students each day so that she can listen to each student during the week.

When she finishes with the fluency work, Ms. Gallegos calls the students to the rug again to reread the weekly story. This time she reads the story one line at a time, and the students repeat each line after her. After they have read the story, Ms. Gallegos goes back to the beginning. She points to the sight words on each page that the class has studied. These are high-frequency words that do not follow regular phonics patterns such as *of, the,* and *one.* The teacher calls on individual students to identify the words she points to. She also introduces two new sight words that appear in the story, *said* and *have.* She gives the students the correct pronunciation of each word and has the class repeat the words after her.

To conclude the 90-minute reading period, Ms. Gallegos asks the students to read the story with her. As they read, she tracks the words with a pointer. She knows that choral reading like this supports her English language learners. The class reads the short story quite easily with the teacher's help. Then they return to their seats and prepare for math instruction.

ANALYSIS OF MS. GALLEGOS' READING LESSON

A careful examination of Ms. Gallegos reading lesson reveals that she holds a word recognition view of reading. All the activities are designed to help students learn to recognize words by either decoding them using their phonics skills or identifying them as known sight words. The exercises in phonemic awareness and phonics build the needed decoding skills, and the work on sight words increases the number of words students can identify as wholes. In addition, students work to improve their fluency. The fluency scores measure students' ability to recognize and pronounce words rapidly and accurately. The part of the lesson during which students drew lines from words to pictures was designed to increase their vocabulary. Ms. Gallegos supported her ELLs by pairing them with native speakers as they found words with the short *a* sound. She also engaged them in choral reading. In addition, she made sure her English language learners had extra time to practice phonics lessons on the computer.

The word recognition view of reading is based on the belief that reading is a process of converting written language into oral language by either decoding written words using phonics skills or identifying written words as known sight words. Once students have changed a written word into its oral form, they recognize the word and comprehend its meaning. By combining the meanings of individual words, students build up a meaning for each text.

This view of reading grows out of the work of a number of researchers. Stanovich (1998) summarized his own studies of the importance of phonemic awareness and studies on eye movement to conclude that there was a "grand synthesis" (p. 44). He claimed that readers see and process every word on a page. Good readers use word recognition skills to identify words accurately and rapidly. Good readers are less dependent on context because they have better word recognition skills than poor readers. Good instruction, then, equips students with the skills needed to decode words or to identify them as wholes. Decoding is facilitated through phonemic awareness and phonics skills. Practice in fluency helps students build the capacity for rapid and automatic word recognition.

An approach to teaching beginning reading that focuses on phonemic awareness, phonics, and fluency poses certain problems for English language learners. Phonemic awareness is the understanding that words are made up of individual sounds or phonemes. Students with phonemic awareness can determine the number of phonemes in a word, they can segment words into their phonemes, they can add or delete phonemes, and they can blend phonemes to form a word. Students engage in exercises to develop these oral language skills. Ms. Gallegos had her students break words like *sad* or nonsense words like *tig* into their component parts.

For ELLs, lessons like these are more difficult than they are for native English speakers. English learners are still acquiring English phonology. The differences between the phonology of their first language and the sounds of English may make exercises in phonemic awareness difficult for students acquiring English. For example, English has two phonemes /d/ and /ð/. These two sounds make a difference in meaning in words like *den* and *then*. However, in Spanish these two sounds are allophones of one phoneme. In a word like *dedo* the first *d* is pronounced like the English *d* and the second like the English *th* in *then*. In addition, the Spanish vowels do not match with the English vowels. For example, the Spanish /i/ falls between the English sounds in words like *beet* and *bit*. This lack of correspondence between English and Spanish makes phonemic awareness exercises and tests difficult for Spanish speakers acquiring English.

Phonics exercises are also difficult for students acquiring English. Phonics rules attempt to capture regular correspondences between sounds and spellings. They are based on the assumption that speakers pronounce words conventionally. However, many L2 students pronounce words in ways that reflect their native language, and, as a result, the phonics rules do not always work for them. Learning the rules is further complicated if the teacher speaks a regional variety of English. Even when they are successful in decoding words and changing the written language to oral language, L2 learners may not recognize the word because it is not yet in their oral English vocabulary. Further, both phonemic awareness and phonics exercises and tests often include nonsense words like *tig*. English language learners may not know whether the words are made up or if they are actual English words they have not yet acquired.

Because English language learners struggle with phonemic awareness and phonics, they are often given additional practice in these areas. Phonemic awareness and phonics are seen as two of the basic pillars needed to learn to recognize words. The idea of giving struggling students additional practice in these skills seems logical. However, the exercises are quite abstract and decontextualized. Students focus on sounds or words in isolation. Little attention is paid to comprehension. In contrast, effective instruction for English language learners involves embedding language in a rich context with a focus on meaning. Good ESL teachers use a number of techniques, such a showing pictures or bringing in real objects, to make instruction comprehensible. Exercises in phonemic awareness and phonics, especially when they include nonsense words, are difficult for ELLs because little or no contextual support is provided and the focus is not on meaningful communication.

Practice in increasing reading fluency is also problematic for ELLs. Often, these students have difficulty in achieving high fluency scores because they mispronounce words, and fluency scores are based on speed and accuracy. In addition, the emphasis on reading rapidly sends the wrong message. Instead of slowing down and trying to make sense of a difficult text, an L2 learner is encouraged to pronounce the words as quickly as possible. As a result, some students develop the idea that reading is a process of saying words aloud rapidly. As English learners move up the grades, they are expected to understand what they read. This early practice with fluency does not prepare them to comprehend. Proficient readers can read rapidly, but they also know that they have to adjust their speed depending on the text they are reading (Flurkey, 1997). Simply reading faster does not lead to better comprehension. All too often, ELLs in classes like Ms. Gallegos's that emphasize phonemic awareness, phonics, and fluency encounter great difficulties as they move into the intermediate and secondary grades where they are expected to understand and apply what they read (Cummins, 2000; Fitzgerald, 1993, 1995). While some teachers, such as Ms. Gallegos, follow a word recognition view of reading, other teachers take a socio-psycholinguistic view.

MR. ROBERTS' READING LESSON

Mr. Roberts also teaches first grade. His class has native English speakers and ELLs whose native languages include Spanish, Farsi, and Punjabi. Mr. Roberts does not speak any of these languages, but he has found ways to support the first languages and cultures of his students. He uses culturally relevant books (Freeman, Freeman & Freeman, 2003), including some bilingual books, he often pairs a native English speaker with an English language learner as they work on projects (Freeman, Freeman, & Mercuri, 2005), and he organizes his curriculum around themes that connect to the backgrounds of his students (Freeman & Freeman, 1998). For example, he started the year with an extended theme on immigration during which students investigated big questions such as, "Why do immigrants come to a new country?" and "What contributions have immigrants made to our country?"

Mr. Roberts has organized his day to include both readers and writers workshops. During the reading workshop he includes read-alouds, shared reading, guided reading, and independent reading. The workshop structure allows him to differentiate instruction and provide the extra support his ELLs need. He begins by doing much of the reading for them through read-alouds and shared reading and then gradually releases the responsibility for reading to his students. He always keeps the focus on constructing meaning from texts. Let's look at a lesson Mr. Roberts teaches in late September.

He begins his readers workshop time by calling the children to the rug in the front of the room. Mr. Roberts sits on his chair to read *Marianthe's Story: Painted Words* (Aliki, 1998). The children enjoy the daily read-alouds because Mr. Roberts reads very expressively. As he reads, he stops the reading at different points in the story. He asks students to turn and talk with a partner about what they think about the story. In *Painted Words,* the little girl, Marianthe, doesn't speak English and doesn't talk at all, but she paints her experiences of coming to America. Mr. Roberts asks the class to discuss why they think she doesn't talk, what they think happened to her, and why her family came to the United States. He writes their ideas on the board. Talking in pairs and writing down key ideas help his ELLs understand the story.

Next, Mr. Roberts puts a color transparency of the cover of *Something from Nothing* (Gilman, 1992) on the overhead projector. He asks the students to predict what this story might be about. As the students call out answers, Mr. Roberts writes them on butcher paper so everyone can see. As the students predict, Mr. Roberts asks them to explain why they made this prediction. Students use the title and the picture to tell him the story is about a boy and his grandfather. They guess that the grandfather might sew something with the blue cloth he has in his hand. They also comment on the hats that the grandfather and boy are wearing. Mr. Roberts asks, "What does this make you think about these characters?"

Juan answers, "Maybe they are from another country because people here don't usually wear hats like that."

"That's a good inference, Juan," replies Mr. Roberts. "We don't usually see people dress like this, so maybe the story is about people from a different country."

Mr. Roberts begins to read this predictable story from transparencies he has made. It tells of a young boy, Joseph, who has a favorite blanket. Mr. Roberts pauses to ask, "Do any of you have a favorite blanket or toy you like to have with you?" Several of the students remember how they had a blanket or toy that helped them go to sleep when they were younger. "Do you remember a story we read about a boy with a favorite toy he needed to help him sleep at night?" asks Mr. Roberts. Derrick recalls a story about a boy with a teddy bear. "That's right," says Mr. Roberts. That story was called *Ira Sleeps Over* (Waber, 1972).

Mr. Roberts continues to read. As Joseph's blanket gets older, his mother urges him to throw it out. Joseph answers, "Grandpa can fix it," and he takes the blanket to his grandfather, who looks at it carefully and says, "There's just enough material here to make . . ." Mr. Roberts stops and asks students to guess what the grandfather will make from the blanket. He records the students' answers. Then he turns the page to finish the sentence ". . . a wonderful jacket." When the jacket gets old and his mother wants him to throw it out, Joseph takes it to his grandfather again, and once more the grandfather creates something new from the cloth.

The pattern of the story is predictable and easy to follow. After a few pages, the children chime in on the repeated section, "Joseph's grandfather took the ___ and turned it round and round. "Hmmm," he said as his scissors went snip, snip, snip, and his needle flew in and out and in and out, 'There's just enough material here to make . . .' " As he reads these parts, Mr. Roberts uses hand motions to show students how the grandfather turns the cloth "round and round," how he rubs his chin as he says "Hmm," how the scissors go "snip, snip, snip," and how the needle flies "in and out and in and out." The children quickly begin to imitate these actions as they repeat the lines.

Each time the grandfather examines the cloth, Mr. Roberts stops and asks the students to predict what he will make next. The students are surprised when he makes Joseph a vest and a tie, but Mr. Roberts reminds them that people in other countries dress differently than they do. He asks his L2 learners to tell something about the clothes people wear in their country.

After the shared reading time, Mr. Roberts asks students to look at the chart and find out what their group will do at centers. The chart has a symbol for each group followed by a series of pictures showing what they will do today. While Mr. Roberts works with one group on guided reading, the other groups will listen to a taped story on headphones at the listening center, read an interactive story on the class computers, complete an art project in response to a story they read yesterday, or practice a readers theatre version of *Something from Nothing* with the help of a parent volunteer. During the week, the groups rotate through the centers, and Mr. Roberts has time to work with each small group on guided reading.

During the guided reading time the students reread a familiar short text. Then Mr. Roberts works with them on a new story chosen to match the group's instructional level. Mr. Roberts assists the students in reading the story and uses the story to teach a short skills lesson. Guided reading allows Mr. Roberts to adjust his instruction to the different levels of his students. He often groups his ELLs together for this time so that he can work specifically with them on the reading skills they need to develop. He makes sure to teach these skills in the context of real books.

Following the centers time, all the students find a book they can read for independent reading. Mr. Roberts has put out many books related to the immigrant theme. The books are in tubs of different colors. He has worked with the students to help them make good book choices during independent reading. They know that the different colors signal different levels of text. The ELLs are encouraged to choose more limited text books with greater picture support. Even though this is independent reading time, some of the students read together quietly. At this point in the year, Mr. Roberts' first graders can read for about twenty minutes. His goal is for them to engage in productive silent reading for a half hour each day, but he knows that it will take time to build the capacity for independent reading so he has started with a shorter time period and plans to increase it gradually.

To end the reading workshop, Mr. Roberts calls the students back to the rug. Five of the students report on what they read during their independent reading. He also asks them to predict what will happen next in their book. During the week, all the students will be given time to report. Mr. Roberts reminds the students that good readers always make predictions as they read and then check to see if their predictions turn out to be good ones. He ends reading workshop time by complimenting his students on the good work they have done this morning.

ANALYSIS OF MR. ROBERTS' READING LESSON

The socio-psycholinguistic view of reading is clearly reflected in Mr. Roberts' lesson. This view holds that reading is a process of constructing meaning from text. Readers use background knowledge and linguistic cues from the graphophonic, syntactic, and semantic systems as they read. The process includes sampling the text, predicting and inferring, confirming or disconfirming predictions, and integrating the new information with previous ideas.

The socio-psycholinguistic theory is neither "top down" nor "bottom up." It is a dual approach similar to the one described by Han and D'Angelo (this volume). All three cueing systems are important. Beginning readers tend to rely more heavily on the graphophonic system while more proficient readers make greater use of the syntactic and semantic cue systems as a source for predicting, inferring, and confirming (Kucer & Tuten, 2003).

Mr. Roberts begins the workshop time by reading a relevant book to his students. He chooses a book related to the theme the students have been studying. Because they have read and discussed several books related to this theme, his students have built background knowledge about immigrants. In addition, many of the ELLs in Mr. Roberts' class are immigrants or children of immigrants, so they have personal experiences they can connect to the immigrant story.

As he reads aloud, Mr. Roberts changes his voice for different characters. He reads expressively so that his students can enjoy the story. Then he has students talk about the story with a partner. This allows ELLs to clarify their understanding of the story. The pairs report back, and the teacher writes their comments on the board. This provides a good summary for his ELLs. Students stay focused on constructing meaning as Mr. Roberts reads. During the read-aloud, Mr. Roberts does all the work of reading, but as the workshop progresses, students take on increased responsibility. In this way, Mr. Roberts scaffolds his instruction to provide the support his ELLs need.

Next, the teacher moves to shared reading. Since he does not have an enlarged version of the text, Mr. Roberts has made transparencies so all the students can see the pictures and the words as he reads. This helps his beginning readers match his voice to the words in the text. Students chime in on the repeated sections of the book. Their understanding is enhanced by the hand motions they use to represent the different actions of the grandfather. In addition, Mr. Roberts uses this book to help students learn to predict and confirm or disconfirm their predictions. Later, during the guided reading time, he involves the small group in making predictions to refine this strategy.

On other days, Mr. Roberts teaches mini-lessons on other aspects of reading. For example, he places Post-its® over some of the words in another predictable book, and as he reads the book aloud, he asks students to predict what word was covered up. Then he slides the Post-it® over to reveal the first letter and asks his students whether their prediction is still a good one. This helps students focus on graphic clues. At one of the centers students complete a cloze activity. They work in pairs to fill in the blanks in a story. Mr. Roberts had deleted the adjectives that preceded nouns from this text. Later, students compare their version with the original and discuss whether they used good descriptive words in their version of the story. This helps his students build vocabulary and also build their knowledge of English syntax. All these activities are designed to help students construct meaning as they read by using linguistic cues and psychological strategies. In each case, Mr. Roberts teaches skills in the context of complete texts so that all the linguistic cues are available. This added context is especially helpful for his ELLs.

Those who hold a socio-psycholinguistic view of reading argue that reading is a universal process (Goodman, K., 1984). All readers use back-

ground knowledge and psychological strategies such as predicting and inferring as they read. They also use their knowledge of graphophonics, syntax,
and semantics. Although there are differences in the order of words and
the sound-letter correspondences, the process of constructing meaning from
text is the same for readers of any language.

Research support for the socio-psycholinguistic view comes from
studies using miscue analysis (Goodman, Y., Watson, & Burke, 1987). Miscue studies have been conducted in a number of languages, including non-
Roman alphabet languages such as Hebrew and non-alphabetic languages
like Chinese and Japanese. Careful analysis of readers' miscues reveal that
all readers rely on linguistic cues from the text and engage in psychological
strategies as they read. In addition, the social context of the reading helps
shape how readers make sense of text.

Although Stanovich (1998) cited eye movement studies to support his
claim that good readers automatically recognize words as they read (see also
Pulido, this volume; Shiotsu, this volume) and that context is not important
for initial recognition since readers see and process every word, a careful
review of studies conducted over the past 100 years shows clearly that readers do not see every word. Instead, they sample text (Paulson & Freeman,
2003). Readers fixate on about two-thirds of the words in a text, and it is
only when a word is fixated that information is sent to the brain. Studies
combining miscue analysis and eye movement suggest that readers use the
redundant linguistic cues that languages provide along with strategies such
as predicting and inferring to make sense of the limited visual input they
receive as they read (Paulson, 2005, 2002; Paulson, Flurkey, Goodman, &
Goodman, 2003).

This evidence, based on careful analysis of children and adults reading texts in different languages, supports the claim that written language,
like oral language, is acquired when readers receive comprehensible written
input. Mr. Roberts and other teachers who hold a socio-psycholinguistic
view of reading plan their instruction to provide the written input their
students need. They make the input comprehensible by scaffolding instruction and gradually releasing the responsibility of reading independently to
their students. They use read-alouds, shared reading, and guided reading to
prepare students to read on their own. At the same time, they teach mini-
lessons designed to strengthen students' use of background knowledge,
linguistic cueing systems, and psychological strategies as they read. They
provide a rich context for reading and keep students focused on making
sense of texts.

All students need to become proficient readers in order to succeed in school. Students who learn to read in their first language can transfer the knowledge and skills they develop to reading in a second language. However, many ELLs receive initial reading instruction in English. These students face a real challenge in learning to read in a language they are still learning to speak and understand. It is crucial for teachers of ELLs to use the most effective methods for teaching their students to read.

One set of methods is based on the view that reading is a process of converting written language to oral language. Good readers decode words automatically and rapidly (cf. Pulido, this volume; Shiotsu, this volume) or they identify whole words. They match the written representations with words in their oral vocabulary to assign meaning to the words. They then combine the meanings of individual words to build meaning for a text. To decode words, students need to develop phonemic awareness and to learn phonics. In addition, they need to practice reading aloud rapidly and accurately to increase their proficiency.

In contrast to the word recognition view, the socio-psycholinguistic view is based on the belief that reading is a universal process of constructing meaning from text by using background knowledge, linguistic cues, and psychological strategies. Those who hold this view use a different set of methods to teach reading. They make written language comprehensible by reading aloud to students and by doing shared and guided reading with students so that students can read independently. At the same time, these teachers provide mini-lessons to strengthen the use of background knowledge, linguistic cues, and psychological strategies.

The methods followed by those who hold a socio-psycholinguistic view of reading are consistent with effective methods for teaching an L2. Teachers enrich the context by organizing curriculum around themes, building or activating background knowledge, using complete texts, pointing to pictures, and varying tone of voice and emphasis to make the input comprehensible. For beginners, they choose texts with just a few words and with supportive illustrations. Gradually, they increase the difficulty of the reading by shifting more of the responsibility to the students and providing them with more difficult texts.

English language learners in classes that follow a word recognition view often develop decoding and word identification skills. They become adept at rapid, accurate pronunciation of the words in a text. However, although their oral reading may sound good, many of these students have difficulty retelling what they have read. They become good word callers who lack comprehension. On the other hand, English language learners in classes that follow a socio-psycholinguistic view may read more slowly. However, since their focus is on constructing meaning, they are better able to retell what they have read. They develop higher levels of comprehension.

Both Ms. Gallegos and Mr. Roberts are experienced teachers who employ a method of teaching reading that is consistent with their view of reading. English language learners in each of their classes learn what is expected of them. Students in Ms. Gallegos' class will learn to recognize words. They may do well on first grade reading tests since those are primarily tests of decoding. Mr. Roberts' students will acquire the ability to construct meaning from texts. They will fare much better as they move up through the grades because the reading tests and tasks they face will demand high levels of comprehension. These students will be better prepared for the challenges they face as they study academic subjects in an L2.

Reflection Questions

Reflection Questions

1. Freeman and Freeman discussed some advantages of teaching students to read in their primary language. What do you see as the pros and cons of primary language reading instruction? Do students who live in your area receive primary language reading instruction? Why or why not?

2. Freeman and Freeman described two different approaches to teaching L2 students to read. They described the lessons taught by Ms. Gallegos and Mr. Roberts and then analyzed them. If you are currently teaching reading, analyze one of your lessons using the model in the chapter. Try to identify specific teaching practices you follow that fit either the word recognition or socio-psycholinguistic view of reading. If you are not currently teaching, observe a reading lesson and analyze it using the two views framework.

3. Interview a teacher to find out how he or she teaches reading to L2 students. Record your results and then try to identify the view of reading that this teacher has. Are this teacher's L2 students becoming proficient readers as the result of the instruction they are receiving?

CHAPTER 6

ACTIVE Reading: The Research Base for a Pedagogical Approach in the Reading Classroom

Neil J. Anderson, Brigham Young University

When developing materials for use in language teaching, authors and publishers often claim that certain materials employ the latest developments in language teaching theory. Is it possible and feasible for theory and practice to meet? Richards (2006) points out that "traditionally there has been very little cross over between those working in either domain" (p. 5). Richards emphasizes his point by encouraging us to look at the types of articles that are published in journals written for practitioners and those written for researchers. The disconnect between the two worlds is often greater than we would hope.

This chapter describes the integration of six principles identified from reading research that have come to form a pedagogical approach appropriate for the reading classroom. These principles identified from the research literature informed the curriculum development process for an L2 reading series, *ACTIVE Skills for Reading*, 2*nd* ed. Each of these six principles is interdependent and dynamic. The integration of theory and practice is framed in the ACTIVE reading approach:

A: Activate prior knowledge
C: Cultivate vocabulary
T: Think about meaning
I: Increase reading fluency
V: Verify reading strategies
E: Evaluate progress

Grabe (2004) identifies 10 areas of research on reading instruction. He points out that "based on extensive and still accumulating research, the following implications for academic reading instruction and curriculum design are reasonably well supported" (p. 46). There is overlap between seven of the ten points with the ACTIVE framework. A comparison of the ACTIVE framework and Grabe's 10 areas of research in reading is provided in Table 6.1.

TABLE 6.1
Comparison between the Research Base for the ACTIVE Framework and Grabe's (2004) Areas of Research on Reading Instruction

Research Base for the ACTIVE Framework	Grabe's 10 Areas of Research on Reading Instruction
Activate prior knowledge	3. Activate background knowledge in appropriate ways.
Cultivate vocabulary	2. Emphasize vocabulary learning and create a vocabulary-rich environment.
Think about meaning	4. Ensure effective language knowledge and general comprehension skills. 5. Teach text structures and discourse organization.
Increase reading rate	1. Ensure word recognition fluency. 7. Build reading fluency and rate.
Verify reading strategies	6. Promote the strategic reader rather than teach individual strategies.
Evaluate progress	
Other issues	8. Promote extensive reading. 9. Develop intrinsic motivation for reading. 10. Plan a coherent curriculum for student learning.

Although Points 8, 9, and 10 are not part of the ACTIVE framework, they play an essential part in connecting theory and practice in the development of reading materials for the L2 classroom.

In the remainder of this chapter, the six elements of the ACTIVE framework will be considered, in turn, in terms of their research base, and suggestions will be made for putting the theory into practice. It would be impossible to cite and incorporate all of the data that supports the research base for the framework as well as cover all of the possible pedagogical applications. I, therefore, have selected from the literature those studies and applications that have had the greatest impact on my thinking as a researcher and teacher of L2 reading.

ACTIVATE PRIOR KNOWLEDGE

Research Base

A reader's background knowledge influences reading comprehension (Bernhardt, 2005; Carrell, 1983a, 1983b; 1984; Carrell & Eisterhold, 1983; Chang, 2005; Chen & Graves, 1995; Clarke & Silberstein, 1977; Coady, 1979; Gross, 2005; Hauptman, 2000; Pritchard, 1990; Shen, 2004). Background knowledge includes all experiences that a reader brings to a text: life experiences, educational experiences, knowledge of how texts can be organized rhetorically, knowledge of how one's first language works, knowledge of how the L2 works, and cultural background and knowledge. Background knowledge is also referred to as *schema* in the reading literature (*schemata* when plural).

A significant amount of research has been conducted by L2 reading researchers indicating that reading comprehension and reading skills are significantly enhanced when prior knowledge is activated. Grabe and Stoller (2002) remind us that "background knowledge (whether understood as linked networks of knowledge, schema theory, or mental models) plays a supporting role and helps the reader anticipate the discourse organization of the text as well as disambiguate word-level and clausal meanings as new information is incorporated into the text model" (p. 27).

The notion of prior knowledge influencing reading comprehension suggests that meaning does not rest solely in the printed word, but that the reader brings certain knowledge to the reading that influences comprehension. Some readers may have weak or no prior knowledge to activate. For example, some readers may not have previous experience with topics in content areas like engineering or business management. In such cases, it will be necessary for the reading teacher to establish background prior to asking the students to read so that they have sufficient information to understand the text.

Another interesting concept to consider related to the role of background knowledge is the negative influence it may have. Incorrect background knowledge can hinder comprehension. For example, some readers may have misconceptions about how AIDS is contracted. Some may believe that you can get AIDS by kissing, swimming in a pool, shaking hands, or by donating blood. If students have these misconceptions, their background knowledge may interfere with a reading passage on AIDS. The teacher may have to correct the background knowledge through a pre-reading activity before reading comprehension can be achieved.

Putting Theory into Practice

Three classroom activities will be illustrated here to draw the explicit link between research and practice. First, the role of pre-reading discussions will be highlighted. Second, knowledge of text structure will be addressed. Finally, the importance of making predictions will be discussed.

Pre-reading discussions provide an opportunity for readers to see what they know about a topic and what others may know. One way to manage a pre-reading discussion is suggested by Dubin and Bycina (1991). They recommend the use of what they call "anticipated guides," which contain "a series of statements, often provocative in nature, which are intended to challenge students' knowledge and beliefs about the content of the passage" (p. 202). The purpose of the anticipation guide is to learn what the readers already know about the topic of the reading.

You can prepare key statements about the content of a reading passage based on the reading skill you are trying to develop. For example, if you are trying to develop the readers' ability to make inferences, prepare five inference questions. Before the students read the passage, they read the inference statements and determine whether they agree or disagree with the statement. The students then read the passage and respond a second time to the same inference statements. We expect that the students will not be able to respond correctly to the inference statements before reading the passage. But, after reading the passage, we expect that they will be able to make correct inferences and respond correctly to the statements. Figure 6.1 contains a blank anticipation guide that can be used as a model.

FIGURE 6.1
Anticipation Guide

Instructions: Respond to each statement twice, once *before* you begin this unit and *again* at the conclusion of the unit.
Write *A* if you agree with the statement.
Write *D* if you disagree with the statement.

Response before Reading	Topic	Response after Reading
	1.	
	2.	
	3.	
	4.	
	5.	

Second, a pre-reading discussion on the type of text structure and what expectations a reader may have about the organization of the material is very valuable for L2 readers. This discussion could include a discussion of the kinds of transition or linking words that the reader can expect to find. Activation of prior knowledge of text organization can facilitate reading comprehension.

Next, if readers will make predictions about what they think the text content will be, they can then read to support or reject their hypotheses. A teacher can give the readers the title of the passage to be used and invite them to make predictions about what they expect to read. While using this activity, the students should be asked to pause at particular points in a reading and predict what information they think will come next. These activities can be followed up with confirmation activities. Check the predictions made earlier in the lesson to verify that what was predicted indeed happened or did not happen. Revised predictions can be made based on the outcome of earlier predictions. Any opportunity to engage readers in making predictions and then confirming or rejecting the predictions will help them draw on their background knowledge.

CULTIVATE VOCABULARY

Research Base

An increased interest continues to be given to the role that vocabulary plays in the reading process (Coxhead, 2000; Folse, 2004; Fukkink, Hulstijn, & Simis, 2005; Gardner, 2004; Grabe, 2004; Hunt & Beglar, 2005; Hyland & Tse, 2007). The word *cultivate* is specifically chosen in order to encourage a long-range plan for vocabulary development.

What comes to mind when you read the word *cultivate*? Four ideas are important from a research and pedagogy perspective. First, *cultivate* implies preparation of the soil for growing crops. Teachers and researchers need to examine ways that readers are prepared for learning new vocabulary. Second, *cultivate* means "to grow a plant." When planting seeds it is important to be aware that they sprout at different rates. For example, it takes approximately 100 days from the time a tomato seed is planted to the time you can eat a tomato. In contrast, it can take a few years from the time an apple seed is planted before you can eat an apple. Learners cannot expect to learn all vocabulary words quickly and easily. Different study techniques should be applied to vocabulary study. Third, certain conditions must exist for proper germination of seeds and plant growth. Temperature, light, oxygen, and water are all necessary in the proper amounts in order for seeds to grow. Thus, researchers and teachers must assure that the proper conditions are in place for L2 readers to learn new vocabulary. Finally, another definition of *cultivate* is to improve or develop something, usually by study or education. Vocabulary can be developed. Vocabulary can grow. Researchers and teachers can work together to identify ways to cultivate the vocabulary skills of L2 readers.

Nation (1990) emphasizes "a systematic and principled approach to vocabulary by both the teacher and the learners" (p. 1) and suggests that in order for instruction to be effective the teacher needs to make informed decisions about how to teach vocabulary. He suggests five reasons why a concentrated focus on cultivating vocabulary is needed:

1. Research findings suggest a great deal "about what to do about vocabulary and about what vocabulary to focus on" (p. 1).

2. A variety of ways are available to classroom teachers for presenting needed vocabulary. Teachers should not ignore

explicit vocabulary instruction simply because they do not like one particular method for teaching vocabulary.

3. Researchers and students alike "see vocabulary as being a very important, if not the most important, element in language learning" (p. 2).

4. Readability research suggests that vocabulary plays a crucial role in development of reading skills as well as academic achievement.

5. "Giving attention to vocabulary is unavoidable" (Nation, 1990, p. 2). Independent of the language teaching methodology employed in the classroom, vocabulary must be addressed in some manner.

The first 2,000 most frequent words from M. West's (1953) General Service List account for almost 80 percent of the words found in average texts (Carroll, Davies, & Richman, 1971; Coady, Magoto, Hubbard, Graney, & Mokhtari, 1993; Cobb, this volume; Horst, this volume). These highly frequent words should be recognized automatically. Coady et al. suggest that because these words occur so frequently, there is justification for significant commitments of instructional or learning time. They suggest that direct instruction of vocabulary is best done by treating words in context.

One of the significant research findings from Gardner's (2004) research is that the type of vocabulary found in children's narrative texts is significantly different from the vocabulary found in expository texts. He emphasizes that to reach an adequate level of comprehension when reading expository texts, learners go through different vocabulary acquisition processes due to the challenging nature of expository texts. This has a significant impact on vocabulary instruction because we must examine the types of materials we are using (narrative and/or expository) and the types of reading materials that our students will encounter outside the instructional setting.

Another consistent finding in the research literature related to vocabulary instruction is that the teaching of common morphological endings in English facilitates word comprehension (Graves, 2004; Mountain, 2005; Nation, 1990). White, Sowell, and Yanagihara (1989) provide a frequency list of prefixed and suffixed words from the *Word Frequency Book* (Carroll, Davies, & Richman, 1971). From this list, four prefixes (*un-, re-, in-* [meaning "not"], and *dis-*) account for 58 percent of the prefix occurrences in English, and three inflectional suffixes (*-s/-es, -ed,* and *-ing*) account for 65 percent of the suffix occurrences. White, Sowell, and Yanagihara

(1989) suggest that these most frequent morphological endings deserve our attention in the classroom.

Perhaps the most consistent finding from vocabulary research over the years is that vocabulary is acquired during reading. Studying vocabulary lists in isolation does not lead to the same rich use of new words as encountering those words through reading. Extensive reading plays an essential role in providing the multiple contexts that readers must have to learn new words and make them their own (Anderson, R.C., 1996; Graves & Watts-Taffe, 2002; Horst, this volume; Nagy, Herman, & Anderson, 1985; Stahl, 1998).

Putting Theory into Practice

Three pedagogical applications provide suggestions for putting vocabulary acquisition theory into practice. First, Nation (1990) recommends that language teachers "make a distinction between direct and indirect vocabulary learning" (p. 2). To do this, he provides four ways that vocabulary instruction can be integrated into language learning. These four principles are listed "from the most indirect to the most direct" way to teach vocabulary:

1. Language learning materials are explicitly prepared through carefully controlling the vocabulary presented in written texts.

2. Unfamiliar vocabulary is discussed as it naturally comes up. Nation indicates that this is perhaps the most common method of vocabulary instruction.

3. Vocabulary should be taught in connection with other language activities. For example, Nation suggests that prior to reading a passage or listening to a text, learners should be provided with essential vocabulary. Vocabulary exercises may also follow language activities. The thrust of Nation's suggestion is that the vocabulary is learned as part of another language activity. As mentioned earlier, this also serves the function of activating the prior knowledge of a reader.

4. Vocabulary is taught independent of other language activities. Actual classroom activities that typically fall into this classification of vocabulary instruction include knowing spelling rules, analyzing word structure, mnemonic techniques, paraphrase activities, and vocabulary puzzles.

A second pedagogical application for vocabulary instruction is word structure analysis skills. Teachers should encourage the learner to study prefixes, roots, and suffixes and use this knowledge to learn new vocabulary. Nation (1990) states that in order for learners to make use of word analysis, three skills are needed: (1) Recognizing the parts of a word, which is best accomplished by asking learners to break words into their parts; (2) Learning the meaning of prefixes and roots; simple memorization of the meanings of key prefixes and roots is recommended; (3) Using prefixes and roots because learners need to be able to combine prefixes and roots to create words and recognize how the combined meanings create the meaning of a word. Nation provides fourteen key words that he recommends be studied. Knowing the meanings of the prefixes and roots of these fourteen key words unlocks the meaning of more than 14,000 words in English. (See Anderson, N., 1999, pp. 27–28 for more information.)

Third, learners should be aware of the differences between massed repetition and spaced repetition. During vocabulary study in massed repetition, a learner usually makes a list of vocabulary on a single sheet of paper, folds the paper in half, and then writes a definition opposite the vocabulary word. Study is done in a short period of time, cramming to learn all of the words. This study technique may work quickly for short-term learning of vocabulary, but the words are gone quickly from memory, usually shortly after the learner finishes taking a vocabulary test. Spaced repetition is a more effective vocabulary study strategy. Using this technique, the learner uses flash cards. The cards can include a wide variety of information, for example, the vocabulary word to be studied on one side of the card with a first language translation and a definition, and a sample sentence on the other side. The learner then studies the vocabulary words in groups of five to seven words. Cards of vocabulary learned are discarded and new cards are added. Discarded words are reinserted into the pile and practiced. The learning of the vocabulary is spaced out over a period of time. This study technique can lead to longer-term retention of vocabulary than massed repetition.

THINK ABOUT MEANING

Research Base

In many reading instruction programs, a greater amount of emphasis and time may be placed on *testing* reading comprehension rather than on *teaching* readers how to think about the meaning of what is read. The ultimate goal of reading is comprehension. Monitoring comprehension is essential to successful reading.

Thinking about meaning is closely tied to comprehension strategy instruction. Both first language and L2 reading researchers have conducted strategy training experiments to see if comprehension can be improved (Carrell, 1985; Carrell, Pharis, & Liberto, 1989; Nunan, 1997; Robinson, Faraone, Hittleman, & Unruh, 1990). Grabe (1991) points out that "this line of research is particularly important because of the promise it holds for reading instruction" (p. 393).

Additional research on comprehension instruction comes from Chung (2000) who reports on the important relationship between signal words and reading comprehension. She focused on the research question: Is there a relationship among transition words, coherence, and reading comprehension? Chung focused, in particular, on two types of transitions: signal words and paragraph headings. She focused on three levels of reading comprehension: total reading comprehension, macro-level comprehension, and micro-level comprehension. The participants were 403 secondary level 6 students in Hong Kong. Three sets of materials were used to address the research question: (1) a battery of reading placement test scores; (2) four versions of a reading comprehension test specifically prepared for this study, which provided different degrees of transition words; and (3) multiple choice comprehension questions to test macro-structure and micro-structure features of the texts. Chung began the research process with three hypotheses: (1) There is no difference in the three kinds of reading comprehension scores; (2) there is no difference in the scores on the three kinds of comprehension among three groups of learners: high performers, medium performers, and low performers; and (3) there is no significant difference among the four versions of text used in the study.

The results indicate that for the micro-structure context, the signal words did not facilitate comprehension. In all other contexts, the signal words facilitated the readers' ability to comprehend the text. The greatest impact of the study is the finding that the signal words proved to be of most use to the less able readers. The implication for reading comprehension instruction is the importance for teachers to explicitly teach signal words to readers in an effort to improve overall reading comprehension.

Putting Theory into Practice

Of the many classroom activities that can be implemented to think about meaning, four are highlighted here. First, get readers to formulate questions of their own. This classroom activity can be implemented in several ways.

Readers can ask questions about material they do not understand and about which they would like to seek clarification from the teacher and/or classmates. This allows each reader to identify what is not understood and thus increases comprehension by obtaining an answer. Often the first step in teaching for comprehension is to ask readers to identify what is not comprehended.

A second classroom activity to engage readers in thinking about meaning is to have them summarize a reading passage or a partial passage. The value of this teaching tool is that, in providing the summary, the reader needs to be able to distinguish between different levels of importance in the text: main ideas, supporting ideas, and details. An effective summary would demonstrate that a reader sees the difference among these different levels and can place emphasis at the proper level.

Third, Questioning the Author is an excellent approach for use in the reading classroom developed by Beck, McKeown, Hamilton, & Kucan (1997). The purpose of the approach is to support teachers in their efforts to engage students in meaningful cognitive and meta-cognitive interactions with text and to assist students in the process of constructing meaning from text. Beck et al. emphasize that this activity is to be done *during* the reading process, *not after* reading. The approach is designed to *teach for comprehension*. The approach requires that the teacher model the reading behaviors of asking questions in order to make sense of what is being read. Students learn to engage with meaning and develop ideas rather than retrieve information from the text. This particular technique is the kind of activity that teachers of reading should engage the class in, rather than asking the students to read a passage and then testing their reading comprehension of the material. Use of this approach engages the teacher and readers in queries about the text as the material is being read. Examples of queries include "What is the author trying to say here? What is the author's message? What is the author talking about? What does the author mean here? or Does the author explain this clearly?" (Beck et al., 1997, pp. 34, 37). Teachers are encouraged to plan ahead carefully by dividing a text into chunks in such a way that they can model how good readers ask questions while they read and then engage the class in asking and answering the questions. The ultimate goal is to move from a class working through the text together to each individual reader working silently with the text and comprehending the intent of the author.

Finally, reciprocal teaching is an effective way to bridge the research/practice gap. This technique was first developed by Palincsar and Brown (1984) and has been applied in a variety of teaching contexts. This technique engages learners in reading groups and includes four key steps for engaging them in thinking about meaning: (1) Learners read the title of the passage and make predictions about what they are going to read. They continually practice making predictions throughout the reading. (Recall the discussion earlier in this chapter on the role of making predictions and the activation of background knowledge.) (2) Readers are encouraged to ask questions while they are reading. There is significant overlap between this step in reciprocal reading and Questioning the Author (Beck et al., 1997) previously discussed. The readers are encouraged to think about meaning by relating what is being read to questions that they have about the text. (3) Readers are encouraged to seek clarifications when they are confused. The readers work together to resolve the confusion by thinking together about the meaning of what is being read. (4) Finally, readers summarize the text they have read together. This summary provides evidence for the readers as well as for the teacher that meaning is understood.

The value of thinking about meaning activities in a reading classroom cannot be underestimated. Multiple choice tests can be developed to test comprehension but what a classroom teacher should focus on is teaching activities which teach rather than test comprehension.

INCREASE READING FLUENCY

Research Base

Data from Segalowitz, Poulsen, and Komoda (1991) indicate that L2 reading rates of highly bilingual readers are "30% or more slower than L1 reading rates" (p. 15). These data are also supported by Weber (1991), who points out that highly skilled bilinguals typically have a slower reading rate in their L2. Jensen (1986) indicates that "at the end of [a reading] course, even advanced L2 students may read only 100 words per minute or less" (p. 106). For many L2 readers, reading is a suffocatingly slow process. Explicit instruction in rapid reading is an area which is often neglected in the classroom. The discussion and activities to increase reading rate suggested here are not designed to have L2 readers read thousands of words per minute, but to increase their reading rate to a satisfactory level to be successful in academic reading tasks.

Nuttall (1982, 1996) describes the frustration that may be part of slower reading in her description of the "vicious cycle of the weak reader" (p. 167). Readers who do not understand often slow down their reading rate and then do not enjoy reading because it takes so much time. Therefore, they do not read much. These readers continue in the vicious cycle. By increasing reading rate, Nuttall suggests that the reader can get into the "virtuous cycle of the good reader" (1982, p. 167). By reading faster, the reader is encouraged to read more and, with more reading, comprehension improves.

Grabe (1991) states that "fluent reading is rapid; the reader needs to maintain the flow of information at a sufficient rate to make connections and inferences vital to comprehension" (p. 378). Conflicting data exist regarding the optimal or sufficient reading rate. Some authorities suggest that 180 words per minute "may be a threshold between immature and mature reading, that a speed below this is too slow for efficient comprehension or for the enjoyment of text" (Higgins and Wallace, 1989, p. 392). Dubin and Bycina (1991) state that "a rate of 200 words per minute would appear to be the absolute minimum in order to read with full comprehension" (p. 198). Jensen (1986) recommends that L2 readers should seek to "approximate native speaker reading rates and comprehension levels in order to keep up with classmates" (p. 106). She suggests that 300 words-per-minute is the optimal rate. This rate is supported by Nuttall (1982), who states that "for an L1 speaker of English of about average education and intelligence . . . the reading rate is about 300 wpm. The range among L1 speakers is very great; rates of up to 800 wpm and down to 140 wpm are not uncommon" (p. 36).

Fluency is currently receiving increased attention in the United States, especially in the public school context. Decisions about what constitutes fluent reading for native speakers of reading is influencing decisions for children who are second language readers. In 1997, the National Institute of Child Health and Human Development (NICHD) convened a National Reading Panel (NRP) consisting primarily of cognitive scientists to conduct a meta-analysis of research in the teaching of reading (see also Han, Anderson, & Freeman, this volume). They examined five areas of reading research: phonemic awareness, phonics, fluency, vocabulary, and comprehension (National Institute of Child Health and Human Development, 2000). These have come to be known as the "fab 5" among teachers and researchers engaged in reading instruction and research.

A major outcome of this work is that reading fluency is being defined and measured as the ability of the reader to read a passage *orally*. Stahl (2004) points out that under this examination of reading fluency, a reader is judged as fluent when engaged in accurate and fast reading with good expression that is common for mature readers. Pressley (2006) cautions us that under this view, readers are not asked about their comprehension of the text but rather are only evaluated on how fast and accurate they read. He warns that "nobody should be interested in or promoting fast reading with low comprehension" (p. 209).

In my previous work (1999, 2008), *reading fluency* was defined as reading at an adequate rate with adequate comprehension. To my knowledge, I am one of the few researchers who states the need to examine the relationship between reading rate *and* comprehension. Adequate rate is defined as 200 wpm and adequate comprehension is defined as 70 percent. Thus, we see that in reality we cannot discuss reading rate in isolation of a discussion of reading comprehension. This combines the T and the I in the ACTIVE approach to reading. Tindale (2003) stresses that "in building reading fluency, it is important to balance reading rate and comprehension: sometimes rate may need to take priority over comprehension in order to develop automaticity in reading" (p. 47).

Putting Theory into Practice

The following five reading rate activities are among the ones I have used in my L2 reading class to increase student reading rate and at the same time help readers be responsible for comprehension. These activities do not require specially developed texts or equipment.

1. Shadow Reading. Shadow reading provides a structured opportunity for learners to read fluently. First, I use the audio CD that accompanies the reading text that I use in class, or if an audio CD is not available, I read the passage aloud. I have learners listen to the reading passage. I do not have them look at the printed text. They are asked to just listen. Following the listening passage, we discuss what we heard.

Next, after the brief discussion, I ask the readers to open their books and follow along silently as they listen to the recording again on the CD. For most of the learners in my class, their eyes are moving faster while following the text and listening to the recording than they would be if they were reading silently by themselves. This is a good practice opportunity. Students begin to realize that the rate of speech in listening is faster than they are accustomed to reading.

Finally, I have the learners read aloud quietly with the CD. Keeping up is often a challenge as learners are not accustomed to reading that fast orally. We may repeat this phase of Shadow Reading more than once during the lesson. Students enjoy the challenge of trying to keep up with the CD.

Following the Shadow Reading activity, readers will answer the reading comprehension questions that accompany the passage. By doing this, readers understand that they are responsible for comprehension as well as reading rate.

2. Rate Buildup Reading. Students are given 60 seconds to read as much material as they can. They then begin reading again from the beginning of the text and are given an additional 60 seconds. They are to read more material during the second 60-second period than in the first. The drill is repeated a third and a fourth time. The purpose of this activity is to reread "old" material quickly, gliding into the new. As their eyes move quickly over the "old" material, the students actually learn how to get their eyes moving at a faster reading rate. The exercise involves more than simply moving the eyes quickly; rather, the material should be processed and comprehended. As students participate in this rate building activity, they learn to increase reading rate (see N. Anderson, 1993a, for more detail).

3. Repeated Reading. Students read a short passage over and over again until they achieve criterion levels of reading rate and comprehension. For example, they may try to read a short 100-word paragraph four times in two minutes. The criterion levels may vary from class to class, but reasonable goals to work towards are criterion levels of 200 words per minute at 70 percent comprehension. Results of repeated reading studies with native speakers of English indicate that

> as the student continued to use this technique, the initial speed of reading each new selection was faster than the initial speed on the previous selection. Also, the number of re-readings required to reach the criterion reading speed decreased as the student continued the technique. . . . [This seems to indicate] a transfer of training and a general improvement in reading fluency. (Samuels, 1979, p. 404; see N. Anderson, 1993b, for more detail)

4. Class-Paced Reading. This activity requires a discussion regarding a class goal for minimal reading rate. Once that goal is established, the average number of words per page of the material being read is calculated. It is then determined how much material needs to be read in one minute in order to meet the class goal. For example, if the class goal is to read 250 words-per-minute and the material being read has an average of 125 words per page, the class would be expected to read one page every 30 seconds. As each 30 seconds elapses, the teacher indicates to the class to move to the next page. Students are encouraged to keep up with the established class goal. Of course, those who read faster than 250 wpm are not expected to slow down their reading rate. As long as they are ahead of the designated page, they continue reading.

5. Self-Paced Reading. The procedures for this activity are very similar to the class-paced reading activity outlined above. During this reading

rate activity, the students determine their own goal for reading rate. They then determine how much material needs to be read in a 60-second period to meet their objective rate. For example, suppose a student's objective rate is 180 wpm and that the material being read has an average number of ten words per line. The student would need to read eighteen lines of text in one minute to meet the goal. The activity proceeds nicely by having each student mark off several chunks of lines and silently read for a period of five to seven minutes with the instructor calling out minute times. Students can then determine if they are keeping up with their individual reading rate goal.

Often, in their efforts to assist students in increasing their reading rate, teachers overemphasize accuracy at the expense of fluency and when accuracy is overemphasized, reading fluency is impeded. The teacher must work towards a balance in reading rate improvement and reading comprehension. During some rate building exercises, the teacher may need to emphasize reading rate over reading comprehension.

VERIFY READING STRATEGIES

Research Base

Strategies can be defined as the *conscious* actions that learners take to improve their language learning. Strategies may be observable, such as someone taking notes during an academic lecture to recall information better, or they may be mental, such as thinking about what one already knows on a topic before reading a passage in a textbook. Because strategies are conscious, there is active involvement of the L2 learner in their selection and use. Strategies are not an isolated action, but rather a process of orchestrating more than one action to accomplish an L2 task (Anderson, N., 2005). This definition underscores the active role that readers take in strategic reading. Students need to learn how to orchestrate the use of reading strategies to achieve the desired result.

I highlight for readers that there are no bad strategies. There is only bad application of strategies. Because there are varieties of strategies that are available to readers, every reader uses a different set of strategies to accomplish his/her purposes for reading.

Researchers have suggested that teaching readers how to use strategies is a prime consideration in the reading classroom (Anderson, N., 1991, 2005; Chamot & O'Malley, 1994; Oxford, 1990; Rubin et al., 2007). While

L2 readers are taught how to use a given strategy, they must also be taught how to determine if they are successful in their use of that strategy.

Chamot and O'Malley (1994) stress the central role of explicit strategy instruction:

> We emphasize repeatedly that students who are mentally active and who analyze and reflect on their learning activities will learn, retain, and be able to use new information more effectively. Furthermore, students will be able to learn and apply strategies more effectively with new tasks if they verbalize and describe their efforts to apply strategies with learning activities. (p. 11)

Rubin, Chamot, Harris, & Anderson (2007) summarize ways that strategy-based instruction can be integrated into the classroom. They point out that the research on ways to integrate strategy instruction into the classroom setting includes the following four phases:

1. raising awareness of the strategies learners are already using
2. teacher presentation and modeling of strategies so that students become increasingly aware of their own thinking and learning processes
3. multiple practice opportunities to help students move towards autonomous use of the strategies through gradual withdrawal of the scaffolding
4. self evaluation of the effectiveness of the strategies used and transfer of strategies to fresh tasks. (p. 142)

Strategies versus Skills

The use of the terms *strategies* and *skills* can be confusing in the literature. Some use these two important terms interchangeably as if there were no difference between them. Important distinctions can be made between strategies and skills (Afflerbach, Pearson, & Paris, 2008; Kawai, Oxford, & Iran-Nejad, 2000). Afflerbach, Pearson, and Paris (2008) point out that "how teachers think about skill and strategy is of utmost importance because we cannot possibly teach well those things that we don't carefully define and fully understand" (p. 14).

A skill is a strategy that has become automatic. As learners consciously learn and practice specific reading strategies, the strategies move from conscious to unconscious, from strategy to skill. Figure 6.2 provides a graphic representation of this concept.

FIGURE 6.2
Strategy to Skill Continuum

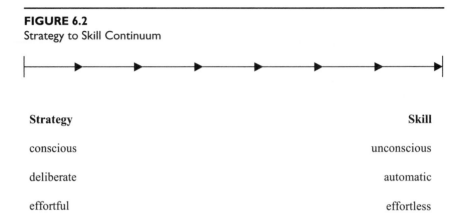

Strategy	Skill
conscious	unconscious
deliberate	automatic
effortful	effortless

This distinction is supported by Afflerbach, Pearson, and Paris (2008). They emphasize that

> reading skills are automatic actions that result in decoding and comprehending of texts with speed, efficiency, and fluency, usually without the reader's awareness of the components or controls involved. Reading skills operate without the reader's deliberate control or conscious awareness. . . . Reading strategies are deliberate, goal-directed attempts to control and modify the reader's efforts to decode text, understand words, and construct meaning of text. The reader's deliberate control of work, the goal-directedness of the work, and the reader's awareness of work define a strategy. (p. 15)

For example, guessing the meaning of unknown vocabulary from context can be listed as both a strategy and a skill in reading texts. When a reader is first introduced to this concept and is practicing how to use context to guess the meaning of unfamiliar vocabulary, he or she is using a strategy. The use of the strategy is conscious during the learning and practice stages. As the reader develops automaticity in the ability to guess unfamiliar vocabulary from context, he or she moves from using a conscious strategy to using an unconscious skill. The use of the skill takes place outside the direct consciousness of the reader. The goal for explicit strategy instruction is to move readers from conscious control of reading strategies to unconscious use of reading skills.

As L2 readers actively monitor their comprehension processes during reading, they will select strategies to assist in getting at the meaning of what they are reading. Meta-cognitive awareness of the reading process is perhaps one of the most important skills L2 readers can use while reading. This indicates that they are able to verify the strategies they are using. Meta-cognition is best defined as thinking about thinking (N. Anderson, 2002, 2005). Verbal reports have been used in many L2 research designs as a method of getting at the mental processes that L2 learners use to understand the language. Verbal reports allow "insight into the dynamic and interactive nature" of the language learning process (MacLean & d'Anglejan, 1986, p. 814). Getting students to think aloud and use verbal reports is a beneficial meta-cognitive activity. Irwin (1991) states that

> when students think aloud or hear others think aloud, their meta-cognitive awareness of options for responding to text increases. It can also help them to become aware of how much thinking goes into comprehending a text. (p. 203)

If we want readers who can easily move back and forth between skills and strategies, we need teachers who can effectively guide them in the process. Instruction must include what Afflerbach, Pearson, and Paris (2008) call a "meta-cognitive layer of discussion" (p. 19). Teachers must be prepared to use instructional time to talk about the strategies and provide explicit practice in how to use them. This will be addressed in the section below on putting theory into practice.

Most strategy research makes use of a survey of some type to elicit learners' reactions to the frequency of use in different strategies. One such survey is an instrument developed by Mokhtari and reported in Mokhtari and Sheorey (2002) and Sheorey and Mokhtari (2001). The Survey of Reading Strategies (SORS) focuses on meta-cognitive strategy use within the context of reading. The SORS was based on a separate meta-cognitive reading strategy survey developed for native speakers of English, the Metacognitive Awareness of Reading Strategies Inventory (MARSI). The SORS measures three categories of reading strategies: global reading strategies (e.g., having a purpose for reading, using context to guess unfamiliar vocabulary, confirming or rejecting predictions), problem-solving strategies (e.g., adjusting reading rate, focusing when concentration is lost), and support strategies (e.g., taking notes while reading, highlighting important ideas in the text). Mokhtari and Sheorey report reliability for the MARSI but not for the SORS. Since it has just recently been completed, more studies need to be conducted using this instrument to determine whether the SORS is as stable of an instrument as the MARSI on which it was based. Additional inventories for identifying L2 learner strategies can be found on the Internet: Language Strategy Use Survey by Cohen and Chi and the Young Learners' Language Strategy Use Survey by Cohen and Oxford, carla.acad.umn.edu. All of these surveys serve as a resource to researchers and teachers alike in identifying the knowledge that learners have of their strategy use.

Being strategic while reading does not guarantee successful comprehension (Afflerbach, Pearson, & Paris, 2008). Readers may apply a variety of strategies, monitor their comprehension, and still not understand what they are reading. But the strategic reader will not give up. One characteristic that distinguishes strategic readers form non-strategic readers is the focus on successful comprehension and doing all that it takes to understand. Non-strategic readers give up too soon.

One final point about strategic reading: Afflerbach, Pearson, and Paris (2008) indicate that there are motivational advantages for students when teachers distinguish strategies and skills as outlined by the continuum in Figure 6.2.

> Reading skills are motivated by goals of fluency, effortlessness, and accuracy; they give rise to the student reader's pride in ability, not effort.... Strategic readers feel confident that they can monitor and improve their own reading so they have both knowledge and motivation to succeed. (p. 19)

Teachers play an essential role in helping learners achieve the goal of successfully balancing strategies and skills. We can only do that if we clearly understand the distinctions between these two commonly used terms in the reading literature.

Putting Theory into Practice

Based on this theoretical input, one approach L2 reading teachers can take for the instruction of reading strategies is by addressing the following six questions suggested by Winograd and Hare (1988). The six strategy instruction questions are applied to a specific reading skill: Main Idea Comprehension (see Baumann, 1984, for additional information).

1. What is the strategy? Being able to identify the main idea is one of the most important reading skills you can develop. It is a skill that you need to apply to the majority of reading contexts.

2. Why should the strategy be learned? If the main idea can be identified, comprehension is facilitated by being able to organize the information presented and by being able to distinguish main ideas from supporting ideas and details.

3. How can the strategy be used? Read to locate the thesis statement of the passage and the topic sentence of each paragraph. Read quickly, don't worry about the details.

4. When should the strategy be used? Main idea comprehension should be used when reading expository passages which contain much new information.

5. Where should the reader look? The reader should read the first and last paragraphs of a passage and read the first sentence of each paragraph. Readers should be reminded to ask themselves the following questions: What idea is common to most of the text? What is the idea that relates the parts to the whole? What opinion do all the parts support? What idea do they all explain or describe?

6. How can you evaluate the use of the strategy? In the early stages of reading comprehension, open discussions with the reader will be the best method to verify whether the strategy is being used appropriately. The use of verbal think-aloud protocols can facilitate the evaluation of the strategy.

Grabe (1991) provides a caution: "effective strategy training is not a simple or easy matter" (p. 393). He points out that the duration of training, clarity of training procedures, student responsibility, and strategy transfer are variables which influence strategy training results.

In addition to these six steps outlined by Winograd and Hare (1988), allowing readers to become more aware of what they actually do while reading is extremely beneficial. Verbal reports and think-aloud protocols were originally designed as a tool for researchers to tap into the unseen and unobservable nature of learning strategies. Today, think-aloud protocols are a common tool for the classroom teacher in getting readers to verify what they are doing while they are reading (see Wilheim, 2001 as an example). A verbal report is produced when a language learner verbalizes his or her thought processes while completing a given task (Ericsson & Simon, 1984). Readers can listen to the verbal report of another reader who has just read the same material and it is often revealing to hear what other readers have done to get meaning from a passage. Rubin et al. (2007) point out that the think-aloud protocol begins with the teacher modeling the behaviors of proficient readers; much like what was emphasized in Beck et al.'s (1997) Questioning the Author technique discussed earlier. As Wilhelm (2001) points out, think-aloud strategies are an excellent tool for improving reading comprehension. This integrates the T (teach for comprehension) and the V (verify strategies) in the ACTIVE approach to reading. Cohen (1990) suggests that as readers verify what strategies they are using, they become more aware of the "full array of options open" to them to improve their reading (p. 73).

The application of verbal reports to the L2 classroom provides an opportunity for a teaching of meta-cognitive strategies in all language skills. Anderson and Vandergrift (1996) and N. Anderson (2004) outline specific suggestions for how think-aloud protocols can be used in the classroom to develop awareness of reading strategies:

1. The teacher demonstrates the use of think-aloud protocols by selecting a passage which he/she has never read before in order to show in as natural a fashion as possible what is going on in the mind while reading. The teacher reads the passage aloud while the students follow silently. While reading, the teacher verbally reports what is going on in his or her mind. Teachers who are fluent, advanced readers, particularly native speakers, may need to slow down their thinking processes in order to be aware of what they actually do while reading.

2. At the conclusion of the demonstration, the teacher encourages the students to add any thoughts that occurred to them during the reading.

3. Additional demonstrations may need to be provided so that students see what is involved in producing a think-aloud protocol.

4. Students are then grouped into pairs or threes and work together to practice reading aloud. One student in the group reads aloud while the other(s) follow silently. The teacher encourages students to verbalize their thoughts and the strategies that they are using during the reading.

5. Students who act as listeners during this activity then add their thoughts to what their classmate has already shared.

6. The activity can also be done in a "reading round robin" format (Irwin, 1991). The class is given a reading passage, and each student is asked to read one sentence at a time and then verbalize thoughts and strategies. This activity works best if the readers cover the passage and reveal only one line of text at a time.

7. A "hot seat" activity can also be conducted. One student reads a short passage and thinks aloud, while the others in the class follow along silently.

8. Think-aloud protocols can also be used in regular silent reading periods. Occasionally during a silent reading activity, students are stopped and asked to verbalize what they are thinking. Alternatively, the think-aloud protocol can be implemented by having students stop at certain points and turn to a partner to verbalize their thoughts.

9. Finally, students can practice this activity while reading silently, outside the classroom. Davey (1983) suggested that students be asked to read silently and then complete a checklist to report the kinds of strategies they were implementing during the silent reading sessions. This can very easily be conducted as a homework assignment.

10. The above technique could be modified for one-on-one conferences with a learner. (Anderson & Vandergrift, 1996, pp. 9–10)

By using this technique in reading classes, students can be taught how to be more aware of what they are doing while they are reading and to see what other readers do when they encounter difficulties. Many of the examples that students come up with during their verbal reports in class provide excellent points of discussion about what good readers do when they read.

In practicing verbal reports in class, a continual focus should be on getting students to "aim for transfer" (Davey, 1983). The objective should be to get students to use this in all their reading activities. The demonstration and practice provides not only a discussion of how to read, but also why and when certain strategies would be used.

EVALUATE PROGRESS

Research Base

Alderson (2000) provides perhaps the most definitive research on the role of assessment and evaluation in reading. He points out several factors that influence the assessment of reading: the difficulty of the reading passage and the questions, the reading skill being tested, being able to look back at the passage during the test, and the length of the test passages.

Perhaps the point that is important for us to consider here is that in the classroom we want to be able to provide multiple opportunities for the readers to evaluate the progress they are making so that when a high-stakes test is taken, the learners are already aware of their strengths and weaknesses.

Although the E in ACTIVE falls at the end of the acronym, this should not suggest that evaluation should wait until the end. Evaluation is an ongoing, continuous process for the learner and the teacher. Teachers should provide opportunities for evaluation. Evaluation should not always come from the teacher. We must help learners be engaged in meaningful self evaluation. We cannot possibly teach everything there is to know about reading in the classroom. Readers must learn to take responsibility for their own learning.

Afflerbach, Pearson, and Paris (2008) emphasize the essential role of evaluation and reading. In specifically addressing the importance of assessment in relation to teaching strategies and skills (see earlier discussion in the Verifying Strategies section), they point out that

> strategy assessments are formative; when done well, they provide diagnostic information that helps shape our understanding of students and plan instruction. In contrast, skill assessments are summative. Too often, teachers try to use skill assessments for diagnostic teaching or fail to assess strategy use so students are given repeated cycles of the same instruction and inappropriate, unhelpful assessments. (p. 22)

A possible first step in that direction that is suggested in the research literature is to help L2 readers learn how to accurately self-assess. The literature provides mixed reviews on learners' ability to accurately self-assess. Strong-Krause (2000) found that learners can provide good self-assessments if they are given adequate input in making the self-assessment. Al-Hamly and Coombe (2005) provide data that suggest that L2 learners cannot make accurate self-assessment. They point out that learners do not have an accurate standard against which to judge themselves.

For self-assessment to be effective, readers must be taught how to engage in healthy but critical self-assessment. Most learners fall on one end of the self-assessment continuum: superficial self-assessors or hyper-critical self-assessors. Most likely, where learners fall on this self-assessment continuum would also be where they would fall on a peer-assessment continuum. Teachers must provide classroom opportunities for readers to be engaged in healthy but critical self- and peer-assessment.

In addition to self-assessment, teacher evaluation is central to effective classroom learning. Reading progress records can be effectively utilized by the teacher to assist readers in keeping track of their progress. Recording progress can become an effective tool in motivating readers to continue to improve. Stoller (1986) points out that progress charts and graphs can facilitate reading improvement and is a "critical aspect of the instructor's responsibilities" (p. 55).

Assessing growth and development in reading skills from both a formal and an informal perspective is often a concern for reading instructors as well as materials developers. Research suggests that both quantitative and qualitative assessment activities should be included in reading materials (O'Malley & Valdez Pierce, 1996). Quantitative assessment will include information from placement tests, in-class reading quizzes, and final examinations. Qualitative information can include student responses to questionnaires about reading strategies, teacher observations during in-class reading tasks, and verbal reports from students regarding their cognitive processes during reading. Such reading materials can have a tremendous impact on reading instruction if there is a healthy balance of both types of assessment activities to evaluate progress.

Putting Theory into Practice

Five classroom record-keeping procedures can be used by classroom teachers for qualitative and quantitative evaluation. First, a reading log provides readers a mechanism of accountability to record what they are reading each day. Students can be encouraged to read for at least 30 minutes outside of class each day and record what they are reading. Another way that this reading log has proved useful is to have students record everything they read during the day and how much time they spent reading. Students are often surprised at how much of their day is spent in reading activities. The log does not require readers to provide a detailed description of their comprehension of what has been read. Some teachers implement a reading log in which the readers must summarize what they have read and/or ask questions to the teacher. Used in this fashion, the reading log can become a tool for teaching for comprehension.

Second, reading rate graphs can be kept to mark improvement in reading rate. Likewise, a graph of reading comprehension scores can be kept. These two graphs become useful tools for the students to use in setting individual goals.

Next, a reading rate record is a tool for readers to calculate reading rate during extended reading periods. This record allows the teacher, as well as the students, to monitor reading rate. For this record, the reader multiplies the number of pages read by the average number of words per page. This gives the total number of words read, which is divided by the number of minutes spent reading to result in the approximate number of words read per minute.

A simple formula for calculating the average number of words per page is to use the following four steps:

1. Count every word on the first five lines of text.
2. Divide the sum in Step 1 by 5. This gives you the average number of words per line of text.
3. Count every line on the page.
4. Multiply the total number of lines per page (Step 3) by the average number of words per line (Step 2). This results in the average number of words per page.

Finally, a record of repeated reading practice is a tool in helping individual readers set goals for reading rate improvement as well as a tool in helping readers see their progress.

The role of the teacher is integral to success of L2 readers. Teachers should view themselves as facilitators helping each reader discover what works best. The ACTIVE reading framework provides a pedagogical tool for the teacher to integrate the principles from reading theory with classroom practice. This integration can lead to more effective reading instruction in the L2 classroom.

On the surface, it appears as if ACTIVE is a linear process, beginning with activation of prior knowledge prior to reading and concluding with evaluation of the reading process. I hope that it has become clear here that ACITVE is an integrated approach to teaching. There are elements of interaction among each of the aspects of the approach.

As L2 educators, we have a great responsibility to make clearer connections between what we learn from our research and how that research gets applied in the classroom. The ACTIVE approach is one such effort.

Reflection Questions

Reflection Questions

1. Review Table 6.1 (page 118). Can you identify a major area of L2 reading research that is not covered in the ACTIVE framework or in Grabe's ten areas of research on reading instruction?

2. Can you think of a specific example from your own reading or from students you have taught where activation of prior knowledge facilitated reading comprehension? What about an example where lack of prior knowledge hindered reading comprehension?

3. If you have access to a group of L2 learners, practice conducting one of the five reading rate building activities outlined in this chapter (shadow reading, rate buildup, repeated reading, class-paced reading, self-paced reading). What did you learn from practicing the activity? What other activities could you use in class to help readers become more fluent readers?

4. Informal assessment is integral to success in the reading classroom. In addition to the ideas presented in this chapter, what additional informal assessments could you use to help learners see their progress? What self-assessment techniques could you use?

CHAPTER 7

Necessary or Nice? Computers in Second Language Reading

Tom Cobb, Linguistique et Didactique des Langues, UQAM, Montreal, Canada

Does the computer have any important role to play in the development of L2 reading ability? One role seems uncontroversial: networked multimedia computers can do what traditional media of literacy have always done, only more so. They can expand the quantity, variety, accessibility, transportability, modifiability, bandwidth, and context of written input, while at the same time encouraging useful computing skills. Such contributions are nice if available, but hardly necessary for reading development to occur. A more controversial question is whether computing can provide any unique learning opportunities for L2 readers. This chapter argues that the role computing has played in understanding L2 reading, and the role it can play in facilitating L2 reading, are closer to necessary than to nice.

This chapter departs from two framing ideas in the introduction, one that L2 reading research continues to borrow too much and too uncritically from L1 reading research and the other that within the communicative paradigm reading is seen as a skill to be developed through extensive practice. The argument here is that L2 reading ability is unlikely to reach native-like competence simply through skill development and practice, and that the reason anyone ever thought it could is precisely because the realities of L1 and L2 reading development have been systematically confused. However, we now have a dedicated body of L2 reading research, along with some more careful interpretations of L1 research, that together provide a detailed task analysis of learning to read in an L2 and show quite clearly why reading has long been described as "a problem" (e.g., Alderson, 1984) and reading instruction a "lingering dilemma" (Bernhardt, 2005). The L2 findings, based on empirical research and supported by the analysis of texts by computer programs, detail both the lexical knowledge that is needed to underpin reading and the rates at which this knowledge can be acquired. Although strong and relatively well-known, these findings tend not to be incorporated into practice because there has seemed no obvious way to do so. However, the same computational tools that helped produce the findings can also help with exploiting them, and indeed that there is probably no other way to exploit them within a classroom context and time frame.

There are four relevant contexts to this chapter. The first is the large body of high-quality L2 vocabulary and reading research, or rather vocabulary in reading research, that has come together since about 1990. The second is the spread of networked computing throughout much of the education system since about 1995. The third is the rapidly increasing number of non-Anglophone students worldwide who are attempting to gain an education through English, which of course largely means reading in English—that is, reading English to learn. At one end, 30 percent of Ph.D. students enrolled in U.S. universities in 2002–03 were international students (almost 50 percent in areas like engineering) according to Open Doors 2003 (Institute of International Education, 2003), and figures are similar or higher in other English-speaking countries like Canada, the United Kingdom, Australia, and New Zealand. At the other end, in the K–12 population 12 percent are currently classified as having limited English proficiency (LEP) (U.S. Census Bureau, 2000), and this figure is predicted to increase to 40 percent by the 2030s (Thomas & Collier, 2002). We owe it to these people to know what we are doing with their literacy preparation.

And finally a less obvious context is the long-standing debate among educational media researchers about the contribution to learning that can be expected from instructional media, particularly those that involve computing. One camp in this debate argues that while such media may improve access or motivation (i.e., they could be nice), they can in principle make no unique contribution to any form of learning that could not be provided in some other way (i.e., they are not necessary; Clark, R., 1983, 2001). Another camp argues that, while the no-unique-learning argument often happens to be true, there are specific cases where media can indeed make unique contributions to learning (Cobb, 1997, 1999, 2008a) and that L2 reading is one of them. Discussed in generalities, there is no conclusion to this debate; discussed in specific cases, the conclusion is clear.

An advance organizer for the argument is as follows: Thanks to the extensive labors of many researchers in the field of L1 literacy, we now know about the primacy of vocabulary knowledge in reading (e.g., R. Anderson & Freebody, 1981). And thanks to the extensive labors of many in the field of L2 reading (as brought together and focused by Nation, e.g., 1990, 2001), we now know about the minimum amount of lexical knowledge that competent L2 reading requires, and in addition, we know the rate at which this knowledge can be acquired in a naturalistic framework. As a result, we can see that while time and task tend to match up in an L1 timeframe (Nagy & Anderson, 1984), they do not match up at all in a typical L2 timeframe. First delineating and then responding to this mismatch is the theme of this chapter, with a focus on the necessary role of the computer in both parts of the process.

The chapter is intended to address practice as much as theory. All of the computational tools and several of the research studies discussed are available to teachers or researchers at my *Compleat Lexical Tutor* website (www.lextutor.ca, with individual pages indicated in the appendix; for a site overview, see Sevier, 2004). These tools can be used to test many of the claims presented here, and to perform concrete tasks in research, course design, and teaching.

THE ROLE OF COMPUTING IN DEFINING THE PROBLEM

How Many Words Do You Need to Read?

Here are two simple but powerful findings produced by L2 reading researchers. The first is from Laufer (1989), who determined that an L2 reader can enjoy, answer questions on, and learn more new words from texts for which they know nineteen words out of twenty. This finding has been replicated many times and can be replicated by readers for themselves by trying to fill the gaps in the two versions of the same text below. The first text has 80 percent of its words known (one unknown in five), the second has 95 percent of its words known (one unknown in twenty). For most readers, only a topic can be gleaned from the first text, and random blanks supplied with effort and backtracking; for the second text, a proposition can be constructed and blanks supplied with clear concepts or even specific words.

The second finding comes from a study by Milton and Meara (1995), which establishes a baseline for the amount of lexical growth that typically occurs in classroom learning. They found the average increase in basic recognition knowledge for 275 words in a six-month term, or 550 words per year. Readers can confirm their own or their learners' vocabulary sizes and rates of growth over time using the two versions of Nation's Vocabulary Levels Test (1990, provided online at Web reference [2]).

Thus, if we have a goal for L2 readers (to know 95 percent of the words in the texts they are reading), a way of determining how many words they know now (using the Levels test), and a baseline rate of progress toward the goal (550 new words per year), then it should be possible to put this information together in some useful way, for example, to answer practical questions about which learners should be able to read which texts, for which purposes (consolidation, further vocabulary growth, or content learning),

---

FIGURE 7.1
Reading Texts with Different Proportions of Words Known (from Nation, 1990, p. 242, and elaborated at Web reference [1])

Text 1 (80 percent of words known – 32:40):

If _____ planting rates are _____ with planting _____ satisfied in each _____ and the forests milled at the earliest opportunity, the _____ wood supplies could further _____ to about 36 million _____ meters _____ in the period 2001–2015.

Text 2 (95 percent of words known – 38:40):

If current planting rates are maintained with planting targets satisfied in each _____ and the forests milled at the earliest opportunity, the available wood supplies could further _____ to about 36 million cubic meters annually in the period 2001–2015.

and how many more words they would need in order to do so. Do learners who know 2,500 words thereby know 95 percent of the words on the front page of today's *New York Times*?

In fact, we cannot answer this type of question yet because there is a hole in the middle of the picture as presented so far. On one side, we have the numbers of words learners know, and on the other we have the percentages of words needed to read texts, but we have no link between words and percentages. Which words provide which percentages in typical texts, and is it the same across a variety of texts? Producing such a link requires that we inspect and compare the lexical composition of large numbers of large texts, or text corpora—so large, in fact, that they can only be handled with the help of a computer.

Corpus and computing are not needed to see that natural texts contain words that are repeated to widely different degrees, from words that appear on every line (*the* and *a*) to words that appear rarely or in specialized domains (*non-orthogonal* in statistics). Before computers were available, researchers like Zipf (Web reference [3]) developed different aspects of this idea, showing, for example, that oft-repeated *the* accounts for or *covers* a reliable five to seven percent of the running words in almost any English text, and just 100 words provide coverage for a reliable 50 percent. Readers can confirm this type of calculation in a hand count of *the* from the previous paragraph, with six instances in 110 words or a coverage of just over five percent. Or they can investigate other coverage phenomena using texts of their own with the help of a text frequency program (at Web reference [4]). It seems quite encouraging that just a few very frequent words provide a surprisingly high coverage across a wide variety of texts, as the recent data from the 100 million–word British National Corpus, provided in Table 7.1, shows. If learners know just these fifteen words, then they know more than a quarter of the words in almost any text they will encounter. Thus, in principle it can be calculated how many words they will need to know in order to achieve 95 percent coverage in any text.

Earlier educators like Ogden (1930, Web reference [6]) and M. West (1953, Web reference [7]) had attempted to exploit the idea of text coverage for pedagogical purposes, but with conceptual techniques alone, in the absence of corpus and computing, this was only a partial success. (For an interesting discussion of early work in the vocabulary control movement, see Schmitt, 2000). The pedagogical challenge was to locate, somewhere on the uncharted lexical oceans between the extremes of very high and very low frequency words, a cut-off point that could define a basic lexicon of a language, or a set of basic lexicons for particular purposes, such as read-

TABLE 7.1
Typical Coverages in a Corpus of 100 Million Words

Word	PoS	Frequency/Million	Coverage (%) Word	Cumulative
1. *the*	Det.	61847	6.18	-
2. *of*	Prep.	29391	2.93	9.11
3. *and*	Conj.	26817	2.68	11.79
4. *a*	Det.	21626	2.16	13.95
5. *in*	Prep.	18214	1.82	15.77
6. *to*	Inf.	16284	1.62	17.39
7. *it*	Pron.	10875	1.08	18.47
8. *is*	Verb.	9982	0.99	19.46
9. *to*	Prep.	9343	0.93	20.39
10. *was*	Verb.	9236	0.92	21.31
11. *I*	Pron.	8875	0.88	22.19
12. *for*	Prep.	8412	0.84	23.17
13. *that*	Conj.	7308	0.73	23.95
14. *you*	Pron.	6954	0.69	24.64
15. *he*	Pron.	6810	0.68	25.33

Source: Leech, Rayson, & Wilson (2001), or companion site at Web reference [5].

ing or particular kinds of reading. This point could not be found, however, until a number of theoretical decisions had been made (whether to count *cat* and *cats* as one word or two), until usable measurement concepts had been developed (*coverage* as a measure of average repetition), and until large text corpora had been assembled and the computational means devised for extracting information from them.

It was only quite recently that corpus researchers with computers and large text samples or corpora at their disposal, like Carroll, Davies and Richman (1971), were able to determine reliable coverage figures, such as that the 2,000 highest frequency word families of English reliably cover 80 percent of the individual words in an average text (with minor variations of about 5 percent in either direction). Subsequent corpus analysis has confirmed this figure, and readers can reconfirm it for themselves by entering their own texts into the computer program at Web reference [8]. This program, *VocabProfile,* provides the coverage in any text of these most frequent 2,000 words of English. Readers will discover that for most texts, 2,000 words do indeed provide about 80 percent coverage. For the previous paragraph, for example, it shows that the 2,000 most frequent words in the language at large account for 81.35 percent of the words in this particular text. Here, then, is the missing link between numbers of words known and percentages of words needed.

With reliable coverage information of words of different frequencies across large numbers and types of texts, we are clearly in possession of a useful methodology for analyzing the task of learning to read in an L2. If learners know the 2,000 most frequent words of English, then they know 80 percent of the words in most texts, and the rest of the journey up to 95 percent can be calculated. But first, do learners typically know 2,000 word families?

What the Coverage Research Tells Us

What the coverage research mainly tells us is that there is no mystery why L2 reading should be seen as a problem area of instruction normally ending in some degree of failure. This is because 95 percent coverage corresponds to a vast quantity and quality of word knowledge and L2 learners tend to have so little of either.

Just within the 2,000 word zone already mentioned, intermediate classroom ESL learners typically do not know such a number of words, even at the most basic level of passive recognition. It is often the case that upper intermediate learners know many more than 2,000 words but not the particular 2,000 complete word families that would give them 80 percent coverage. They often know words from all over the lexicon, which is a fine thing in itself but nonetheless does not cover the basic level that gives them four words known in five. In several studies conducted by the current writer in several ESL zones (Canada, Oman, Hong Kong), academic learners were tested with different versions of Nation and colleagues' frequency-based Levels Test, and a similar result was invariably produced: through random vocabulary pick-up, intermediate learners have at least recognition knowledge of between 4,000 and 8,000 word families, but this knowledge is distributed across the frequency zones—say, following interests in sports, hobbies, or local affairs—but is incomplete at the 2,000 frequency zone.

A study by Zahar, Cobb, and Spada (2001) shows the results of frequency-based vocabulary testing with Francophone ESL learners in Montreal, Canada. The test samples word knowledge at five frequency levels, as shown in Table 7.2. The high group (Group 5) are effectively bilinguals, and Groups 1 and 2 are intermediate learners. The total figure on the right of the table refers to the total number of word families out of 10,000 that these learners know, so that learners in Groups 1 and 2 have recognition knowledge of 3,800 and 4,800 words respectively. But despite this, these learners only know about half the words at the 2,000 level. These skewed profiles are the typical products of random pick-up, with a possible contribution in the case of Francophone or Spanish ESL learners from easy-to-learn (or anyway easy-to-interpret) loan words or cognates which are mainly available at level 3,000 and beyond (*absent, accident, accuse, require*), the 2,000 level itself consisting largely of Anglo-Saxon items (*find, need, help, strike*) that are non-cognate.

Are the learners in Groups 1 and 2 in good shape for reading texts in English? Despite the number of L2 words they apparently know, the answer is probably no, as was confirmed empirically with these particular learners, but probably no in principle. That is because the words they know are mainly medium frequency, low coverage words that do not reappear often in new texts and hence do not increase the known-to-unknown ratio.

There is a rapid fall in text coverage after the 2,000 mark on any standard corpus frequency list, as can be seen in Table 7.3 and its graphic representation in Figure 7.3. While 100 words give just under 48 percent coverage, and 2,000 words give 78 percent coverage, after that the curve flattens out rather dramatically, so that learning another 1,000 word families gives only a further 6 percent coverage, another 1,000 only a further 3

TABLE 7.2
Levels Scores by Proficiency: Many Words, Low Coverage for Some

| Group by Proficiency | Vocabulary Level Scores (%) | | | | | Words Known |
	2,000	3,000	5,000	UWL	10,000	Total
1 (low)	50	56	39	33	17	3800 wds
2	61	72	44	39	22	4800 wds
3	72	83	56	56	39	6000 wds
4	83	89	67	62	39	6900 wds
5 (high)	94	100	83	72	56	8000 wds

TABLE 7.3.
Average Coverage Based on Lemmatized Brown Corpus of 1 Million Words

Number of Words	Coverage Provided
10	25%
100	48%
1,000	72%
2,000	78%
3,000	84%
4,000	87%
5,000	89%
6,000	90%
10,000	94%
15,000	97%
85,000	100%

percent, and so on. In other words, knowing a substantial number of even slightly lower-frequency words does not necessarily affect the key known-to-unknown word ratio. As they read, these learners are facing texts with *at least* one unknown word in five, in other words with more dark spots than the first of the Forestry texts in Figure 7.1. With such a small lexical knowledge base, both comprehension and further lexical growth through reading can only be sporadic.

But if the coverage figures expose potential problems at the 2,000 level, they expose far worse problems beyond the 2,000 level. Suppose a learner were attempting to reach 95 percent coverage on the basis of naturalistic expansion, a prescription which of course is implicit in the skills and practice model. Figure 7.2 predicts a rather slow climb from the 80 percent to the 95 percent mark, which on the basis of naturalistic growth or extensive practice would require the learning of some additional thousands of words, specifically well more than 10,000 word families, to reach 95 percent coverage. Let us now build a logical scenario for how this further growth could happen. Large numbers of post-2,000 words would clearly need to be learned, but unfortunately these words present themselves less and less frequently for learning. How infrequently? Again this can be determined by corpus analysis. Let us take the Brown Corpus as representing a

FIGURE 7.2
Graphic Representation of Coverage Figures

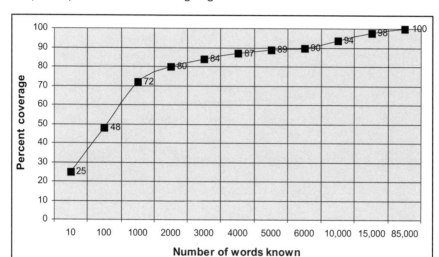

(rather improbable) maximum amount and variety of reading that an L2 learner could do over the course of a year. The Brown Corpus is just over one million words sampled from a wide variety of not very technical subjects. A description of this corpus can be found at Web reference [9], and the concordance analysis program used in this part of the analysis, called Range, at Web reference [10].

Range takes a word or word-root (roughly, a family) as input and returns the number of times and the number of sub-domains in the Brown corpus (from a total of fifteen) in which the input appears. Together, these counts give a maximum estimate of the number of times the input would be likely to appear in even the most diligent L2 learner's program of extensive reading. Table 7.4 shows the number and range of occurrences of a sample of words from below 2,000 and above 2,000 on the frequency list (see Web reference [11] for all lists discussed in this chapter). It seems quite clear that below 2,000, words appear often and in a wide variety of domains, but that at some point quite soon after 2,000, words appear much more rarely and only in some domains. Members of the *abort'* family appear only ten times in one million words, and in fewer than half of the sub-domains. Readers can extend and test this information on Range by entering their own words of different frequency levels. The conclusion seems obvious, that words

TABLE 7.4
Decreasing Likelihood of Meeting Words

0–1,000			1,000–2,000			4,000–5,000		
Word Family	Occurrences	Domains / 15	Word Family	Occurrences	Domains / 15	Word Family	Occurrences	Domains / 15
able	216	15	accustom'	15	10	abort'	10	7
accept'	270	14	admir'	66	14	adher'	26	9
agree'	286	15	afford'	58	12	ambigu'	40	7
answer'	277	15	amus'	38	13	analog'	29	8
appear'	426	15	annoy'	26	9	arbitrar'	27	7
arriv'	134	15	argu'	158	15	aspir'	28	9
MEAN	268.17	14.83		60.17	12.17		26.67	7.83
(SD)	(96)	(0.41)		(51.59)	(2.32)		(9.63)	0.98

will be encountered more and more sporadically after 2,000 and progress toward 95 percent coverage will be slow to non-existent (with the possible exception of cognates, as mentioned). And the picture presented in Table 7.4 may be even more dire than it appears, since counts are based on families, as indicated with apostrophes (*arriv'* = *arrive, arrives, arrival*), yet as Schmitt and Zimmerman (2002) have shown, learners cannot be assumed to recognize the different members of a family as being related.

The number of possible encounters with words clearly decreases, but does it decrease to the point where there is a learning problem? Are ten occurrences many or few? Vocabulary acquisition research has by now told us quite a bit about the conditions of L2 word learning, and of the various kinds of lexical knowledge that are produced by different kinds and numbers of encounters. The number of occurrences question is reviewed in Zahar, Cobb, and Spada (2001), and the overall determination seems to be that at minimum, ten occurrences are needed in most cases just to establish a basic representation in memory (cf. Horst, this volume). As Table 7.2 suggests, after the 2,000 point this many encounters could not always be guaranteed even with one million words of wide reading. However, that is not the end of the problem.

But of course just having a basic representation for words in memory or a vague sense of their meaning in certain contexts is not quite all that is needed for their effective use, especially in oral or written production, but also in effective reading comprehension. A common theme in the L1 reading research of the 1980s was that certain types of word knowledge, or certain ways of learning words, somehow did not improve reading comprehension for texts containing the words (e.g., Mezynski, 1983). These ways of learning mainly involved meeting words in single contexts, looking up words in dictionaries, or being taught words in a language classroom. In fact, the only learning method that did affect reading comprehension was meeting new words not only several times but also in a rich variety of contexts and even a rich variety of distinct situations. The reason appears to be that most words have a range of facets or meanings, such that if only one of these is known, then it is unlikely to be fully applicable when the word is met in a new text.

In the L1 research, however, inert learning was only a problem of passing interest. Direct vocabulary instruction and dictionary look-ups are relatively rare in L1 language instruction, and most L1 learners who are reading at all are doing so roughly within their 95 percent zones and meeting words in varied contexts as a matter of course. It is rather L2 learners who are quite likely to be learning words from infrequent, impoverished contexts, in texts chosen for interest rather than level or learnability, aided (or not) by dictionaries of varying qualities, one-off classroom explanations, and so on. In other words, here is a case where L1 reading research is more relevant to L2 than to L1. Some of my own research (e.g., Cobb, 1999) extends this line of investigation to an L2 context and indeed finds that learning new words in rich, multiple contexts and situations, compared to learning the same words from small bilingual dictionaries, reliably produces about 30 percent better comprehension for texts that incorporate the words. The problem, of course, is where to find a steady supply of such contexts for relatively infrequent words in a time frame of less than a lifetime. For the purposes of the experiments, the contexts were artificially assembled; in nature, even a million words of reading per year would not necessarily provide them in the case of post-2,000 words.

A further dimension of post-2,000 word knowledge that could be predicted to be weak on the basis of insufficient encounters is lexical access. Rapid lexical access is vital for reading ability, and its development is mainly a function of number of encounters with words. Vast numbers of encounters are needed to produce instantaneous lexical access for words (Ellis, N., 2002). With testing that relies on basic recognition as its criterion of word knowledge, learners may look as if they are well on the way to 12,000 word families, but how accessible is this knowledge? Again some of my own research may suggest an answer.

The importance of lexical access in reading was a landmark discovery in L1 research (e.g., Perfetti, 1985) and is now being adapted to the contours of L2 reading by Segalowitz, Segalowitz, and Wood (1998) and others (Fukkink, Hulstijn, & Simis, 2005; Segalowitz & Segalowitz, 1993). A good measure of how well a word is known is the length of time in milliseconds (ms) that it takes a reader to recognize the word or make some simple decision about it. Educated L1 readers produce a baseline reaction time of about 700 ms for common words, a time that rises slightly with frequency to about the 10,000-word mark, rarely surpassing 850 ms. But for even advanced L2 learners, the base rate is not only slower, at about 800 ms for the most common words (Cobb, 2008b; Segalowitz & Segalowitz, 1993), but also rises as words become even slightly less frequent, including between the 1,000–2,000, and 2,000–3,000 word levels. Results from an experiment with 19 advanced francophone L2 learners are shown in Figure 7.3. As can be seen, even medium frequency words (in the 3k or 3,000 word zone) are taking just under 1,000 ms, almost a full second, to recognize; this is 30 percent over the L1 baseline. These are times associated with "problem reading" in L1 (Perfetti & Roth, 1981); that is because lexical access is stealing resources from meaning construction. There is no reason to think the situation is any different in L2 reading. Teachers can test for frequency effects in their own learners' reaction times, for L1 or L2 words or both, using tools available at Web reference [12].

In other words, the prospects for arriving at 95 percent coverage by slogging through the outer reaches of the lexicon are not good, as can be predicted logically, and confirmed empirically. With words distributed as they

FIGURE 7.3
Reaction Times in L1 and L2 at Three Frequency Levels

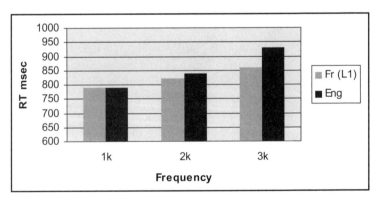

Note: L1 differences n.s.; all Eng (L2) differences significant at $p < .05$

are in the print lexicon, as shown by coverage analysis, sufficient encounters for deep learning can only happen over extremely long periods—in fact, as long as it takes to grow up in a language.

Learning to Read in L1 and L2: More and More Different

Much of the shared knowledge of a culture is stored in its lexicon, and much of a lexicon is stored in written texts. Spoken language, especially conversation, does not normally require a great number of lexical items, because distinctions of meaning can be conveyed extralinguistically or pragmatically or can be co-constructed through negotiation. The sparse nature of the conversational lexicon can be confirmed by running conversational texts through *VocabProfile* (Web reference [8]), which typically shows 90 percent or greater coverage from just 1,000 or even fewer words (cf. 80 percent for 2,000 words in written texts).

Because lexicons attempt to encode all of the possible distinctions that are relevant to successful functioning in their typical environments, they can grow to considerable sizes. In the case of English, and other languages with significant written components, this has led to the evolution of truly enormous lexicons. Limiting the proliferation of lexicons, however, is the competing requirement of learnability. A lexicon cannot become so enormous that no child can learn it. Borrowing from the analysis above, we can infer that the literate adult lexicon must be minimally sufficient to provide 95 percent coverage within a wide variety of texts, such that almost any but the most specialist texts can be read and the literally hundreds of thousands of low frequency items at the peripheries of the lexicon interpreted with varying degrees of effort in context. As already suggested, about 12,000 word families seems to be the minimum number needed for this, with most literate adults having well more than that. How much more? Empirical size estimates are compatible with this proposal in that they typically determine the vocabulary size of literate adults to be 20,000 word families in their L1s (Nation, 2001). This seems, then, to be the zone where the demands of proliferation and learnability intersect—somewhere between 12,000 and 20,000 word families.

And how long does it take to learn either number of word families to the degree that they are useful in reading comprehension? A classic study by Nagy, Herman, and Anderson (1985) detailed rates and sources of lexical growth, showing that while the average probability of learning any word from a single contextual encounter was rather low, it was nonetheless sufficient to account for the measured lexical growth of first-language learners on the basis of an average reading intake of 1 million words per year over 10 years of schooling. Between the ages of six and sixteen, an average of 3,000 to 4,000 literate words per year are learned, which adds up to far more than 20,000 word families. The L2 learner, in contrast, as we remember from the Milton and Meara (1995) study, learns on average 550 words per year, as measured on a basic yes-no vocabulary test (Do you know this word? Yes or No), that is, with no clue as to whether this knowledge was of the rapid-access, multi-contextual variety that can affect comprehension or provide the basis for further learning. In other words, the L1 rate is greater than the L2 rate by a factor of at six or seven. At best, L2 learners can end up with 5,000 or so word families in total, often not known very well, as already shown, and with gaps in high coverage zones, again as already shown. Even with 5,000 well-known words and no gaps, L2 learners are working with only 90 percent coverage, that is, with one word missing in ten—or one per line of printed text, as opposed to one per two lines at 95 percent. If we do the math (words needed, learning opportunities, learning rates) the numbers might add up for L1 learners, but they do not add up for L2 learners.

So the task of acquiring a literate lexicon is radically different for L1 and L2 learners, such that becoming a fully competent L2 reader is effectively impossible on the basis of input and practice alone. This runs against the assumption of communicative approaches to reading, namely the sufficiency of input and practice, which in turn is based on the assumption that learning to read in L1 and L2 are essentially the same. *Impossible* is of course a word the needs interpretation. Clearly some form of L2 reading does take place in the worlds of school and work, although probably with far larger infusions of top-down knowledge or other forms of guesswork than characterizes proficient L1 reading. And impossible only if we assume that input and practice must take place in L2 as it did in L1—that is, letting nature run its course, assigning to teaching a relatively minor, mainly facilitative role, and assigning to instructional design almost no role other than to ensure a wide range of text inputs for self-selection.

In L2, we apparently cannot rely on nature to do our teaching for us but must resign ourselves to mundane prospects like task and needs analysis, the establishment of feasible objectives, possibly different for different learners, and the usual processes of instructional design and materials selection—rather than pretending that reading will happen by itself as it appeared to in L1. But wait a minute: Wasn't it L1 reading researchers who warned educators that reading, unlike speech, is an "unnatural act" that is inherently difficult and will leave many behind unless steps are taken to prevent it (Gough & Hillinger, 1980, cited in Adams, 1990)? Somehow, this was not one of the L1 ideas that got imported into L2 thinking.

To summarize, the chapter has so far argued that the computer has played a vital role in the task analysis of L2 reading. This role derives from the fact that only a computer can hold enough textual or other information in memory to disclose relevant patterns, whether in the vast expanses of the collective lexicon (e.g., coverage information) or the minutiae of individual word processing (e.g., reaction times). To the naked eye, either is as invisible as the role of bacteria in disease must have been 100 years ago. And just as computing has played a vital role in defining the reading problem, so can it play a vital role in solving it. That is because the problem the computer solves for researchers is essentially the same one it can solve for prospective L2 readers—exposing the patterns buried in overwhelming data.

THE ROLE OF COMPUTING IN SOLVING THE PROBLEM

As discussed already, the obstacles to reading in a second language are predictable. But any problem that is predictable is in principle solvable. This part of the chapter deals with solutions to the problems outlined above, and proceeds with a problem and solution framework.

How Can Gaps in High-Coverage Lexical Zones Be Prevented?

While any L2 reading course should offer large amounts and variety of reading—that is, practice—it should also include some sort of direct, frequency-based vocabulary component which will expose learners at the very least to the 2,000 words that will reduce the dark spots in L2 texts to one word in five. This is not something that will happen by itself for all learners. It is common for L2 learners to know many words they will rarely see again yet still have gaps in the zones that provide high coverage in new texts (see Table 7.2). This situation can be prevented by making a level-appropriate, frequency-based vocabulary course a standard part of any L2 reading program, and at the same time making a pedagogical lexis course a standard part of any L2 teacher training program. In my experience, neither of these is particularly common at present, certainly less common than the ubiquitous pedagogical grammar course (despite the fact that grammar has never been shown amenable to pedagogy while vocabulary clearly is).

A point to note regarding vocabulary courses is that commercial vocabulary courses are not necessarily frequency-based; in fact, they are often devoted to "increasing your word power" precisely through the random pick-up of odd but interesting low frequency items that learners are already proficient in. A vocabulary course for learners could use a computer or not but, either way, if it is done according to principles previously discussed, it is likely to be homemade rather than store-bought. An idea for a full computer version of such a course is described in Cobb (1999), in which learners used corpus materials to build their own dictionaries for a complete 1,000-level frequency list and were tested using level-specific cloze passages (which can be built by anyone providing their own texts at Web reference [13]). Some principled, frequency-based course books are now beginning to appear, including one developed for "mastering the AWL" (or Academic Word List, to be discussed) by Schmitt and Schmitt (2005) that exemplifies many of the principles discussed above. A computer version of these materials providing maximum recycling and corpus back-up will be available at Web reference [14].

How Can Reading Texts Be Chosen to Maximize Learners' Skill Development, Vocabulary Growth, and Pleasure?

These benefits can be provided by matching texts to learners, that is, by providing them with texts bearing 95 percent of words they can be reasonably expected already to know and only 5 percent to be handled as new items (looked up, worked out from context, etc.). While such proportions are clearly impossible to calculate with total precision, they can be approximated well enough by matching learners' Levels Test scores to texts that are one level in front of them, as indicated by running the text through the computer program *VocabProfile* (Web reference [8]). For example, learners who are strong at the 1,000 word level but weak at 2,000 should read texts with five percent of their lexical items drawn from the 2,000 level. The texts could be either found texts or modified texts. It would be an understatement to say that finding or writing such texts would be difficult without the help of a program like *VocabProfile*.

Are There Any Shortcuts on the Long Climb to 95 Percent Coverage (12,000 Word Families)?

The short answer is yes, and again the shortcuts have been discovered through various types of computer text analysis and confirmed in empirical studies. Three of these will be outlined. First, Hirsch and Nation (1992) used *VocabProfile* to determine how many words would be needed to read a specific kind of text, unsimplified fiction for young adults, with pleasure and with further vocabulary learning. They found that texts in this genre typically present 95 percent known-word conditions for learners with a vocabulary of only 2,000 word families. This is because of a distinct feature of this particular genre, namely a predominance of names and other proper nouns which reduces the density of novel lexis, since names are not normally words that require any learning. So these texts are an excellent source of consolidation reading for learners who know 2,000 words, or acquisition reading for those who know 1,000 but are weak at 2,000. A limitation of this finding, of course, is that learners may have other reading goals.

Another approach and one of the most exciting research programs in L2 reading involves the creation of dedicated frequency lists for particular reading objectives. One of these is the already mentioned Academic Word List (AWL), which is intended for learners who are planning to undertake academic study through English. The AWL is a list of word families that are not included among the 2,000 most frequent families and yet are reasonably frequent across a minimum number of specialist domains within a large corpus. It was constructed by first isolating all the post-2,000 words of a large corpus with *VocabProfile,* and then determining which of these occurred a minimum number of times in all of four academic domains (arts, law, commerce, and science). The resulting list comprises just 570 word families (words like *access, abandon,* and of course *academic*) but, when added to the 2,000 list, makes a combined list of 2,570 word families that typically provide a coverage of about 90 percent in academic texts (which is otherwise achieved somewhere beyond 5,000 families, as shown in Figure 7.2).

Further shortcuts can be found beyond the AWL through the construction of frequency lists within particular domains. This was shown by Sutarsyah, Nation, and Kennedy (1994) in the domain of economics. Briefly, an economics corpus was assembled, the 2,000 and AWL lists subtracted out of it using *VocabProfile,* and each item in the remainder evaluated for number and range of occurrences across the chapters of a substantial economics text, yielding an "economics list" in the vicinity of 500 word families. This word list, in conjunction with the 2,000 list and AWL, typically raises coverage for texts *in this domain* to fully 95 percent in return for knowing just 3,070 word families. The development of such technical lists is one of the most exciting areas of current research and development.

Is There Any Way to Speed Up the Acquisition of Large Numbers of New Words?

Notwithstanding shortcuts, 2,000 or 3,070 word families are still substantial learning tasks. Medium-frequency words appear in texts only as often as they appear, and there is little that can be done to increase their numbers. But it is possible to increase the number of people looking for them, and then to share the findings. Something like this is often done by good teachers on their blackboards, but it can be done more effectively by learners themselves with a shared database on a computer network. The program *Group Lex* (Figure 7.4, Web reference [16]) is such a database. Hundreds of words can be entered into a simple database from the learners' reading materials, on whatever basis the group or teacher decides, and then sliced, diced, and recycled in several different ways. The program can encourage shared learning, domain-specific learning, and can generate quizzes online or on paper. Hundreds of words per month can thus be accumulated and encountered, either in a single sentence context and definition or in several contexts if this is encouraged. Learning results from an earlier version of this collaborative tool showed the learning rate increasing 40 percent over Milton and Meara's average (Cobb, 1999). Learning results from *Group Lex* and the story of its incorporation in a real language course are reported in Horst, Cobb, and Nicolae (2005).

Can Contexts Be Multiplied by a Computer in Any Learning-Useful Way?

Rich word knowledge depends on meeting words in several contexts. The answer is yes, through the use of an adapted concordance program. A concordance is a computer program that assembles all the contexts for a given word or phrase from different locations throughout a corpus, in the format of a central keyword and chopped-off line endings (although with an option to request a broader contextualization; see Web reference [18]). There is a question, however, whether any "rich" learning benefits can be derived from this form of multi-contextualization. This was the question of a research

FIGURE 7.4
Group Lex: Learning Words Together

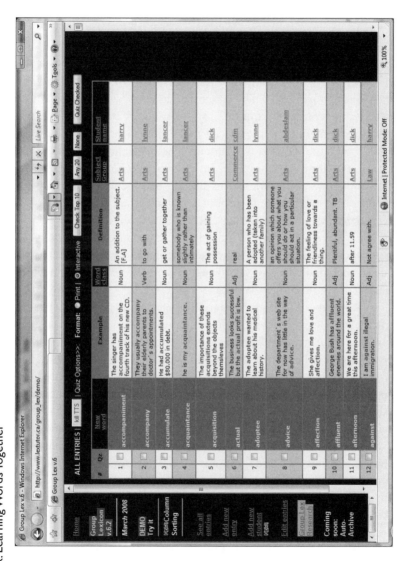

study (already briefly mentioned) in which university-bound learners in Oman built personalized glossaries of the entire second thousand word list, in which testing had shown them to be deficient. Each word in the glossary had to be accompanied by at least one clear example sentence found in a specially built corpus, and this entailed searching through several contexts for one that made sense to the learner. The corpus was a purpose-built collection of all the learners' course materials for one year. A control group performed a similar exercise but without the concordance work. The test of rich learning was to transfer several sets of learned words to gaps in level controlled, novel texts. The concordance users were 30 percent more successful than controls in this task, and therefore it appears that working with computer-generated contexts can make up at least to some extent for the lack of time to meet enough contexts in a more natural fashion (for a report on this research, see Cobb, 1997a, 1999; Cobb & Horst, 2001).

But how applicable is this finding to practical contexts? A purpose-built corpus while able to produce an interesting research result might be considered somewhat impractical. Building even a small special corpus is a rather large task. On the other hand, as a source of learning contexts, a natural corpus such as the Brown surely breaks the 95 percent known-word rule rather badly; many words are unlikely to be known in the inference base. Is there nothing in between?

A number of different sources of electronic text are being considered for their ability to provide comprehensible multi-contexts for intermediate learners. One is a trial learning corpus currently being constructed in Montreal from a collection of about 100 simplified readers. Such texts typically have more than 90 percent of their lexis in the 1,000 word–frequency zone, so virtually all contexts should be comprehensible for intermediate learners. Another idea involves providing concordances from within a single text or within the canon of a single writer, which should provide a consistency of style and substance that learners can gradually become accustomed to, so that as reading proceeds, the contextual information becomes more and more clear.

For example, Figure 7.5 shows a screen from Lextutor's Resource-Assisted Reading version of Jack London's tale *Call of the Wild* (Web reference [19]), wherein a reader has clicked on the curious word *bristling* in chapter 3 only to be reminded that there was already an occurrence of this word in chapter 1 and that there will be several more in chapters to come. This information is provided without the reader leaving the text he or she is reading, that is, without the text disappearing from view behind another window.

FIGURE 7.5
Interactive Story Concordance—I

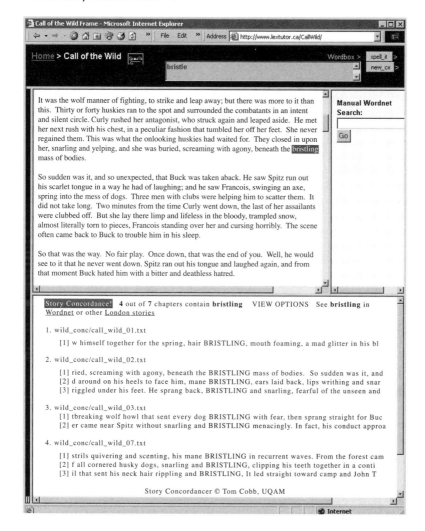

Story Concordancer © Tom Cobb, UQAM

One of the concordance lines in Figure 7.5 features a further unknown word, *mane*. Learners who were curious about that word, or felt it might give a clue to the meaning of *bristling*, could just wait until it cropped up somewhere later in the text, when they might or might not remember why they were interested in the word, or they could just click on it in the concordance window itself, which is also a live window that produces concordances of its own. Another option is to drag the mouse across both words, *mane* and *bristling*, to see further occurrences of the phrase in the story, if any, and in a larger context (as shown in Figure 7.6).

Still more contexts for either words or phrases can be produced by clicking the link *other London stories;* doing this will produce other uses of the same word or phrase in other works by the same author. Sure enough, I have employed this same expression in another story of his repertoire (see Figure 7.7). The point is that multiple contexts drawn from within a single canon should be more comprehensible than contexts drawn from random texts (like those of the Brown corpus), and moreover, this comprehensibility should increase with familiarity. Several screen shots have been provided so that readers can decide for themselves if the author-familiarity argument has any value. At what point 95 percent familiarity is achieved using this method is an empirical question.

The fully wired version of this particular story, Jack London's *Call of the Wild,* can be tested at Web reference [19], and a similarly wired French story (de Maupassant's *Boule de Suif,* at Web reference [20]). *Call of the Wild* and *Boule de Suif* are of course just two randomly chosen stories,

FIGURE 7.6
Interactive Story Concordance—2

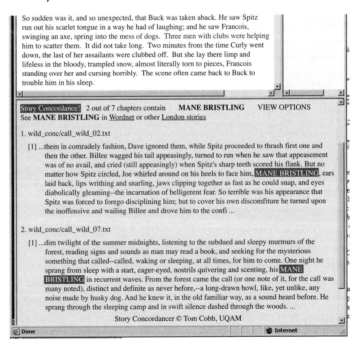

Story Concordancer © Tom Cobb, UQAM

FIGURE 7.7
Interactive Story Concordance—3

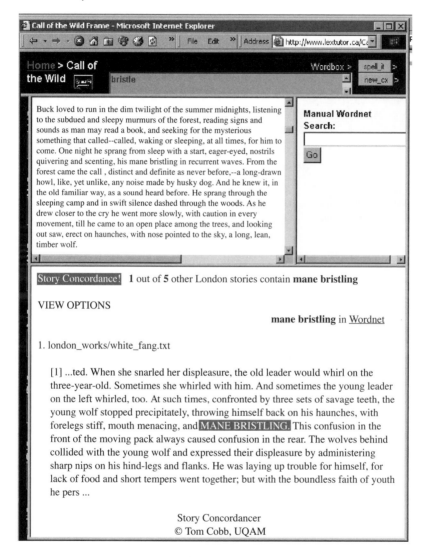

Story Concordancer
© Tom Cobb, UQAM

developed for purposes of demonstration and experimentation, and probably not all that useful for typical L2 readers ("bristling manes" are hardly to be met very often outside certain types of fiction). Teachers and learners would thus want to use these resources with texts of their own choosing, which they can do (for most of the resources described) at Web reference [21].

Is there any learning result from resource-assisted reading? A preliminary single-subject study by Cobb, Greaves, and Horst (2001a, 2001b) showed 40 percent superior vocabulary acquisition from resource-assisted over unassisted reading, and of course, vocabulary growth from reading is a good indication of text comprehension as well as an end in itself.

Isn't the Final Goal to Transfer Word Knowledge to Novel Contexts?

Working with familiar contexts is important at one stage of learning. At some point, of course, any newly learned words will have to be applied in contexts beyond those of a particular writer. Transfer is the final step in most theories of learning, and transfer, as we know, is unlikely to happen unless provisioned in the design of instruction. How it is provisioned in the story concordance is as follows. When learners have identified an interesting word that they want to work on, they can record it for later attention simply by clicking on it with Alt-key held down. Doing this places the word in the silver box that can be seen at the top of Figures 7.5 or 7.7, and reading can proceed uninterrupted. Then, at some convenient point like the end of a chapter, all these words can be recycled in various ways—added to the learner's private database, pasted into *Group Lex*, or sent automatically to a program that generates novel-context quizzes using concordances from the Brown. This program is *Multi-Concordance* (Web reference [18]). Figure 7.8 shows words gathered from a chapter in *Call of the Wild (bristle, howl, growl,* and *leap)* ready to be recycled in quite different sorts of contexts. The learner looks at the words around the gaps and tries to decide which of the targets will fit into each. Other options within *Multi-Concordance* can be used to prepare learners for this activity.

The vision presented here, then, is one where L2 learners undertake systematic vocabulary growth, read texts with known proportions of unknown lexis chosen in accordance with existing knowledge and learning goals, and maximize the vocabulary learning opportunities (recycling, recontextualization, and transfer) within these texts through the use of technology. The ideas presented here barely scratch the surface of what can be done with computers to develop and encourage vocabulary growth in designed L2 reading development. As mentioned, the computer and the L2 reader are a natural match. Instances and teaching ideas could be multiplied, but by now the point is probably made that the computer's ability to take in, relate, and organize large spans of written language, whether single texts or 100-

FIGURE 7.8
Transfer of *Call of the Wild* Words to Novel Contexts

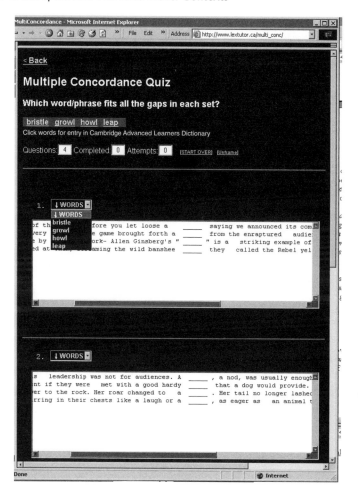

million word corpora, can compensate for many of the inherent difficulties of learning to read in a second language and, in principle, can play a very significant role in the development of L2 reading instruction. And in this context the question of whether media can have any unique effects on learning seems to belong to a simpler time.

But will the computer ever play such a role in L2 reading in fact? It is not impossible, although a number of things are working against it. First, as Bernhardt (2005) recently pointed out, a faithful 20 percent of the variance in L2 reading can be attributed to L1 reading level (cf. Freeman & Freeman, this volume), and "it is a rare L2 [intervention] study that appears to have an effect size large enough to overcome a 20 percent (or even a 10 percent) variance attributable to first language literacy" (p. 142). In other words, some L2 readers will always be weak for reasons neither learner nor teacher has any control over, and it is doubtful if any amount of vocabulary recycling or recontextualizing will produce a competent reader in an L2 who was not a competent reader in the L1. Thus, a good-enough definition of success in L2 reading is likely to prevail, and designs for systematic, goal-oriented improvement such as those proposed here are likely to be seen as wishful thinking. Second, the institutional infrastructure for a thoroughgoing computational approach like the one suggested here is not simple to achieve. If 30 learners are going to spend two hours a week on *Group Lex,* and read twenty pages of text designed by a teacher with the help of *VocabProfile* and linked to learning resources, for a long enough period to make any difference, this will only happen, on other than a one-off basis, in the most supportive of institutions. And third, while most learners are comfortable with screen reading, e-learning, and computing generally, many teachers are doubtful, resistant, or hostile to it. Any systematic use of computing in L2 education probably awaits a generational change. All in all, the role envisaged for the computer in this chapter can probably only develop in conjunction with solutions to broader problems.

On the bright side, the best L2 reading researchers tend to endorse a strong role for computing in reading instruction, albeit often without specifying much detail. Koda (2005) concludes her recent book on reading research with the thought that "The enhanced capabilities of advanced computer technology . . . hold strong promise for major breakthroughs in L2 reading instruction" (p. 273). But the brightest spot on the bright side is some grassroots developments that do not normally make it into the research journals. Lextutor's records show that many individual teachers and even learners are bypassing their institutions and using the website to design their own principled instructional materials. Thousands of users throughout the day and night, from all over the world, log on to take levels tests, run texts through *VocabProfile,* build resource-assisted hypertexts on literally thousands of topics, reconfigure hypertexts as cloze passages, and run many, many concordances for words and phrases of interest. If this is where the researchers, teachers and learners are heading, can the institutions be far behind?

ACKNOWLEDGMENTS

This chapter is based on two invited presentations from 2004, one at the reading symposium preceding TESOL 2004 in Long Beach, California, entitled "Computer solutions to classic L2 reading problems," and the other at the English Language Institute of the University of Michigan entitled "The logical problem with acquiring second lexicons and how networked computing can solve it."

Reflection Questions

1. In what sense is L2 reading often considered "a problem"?

2. With regard to whether computing is a necessity or a nicety in L2 reading, summarize the arguments for necessary, the arguments for nice, integrate each with your own experience, and assess which case is stronger.

3. What is coverage and what does the coverage research tell us about learning to read in a second language?

4. What are the "shortcuts" to competent L2 reading Cobb refers to, how has text computing been used to identify them, and how can text computing be used to exploit them?

Appendix: Web References

[1]   Lextutor Research   www.lextutor.ca/research/

[2]   Levels Tests   www.lextutor.ca/tests/

[3]   Zipf Website   www.nslij-genetics.org/wli/zipf/

[4]   Lextutor Frequency Indexer   www.lextutor.ca/freq/

[5]   Lancaster BNC Lists   www.comp.lancs.ac.uk/ucrel/bncfreq/
      lists/1_2_all_freq.txt

[6]   Basic English Website   ogden.basic-english.org/basiceng.
      html

[7]   General Service List   jbauman.com/aboutgsl.html

[8]   Lextutor VocabProfile   www.lextutor.ca/vp/

[9]   Brown Corpus   helmer.aksis.uib.no/icame/brown/bcm.html

[10] Lextutor Range   www.lextutor.ca/range/

[11] Lextutor Linked Lists   www.lextutor.ca/list_learn/

[12] Lextutor RT Builder   www.lextutor.ca/rt/

[13] Lextutor VP Cloze Builder   www.lextutor.ca/cloze/vp/

[14] Lextutor Schmitt Book   www.lextutor.ca/mastering_awl

[15] Lextutor Text Compare   www.lextutor.ca/text_lex_compare/

[16] Lextutor Group Lex   www.lextutor.ca/group_lex/demo/

[17] Lextutor Concordancers   www.lextutor.ca/concordancers/

[18] Lextutor Multi-Concordance   www.lextutor.ca/multi_conc/

[19] Lextutor Call of Wild   www.lextutor.ca/callwild

[20] Lextutor Boule de Suif   www.lextutor.ca/bouledesuif/

[21] Lextutor Hypertext Builder   http://www.lextutor.ca/hypertext/

[22] Lextutor Cloze Builder   www.lextutor.ca/cloze

CHAPTER 8

Balancing between Comprehension and Acquisition: Proposing a Dual Approach

Zhaohong Han and Amy D'Angelo,
Teachers College, Columbia University

The teaching of L2 reading over the past 30 years, following the communicative movement, has displayed an overriding focus on extracting meaning from the text—that is, comprehension (see, e.g., Aebersold & Field, 1997; Morrow, 1981; Morrow & Schocker, 1987). As a result, in many classroom settings, developing reading skills and strategies has become the sole priority. Such an approach primarily, though not exclusively, encourages top-down processing of reading materials via nonlinguistic, rather than linguistic, means such as contextual support by virtue of pictures (see Freeman & Freeman, this volume) and learners' background knowledge, the so-called *schemata* (see Anderson, this volume).

However, the communicative approach, as many have come to realize, is inadequate on a number of grounds (cf. Cobb, this volume). Most notably, it leads to unbalanced development in the L2 ability. Learners trained through this approach typically are adept at deriving global comprehension of texts (i.e., general understanding) but weak in local comprehension (i.e., understanding details). Of even more concern is that their grammatical ability on the whole suffers slow or minimal progression (cf. Johnson & Johnson, 1998), as does their lexical development (Cobb, this volume).

This chapter proposes a dual approach to teaching L2 reading that aims to balance reading for communicative and for acquisitional purposes. The communicative approach will be briefly compared and contrasted with its historical predecessor, the structural approach, to show that both are biased in terms of promoting L2 development. Drawing on findings from the SLA literature, we then will argue that reading for comprehension does not automatically lead to language development—acquisition—and, hence, the need for external facilitation of syntactic processing in a communicative context. Next, the main features of the dual approach are presented, followed by three research-based strategies to help its implementation in the classroom.

STRUCTURAL VERSUS COMMUNICATIVE APPROACHES

The structural approach (e.g., the grammar-translation method), which was the most prevalent pedagogical framework in the last quarter of the nineteenth century and which continued to dominate L2 classrooms for several ensuing decades, employs reading in service of grammar teaching and learning. Subsequently, this approach has, since the late 1960s, been superseded by the communicative approach.

Under the communicative approach, reading is conceptualized as a meaning-construction process, and instruction revolves around the following aspects:

> Teaching students how to utilize the skills and knowledge that they bring from their first language, developing vocabulary skills, improving reading comprehension, improving reading rate, teaching readers how to successfully orchestrate the use of strategies and how to monitor their own improvement. (Anderson, N., 1999, p. 1)

In sum, the goal of teaching under this approach is to develop skilled readers.

The contrast between the structural and the communicative approach is illustrated in Table 8.1 by two sample units taken from ESL/EFL textbooks.

TABLE 8.1

The Structural vs. Communicative Approach to Teaching Reading

Textbook A (Structural)	Textbook B (Communicative)
Unit 1	Unit 1 Reading Body Language
• Reading: Hidden Treasure	• Chapter openers
• Exercises:	i. Discussion questions: Communication without
i. Complete the sentences. Add any number of words (e.g., *There has always been ___ beside the sea.*).	words (e.g., *Think about these questions. Share your ideas with a partner or with a small group.*)
ii. Complete the sentences. Add any number of words (e.g., *Diamonds make women ___.*).	ii. Getting information from illustrations (e.g., *For each of these sentences, write its number on the line under the illustration that matches*
iii. Use *during* or *for* or *since* to complete these sentences (e.g., ___ *1492 we have known it.*).	*it best.*)
iv. Use of any of these words in each space: *at, for, in, near, of, on, to, with* (e.g., *The cargos ___ the Spanish galleons are not the only treasures ___ the bottom ___ the sea.*).	• Understanding and exploring reading
	i. Previewing the titles (e.g., *Look at the titles in the reading. Check the titles that you find in the following list.*)
	ii. Understanding details (e.g., *Complete the statements with the correct information from the reading.*)
v. In this exercise, one of the answers is better than the others. Do not write anything except the number of the question and the letter of the best answer. For example, to answer No. 1 you write down: '1c'.	iii. Matching ideas and details (e.g., *Match the activity with some part of the body.*)
E.g., 1. *Who wrote* <u>Treasure Island</u>?	• After reading
a. *An unknown writer.* b. *Sir Walter Raleigh.* c. *Robert Louis Stevenson.* d. *Henry Morgan.*	i. Reacting to the reading (e.g., *How do you send these messages non-verbally?*)
	ii. Solving a problem/Applying the information (e.g., *Think about the ideas in the chapter reading. What kinds of problems could people in the following situations have?*)
	• Vocabulary building
	i. Vocabulary in context (e.g., *Complete each sentence with one of the nouns from the following list. Use the words in boldface to help you choose your answer.*)
	ii. Categorizing (e.g., *Circle the word that does not belong in each of the following groups. Prepare to explain the reason for your choice.*)
	• Expanding your language
	i. Speaking (e.g., *Questionnaire: Answer these questions.)*
	ii. Writing (e.g., *Personal writing: Write six to ten sentences about how you use non-verbal language when you communicate.*)

Sources for some content in the table: Lewis, R. (1971). *Reading for Adults*. London: Longman; Wholey, M. (2000). *Reading Matters*. Cengage.

TABLE 8.2
The Structural vs. Communicative Approach: Characteristics of Learners

Learners	Approaches	Characteristics
Type A	Structural	Having "default" metalinguistic orientation,[1] but being poor readers; having a monotonous style of reading
Type B	Communicative	Being fast readers and able to read for different communicative purposes, yet having a poor command of L2 grammar

It is clear from Table 8.1 that there is a great deal of disparity between the two units. First, in [A], the focus is on grammar, but in [B], it is on (a) content, (b) skills (e.g., identifying main ideas and details, understanding the meaning of unknown words in context), and (c) transfer of skills (e.g., solving a problem). Furthermore, [A] manifests a product-orientation. In contrast, [B] features a process-orientation. Additionally, in [A], the learners' ability to read is tested, as is made apparent by the sequence of the reading text and the exercises (cf. Anderson, this volume), whereas in [B], it is explicitly taught. The latter is demonstrated through the pedagogical tasks clustering into three phases: (1) before reading (e.g., chapter openers), (2) while reading (e.g., understanding and exploring reading), and (3) after reading (e.g., reacting to the reading).

Thus, both approaches, by virtue of their respective concerns with one aspect of L2 learning almost to the exclusion of the other, are biased in promoting L2 development, resulting in learners that are strong in one aspect but weak in another. A brief summary is provided in Table 8.2 of what we perceive as major characteristics of learners trained under these approaches.

Apparently, Type A and Type B learners both have advantages and disadvantages to their L2 development. Type B learners, for example, may read more, due to their ability to read for a variety of purposes, hence potentially receiving more exposure to the target language.[2] Type A learners, on the other hand, due to their highly monotonous style of reading, often read less and have restricted experience with the target language (TL). However, this asymmetry in favor of Type B learners may be reversed if viewed from

---

[1]Here "orientation" is used in Tomlin and Villa's (1994) sense, namely, sensitivity to features of incoming linguistic stimuli.
[2]It is as yet an empirical question whether or not Type B learners do indeed have more experience with target language input.

a different vantage point. For example, from the perspective of construction of L2 knowledge, Type A learners may have better sensitivity to L2 grammatical features (cf. Leow, this volume) because of their repeated training in attending to form while reading. Quite often they have better accuracy in their L2 production than Type B learners whose preoccupation has been with construction of meaning from what they read (cf. Bardovi-Harlig, 1995). Hence, even though Type B learners are able to read more, a lot of what they read may fail to serve as useful input. By "useful input," we mean input that may potentially turn into intake. Put differently, the input that Type B learners receive through reading would not necessarily stimulate their construction of relevant L2 knowledge.

To recapitulate a major contrast between the two approaches in more straightforward terms, the structural approach has primarily sought to engage learners in syntactic processing (processing reading materials for their grammar), while the communicative approach focuses learners on semantic processing (processing texts for their propositional content).[3] Clearly, neither approach is sufficient for L2 development. SLA research over the past four decades has established that both types of processing are necessary for balanced—and *crucial* for *continuous*—L2 development (see, e.g., Lightbown & Spada, 1990; Long & Robinson, 1998; Swain, 1985). As VanPatten and Sanz (1995) have pointed out, "if the language is to be learned, the internal processor(s) must eventually attend to how the propositional content is encoded linguistically" (p. 171). It follows that being able to make targetlike form-meaning connections should be the goal of L2 learning. A crucial question, if not the crux of the issue, then, is: How can this goal be best facilitated through the teaching of reading? A necessary point of departure for any attempt to address this issue would require an understanding of the nature of L2 reading, to which we now turn.

L2 READING AS A DUAL PROCESS

That L2 reading can lead to a linguistic as well as an informational outcome has long been recognized (see, e.g., Lee, 2002; Freeman & Freeman, this volume). Krashen (1993), for example, refers to it as the power of reading.

---

[3]Although semantic processing does not preclude syntactic processing, the levels of syntactic processing activated during semantic processing may be insufficient for intake to occur. Comprehension, according to SLA research, may occur at various levels involving either or both the semantic and structural components of the text available to be comprehended, and these levels of comprehension may not interact with one another (Doughty, 1991; Gass, 1988).

However, unlike Krashen, who views the dual outcome as deriving from a unitary process, that is, through exposure to comprehensible input, many researchers have entertained the notion that the dual outcome is subserved by two distinct processes: comprehension and acquisition (Chaudron, 1985; Cook, 1997; R. Ellis, 1994; Faerch & Kasper, 1986; Gass & Selinker, 2001; Lightbown, 2000; Sharwood Smith, 1986; VanPatten, 2004). Gass and Selinker (2001), for example, assert that "comprehension and acquisition are not synonymous" (p. 316). Similarly, VanPatten (1996) speaks of processing input for meaning versus processing input for form, where form is associated, by and large, with forms that carry little communicative meaning such as grammatical morphemes.

The dual-process conception is premised on several established facts. First of all, there exists a fundamental difference between first and second language acquisition (e.g., Bley-Vroman, 1989; Cobb, this volume). First language learners are able to learn language implicitly through experience with the target language (TL). L2 learners, on the other hand, are in general less able to do so; rather, they depend their learning on explicit instruction—external assistance (Bley-Vroman, 1989; DeKeyser, 2000; R. Ellis, 1994; Schmidt, 1990; Swain, 1985; Terrell, 1991). Second, L2 learners, adults in particular, due primarily to first language interference and maturational constraints (Han, 2004), are not easily susceptible to the influence of mere exposure to TL input. Hence, even when afforded abundant input (e.g., many opportunities to read texts in the TL), it does not necessarily follow that they will utilize it to restructure their interlanguage (Harley & Swain, 1984; Swain, 1991). Last but not least, when processing input, oral and written, L2 learners are naturally biased toward meaning (e.g., Faerch & Kasper, 1986; Sharwood Smith, 1986; Skehan, 1998; VanPatten, 1996, 2004). In other words, their focal attention defaults to reconstructing meaning from input.

While the inclination to process input for meaning (i.e., informational content) is arguably true for first language learners as well, the strategies employed by first and second language learners are qualitatively different. First language learners, as Peters (1985) notes, "pay attention to utterances that have a readily identifiable meaning. Extract and remember sound sequences that have a clear connection to a clear context" (p. 1034). Put simply, their processing entails a form-meaning mapping process whereby there is a synchronous processing of form (i.e., language) and meaning. This, however, is not what typically happens when L2 learners process input for meaning; rather, they tend to rely on non-linguistic information such as contextual clues and world knowledge for inferring meaning (for a recent study, see Nikolov, 2006; cf. Cobb, this volume). In consequence, their processing of form occurs only at a minimum. Thus, it is often observed that L2 learners' ability to understand language in a meaningful context surpasses their ability to comprehend decontextualized language and produce language of comparable complexity and accuracy (Lightbown, 2000). This is not to suggest, however, that for L2 learners, processing for form never occurs.

L2 learners, as VanPatten (1990) notes, are able to process input for form in and of itself, but the question is "whether or not they can do this while they process input for meaning" (p. 288). Thus, the issue of attention to form arises only when the input is communicative in nature. SLA research from an information processing perspective has suggested that when focal attention to form occurs, it is often asynchronous with processing for meaning. Skehan (1998; cf. McLaughlin, Rossman, & McLeod, 1983), for example, argues that learners' attentional capacity is limited and, hence, that they need to prioritize cognitive tasks such that processing for meaning takes precedence over processing for form. Similarly, VanPatten (1996, 2004) asserts that not only do learners process input for meaning before they process it for form, they also do so by following some principles, such as:

1. They process content words in the input before anything else.
2. They prefer processing lexical items to grammatical items (e.g., morphology) for semantic information.
3. They prefer processing "more meaningful" morphology before less or nonmeaningful morphology.
4. For them to process form that is not meaningful, they must be able to process informational or communicative content at no or little cost to attentional resources. (1996, pp. 14–27)

These principles reveal another crucial dimension to learners' ability to process input for form, and that is that simultaneous meaning and form processing can only occur when the forms to be processed carry significant information (e.g., lexical items), but not when the forms are not related to sentence or discourse meaning (e.g., morphological agreement).

Taken together, the research-based insights illuminate the inadequacy of an exclusively meaning-based approach to reading instruction: Due to its overriding focus on meaning-oriented comprehension, such an approach offers limited opportunity for students to process texts for an understanding of how meaning is encoded linguistically. As Loschky (1994) aptly points out, "one may generally comprehend input at $i + 1$ by using comprehension strategies without turning it into intake, if one does not pay attention to linguistic forms while interpreting the input" (p. 319). Similarly, Gass (1988) comments that "what is comprehended can either feed into the intake component or alternatively, it may not be used by the learner for anything beyond immediate communication" (p. 205). Clearly, intake, a subset of input that has been attended to and processed by the learner, is what needs to occur for a linguistic system to be built and to be then put to use in comprehension and production. The problem with an exclusively meaning-based approach, then, boils down to the fact that it generates some comprehension but little intake, and hence little acquisition.

An issue that is often neglected by advocates of an exclusive focus on content/meaning is that lack of intake may, ultimately, constrain and compromise comprehension, since use of non-linguistically related comprehension strategies can aid, only to a limited extent, inference of *context-dependent* meaning (cf. Lightbown, 2000). By the same token, reliance on lexical items that carry heavy semantic value may, at best, enable some coarse-grained comprehension. These consequences have been empirically proven. In their study of university students of Spanish as a foreign language, VanPatten and Cadierno (1993), for example, observed that their subjects used contextual clues for comprehension, creating the appearance that they understood the flexible word order rules of Spanish. However, when they were forced to rely on language alone, they made all sorts of errors due to their lack of knowledge of Spanish word order. This same finding was replicated in a later study by VanPatten and Oikkenon (1996).

Language, as we know it, is both context-dependent and *context-independent*. A prime example of the latter is many a morphological and syntactic rule that is "frozen" and that must therefore be strictly adhered to regardless of context. Some of these morphological and syntactic forms carry communicative meaning (e.g., tense and aspect), but others are purely formal (e.g., third person singular form in English)—communicatively redundant, so to speak. Nevertheless, a sound knowledge of both types of forms is clearly necessary for achieving accurate comprehension.

Such, however, has not been the understanding of many teachers working with ESL or EFL learners, nor of many methodologists. By way of illustration, in a *Complete K–12 Reference Guide*, Diaz-Rico and Weed (2002) offer the following recommendation:

> Regardless of what is chosen . . . the teacher must consider two main criteria: Are the content objectives for the lesson adequately presented by the material? Is the material comprehensible to English learners? (p. 122)

[One] means of modifying input is by exaggerating intonation and placing
more stress on important new concepts. Again, this is similar to caretaker
speech, in which nouns and verbs in a sentence are emphasized more than
the smaller function words (*the, a, in, on*). . . . Teachers also monitor their
vocabulary usage and sentence structure. They control their use of idioms
and/or teach idiomatic expressions. They simplify their syntax, often keeping to a subject-verb-object structure with little or no embedded clauses.
(p. 129)

This kind of recommendation reveals several assumptions. First, comprehensible input leads, *ipso facto*, to linguistic development. Second, modified
input—including simplification—facilitates comprehension. Third, content
words are more important than function words. These assumptions mirror
to a great extent Krashen's view, in particular his Input Hypothesis. They
are largely false, nonetheless. SLA researchers over the last twenty years
have empirically shown (a) that acquisition does not necessarily follow as
a byproduct of comprehension (Gass & Selinker, 2001); (b) that modified
input does not necessarily improve comprehension or acquisition (e.g., Lee,
1998, 2002; Leow, 1993, this volume); and finally, (c) that L2 learners have
particular difficulty acquiring, on their own, linguistic items that "are rare,
and/or semantically lightweight, and/or perceptually non-salient, and/or
cause little or no communicative distress" (Long & Robinson, 1998, p. 23).
Although space constraints do not permit an exhaustive review of relevant
empirical studies, four studies are summarized to illustrate the first two
points (cf. Leow, this volume).

Blau (1982) studied the effects of modified input on reading comprehension. For this purpose, three versions of the same paragraph of text—
with the same vocabulary and content—were created of varying length
and syntactic complexity. They were subsequently administered to college
students and eighth graders. The subjects were then given multiple choice
questions immediately following their reading. The results showed that for
neither group did the syntactically modified input facilitate comprehension.
Similar findings were reported in Ulijn and Strother (1990), a study examining the effects of input modification, background knowledge, and linguistic
knowledge. The subjects were humanities and computer science majors for
whom English was an L1 and an L2. A computer science article was chosen
for the experimental text, from which a syntactically modified version was
derived. The results showed that input modification did not facilitate text
comprehension, but background knowledge and linguistic knowledge did.

While both studies examined the effects of input modification on *comprehension*, Leow (1993, this volume) tested a widespread claim, namely that the comprehensibility of input directly determines the amount of intake. Using simplification as a means of input modification and controlling for type of linguistic item and L2 experience, Leow created four input conditions: (a) a simplified reading passage with the Spanish present perfect tense form; (b) an unsimplified reading passage with the present perfect tense form; (c) a simplified reading passage with the present subjunctive form, and (d) an unsimplified passage with the present subjunctive form. One hundred and thirty-seven undergraduate students enrolled in the first and fourth semesters of Spanish language study served as subjects. Through a pre- and post-test design, and using a multiple choice recognition task as a measure of intake, Leow was able to gauge the effects of simplification and language experience on the subjects' intake. Results indicated that simplification of a written authentic text did not have a significant effect on subjects' intake of either of the two linguistic items investigated, but that language experience did. This finding led Leow to conclude:

> If we consider the rather small increase in intake in this study by learners exposed to simplified passage and the amount of time, effort, and expertise needed to modify texts for the classroom, it can be strongly argued that the use of authentic texts provides a more practical alternative to simplified texts. (p. 344)

Leow's study, thus, challenges a popular assumption that simplified input may facilitate comprehension, and that it, in turn, may facilitate intake (cf. Issidorides & Hulstijn, 1992; Long, 1996; Sharwood Smith, 1986; VanPatten, 1990).

That there is no significant correlation between comprehension and intake has been further confirmed in a number of more recently conducted SLA studies. Of note is Lee (1998) for its unique design. Previous studies, as shown, have looked at the effects of input modification on either comprehension (e.g., Blau, 1982; Ulijn & Strother, 1990) or intake (e.g., Leow, 1993), but Lee's study examined both comprehension and intake in one single design, thereby providing a more direct picture of the link (or the lack thereof) between comprehension and intake. Following Leow (1993), in modifying the input Lee targeted a specific linguistic element, verb morphology in Spanish. As in previous studies, different input exposure conditions were created for subjects via three different versions of an experimental text. Two of them contained verb morphological modifications of varying complexity. In the study, comprehension was evaluated through a written recall task immediately following the reading, and intake through a word recognition task immediately after the recall task. Subjects were 71 students from four classes of a second-semester Spanish course at a large, public Midwestern university, and the experiment took place during their regular class time. The three different versions of the reading passage were distributed randomly to each of the four classes. The study led to the following findings:

> When naturally attending to meaning, learners: (a) comprehend better when the forms in the input are less complex than when they are more complex, (b) detect the forms in the input, and (c) comprehend informational content and process the forms via different processes. (p. 42)

Of these findings, two are particularly worth highlighting for our purposes. The first is that input modification by means of morphological simplification—as opposed to morphological complexification—aids comprehension, thus offering a granular understanding of the effects of morphological modification of input for comprehension. The second is that comprehension and intake invoke different sets of cognitive processes. Based on this finding, Lee concluded that "good comprehenders are not necessarily good input processors" (p. 41).

The hitherto rather consistent evidence of a dissociation of comprehension and acquisition validates Sharwood Smith's (1986) theory of language input as having dual relevance, which states:

> At moment X, the learner's main aim may be to extract meaning and survive or succeed in a given interchange of messages. In this case, only those aspects of input which will aid the learner in this communicative endeavor (linguistic or otherwise) will be relevant in this first sense: *the learner will interpret for meaning.* At the same time, there will be linguistic input which is relevant to the current state of the learner's competence. It may contribute to the substantiation or reflection of some current hypothesis about the target language system: *the acquisition device will 'interpret' for acquisition.* (p. 243; emphasis in original)

On this view, language input may be relevant to the learner for comprehension/communication, but it may also be relevant to the learner for intake/acquisition. Figure 8.1 illustrates processes related, respectively, to acquisition and comprehension.

FIGURE 8.1
Input Processing and Dual Relevance (reproduced from Sharwood Smith, 1986, p. 250)

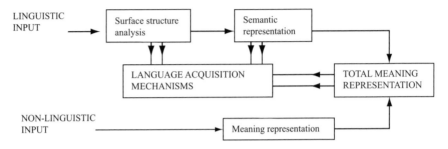

The double arrows in the diagram indicate the course of acquisition-ally related processes; the single arrows show the here-and-now, communicatively related processes. As illustrated, for communicative purposes, the learner potentially has two ways of deriving meaning. One option is to use non-linguistic input, and the other to perform surface structure analysis. In the second case, memory for surface structure can be short-lived; that is, "surface structure is just briefly registered, recoded for meaning alone and then discarded forthwith, [and] the acquisitional mechanism would have little or no access to crucial information for the further development of [grammatical] competence" (Sharwood Smith, 1986, p. 250; cf. Lee & Valdman, 2000). For acquisition to occur, on the other hand, "the surface structure must first be held in an acquisition-specific memory store and not simply discarded after semantic processing has taken place" (p. 251). When such a cognitive condition obtains, the acquisitional mechanisms will perform what is described as a five-stage procedure whereby they

1. compare the semantic representation (derived purely from current competence) with the total meaning representation (semantic representation plus meaning derived via other means like real-world knowledge . . .) and note any discrepancy

2. adjust semantic representation to fit the facts where a discrepancy is noted, i.e., where current competence has apparently generated a semantic representation that is in violation of the facts of the situation

3. generate a surface structure from the adjusted semantic representation according to the rules of the current grammar

4. compare the original surface structure with the new surface structure (in 3) and note any discrepancy

5. restructure current competence system (grammar) so that the adjusted semantic representation may be derived from the original surface structure, if there was indeed a discrepancy (in 4). (p. 251)

Clearly, the implementation of these cognitive procedures requires that the input be sufficiently robust, which means, in this context, consistent and frequent (cf. Larsen-Freeman, 1975).

The dual relevance theory also implies that the input to which learners are exposed must be communicatively complex or 'diversified' so that it may provide for both communicatively driven comprehension and acquisition (cf. Cobb, this volume). Viewed in this light, input modification, especially simplification, may, at best, serve one purpose (i.e., comprehension) at the expense of the other (i.e., acquisition). As Sharwood Smith (1986) aptly points out, "input that has been specially packaged for optimal comprehension may actually deprive the learner of useful structural information about the target grammar" (p. 250). Authentic input, it therefore follows, should be preferred to modified input. For one thing, authentic input naturally contains features that are needed for acquisition to take place.[4] For another, using it would be in keeping with the ultimate goal of communicative teaching, namely, to enable students to develop an ability to work with unmodified texts.

Summing up, research has established eight major findings on input processing as it occurs in the L2 reading process:

1. Meaning takes priority.

2. Comprehension and acquisition are not synonymous.

3. L2 learners need to attend to form for linguistic development.

4. L2 learners are unable to develop a targetlike linguistic system on their own, solely through exposure to comprehensible input.

5. Due to limited cognitive processing capacity, early-stage L2 learners are only able to perform one type of processing at a time.

---

[4]At this stage of understanding, we, as a field, are not yet able to pinpoint the features that would trigger acquisition. Yet precisely for this reason, authentic input—with nothing artificially modified or removed—stands a better chance of meeting the learners' acquisition needs than does modified, especially simplified, input. In this case, the difference between authentic and modified input is that the former leaves the decision on what can become intake to the language acquisition device, while the latter makes the decision for the learner.

6. Acquisition entails form-meaning mapping.

7. Semantic processing is a prerequisite to syntactic processing and syntactic processing a prerequisite to acquisition.

8. Authentic input may be more facilitative of acquisition than simplified input.

Together, these findings form the theoretical foundation for the dual approach to instruction to be recommended in the next section.

A DUAL APPROACH TO TEACHING L2 READING

In this section, we propose, as an alternative to the communicative approach to L2 reading instruction, a dual approach, which aims at fostering both semantic and syntactic processing, as illustrated in Figure 8.2.

As shown in Figure 8.2, the dual approach comprises two major components: *comprehension* and *acquisition*, with *comprehension* identified with *semantic processing* on the one hand, and *acquisition* with both *semantic processing* and *syntactic processing*, on the other. Further, *comprehension* subsumes two sub-processes: *achieving comprehension* and *developing efficiency*. Similarly, *acquisition* has two aspects to it: *developing metalinguistic awareness* and *understanding form-meaning connections*. Note the sequence between semantic processing and syntactic processing: the dual approach stipulates that semantic processing must precede syntactic processing. This is indicated by the one-way arrow between the two. Thus, instruction should begin with a focus on comprehending the meaning of the

---

FIGURE 8.2
A Dual Approach to Teaching L2 Reading

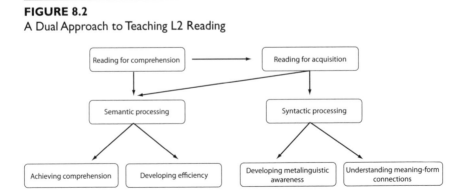

text before it proceeds to exploring some of its grammatical features. This sequence is purported in part to capitalize on learners' natural processing tendency (see earlier discussion) and in part to create a meaningful context for acquisition. Research has shown that "learners/readers make meaning from the form better when they have more opportunities to process the form in the meaningful context of reading a passage" (Lee, 2002, p.132; cf. Doughty, 1991; Lightbown & Spada, 1990).

The dual approach has a number of characteristics: (a) process-orientation, (b) natural integration of semantic and syntactic processing, and (c) specific attention to each type of processing. A brief explication follows.

Process-Orientation

Under the dual approach, the goal of teaching is not testing reading comprehension, but rather equipping learners with skills for comprehending L2 texts as well as facilitating their mental processing of the TL input (i.e., provided by the texts; cf. Anderson, this volume). In other words, the focus of attention is on assisting learners in semantic and syntactic processing.

Natural Integration of Syntactic Processing and Semantic Processing

The dual approach supports a natural integration of semantic and syntactic processing activities. With carefully selected texts, learning tasks are constructed such that skills necessary for comprehension are taught and learner attention is drawn to linguistic features as they naturally appear in the discourse contexts (as provided by the texts). In addition, special pedagogical procedures are deployed to aid learners in processing hard-to-acquire grammatical features.

Giving Due Attention to Each Type of Processing

Under the dual approach, while the two types of processing are naturally integrated within the framework of well-selected texts, due attention is given to the training of each type of processing. Specifically, for semantic processing, tasks are developed to equip learners with strategies, top-down and bottom-up (see Freeman & Freeman, this volume), for comprehension, and skills (e.g., skimming, scanning, and inferring the meaning of unknown words from context) are taught to help learners develop an ability to read for a variety of authentic, communicative purposes. For syntactic processing, on the other hand, explicit and implicit pedagogical strategies are employed to facilitate learners' processing of certain grammatical features and construction of relevant linguistic knowledge about the TL. The next section introduces three strategies culled from the SLA literature: (a) input enhancement, (b) processing instruction, and (c) narrow reading. These strategies are purported to promote intake in a meaning-oriented environment, and hence can be adapted for classroom use within the dual approach framework.

PEDAGOGICAL STRATEGIES

Input Enhancement

The notion of 'input enhancement' comes from Sharwood Smith (1991,1993), referring to pedagogical means by which L2 learners' attention is drawn to linguistic features in the input, such as word order, prepositions, adverb placement, subject-predicate agreement, and so forth (see also Leow, this volume). The notion was put forward on the basis of a number of observations. First, L2 learners are generally found to lack sensitivity to natural input. As a consequence, even when a large amount of it is available in their learning environment, they are unable to take advantage of it. Second, certain linguistic features in the input to which learners are exposed are inherently non-salient, and hence their presence often evades learners' attention. Third, learners' L1 may act as hindrance to their ability to notice certain linguistic features in the input (cf. Shiotsu, this volume).

Input enhancement applies to both oral and written input. Oral input can be enhanced through, for example, adjusting the volume of voice, varying the intonation, intensifying word and sentence stress, inserting pauses, and adjusting the speed for delivering utterances. Similarly, written textual input can be enhanced via typographical means such as capitalizing, underlining, italicizing, and so forth.

Input enhancement is, therefore, about manipulating the input to make certain L2 features salient in order to facilitate their noticing by the learner; it is an implicit, rather than explicit, way to 'teach' grammar. Illustrations of the input enhancement strategy can be found in Alanen (1995) and J. White (1998), among others.

Processing Instruction

"Processing instruction," proposed by VanPatten (see, e.g., VanPatten & Cadierno, 1993), teaches grammar explicitly. It seeks to guide learners' mental processing of input. More specifically, it is about changing the way input is perceived and processed. Research has shown that a processing-instruction approach to teaching reading may enhance both L2 knowledge and use (see, e.g., VanPatten & Sanz, 1995).

Processing instruction takes as its point of departure an attempt to understand how learners are processing a specific linguistic feature of input. It then determines whether the strategies employed will lead to a correct mental mapping of its form and meaning. It is comprehension-based, yet it goes beyond to enable an understanding (i.e., on the part of the learner) of how a given meaning is conveyed via a particular linguistic structure and vice versa. Readers are referred to VanPatten (2004), VanPatten and Cadierno (1993), and VanPatten and Sanz (1995) for illustrations of input processing strategies.

Narrow Reading

Narrow reading is a strategy advocated by Krashen (1981) for providing comprehensible input to facilitate acquisition. It involves providing students with multiple reading texts/multiple messages on the same or a similar topic (see Cobb, this volume, for a similar strategy). As such, it can facilitate comprehension and acquisition in at least three major ways. First, the fact that the same topic is dealt with in multiple texts from (usually) multiple perspectives creates content-familiarity, which, in turn, not only facilitates comprehension but also allows students to free up attentional resources (that would have otherwise gone entirely into semantic processing) for syntactic processing. Second, the recurrence of some linguistic structures and vocabulary increases their saliency, thereby lending them readily to noticing. There is now a general consensus that noticing is a necessary condition for second language acquisition (see, e.g., Schmidt, 2001; cf. Leow, this volume). Third, and most importantly, narrow reading naturally affords focused input that facilitates understanding of form-meaning connections.

The communicative approach to teaching L2 reading instruction facilitates semantic processing, but not syntactic processing, and the structural approach does just the opposite. Each results in a lack of balance in L2 development, and neither is therefore fully conducive to L2 acquisition, acquisition construed as making targetlike form-meaning connections. Considering that L2 learners, in general, are inadequate at implicit learning (i.e., learning from comprehensible input alone), we recommend that a dual approach be employed in teaching L2 reading that gives due attention to both content and language. Under this approach, instructors teach comprehension skills *as well as* raise learners' metalinguistic awareness of linguistic features and form-function relations—importantly, in context. Such an approach, we reason, is likely to realize the potential of L2 reading as a dual process, and, hence, to result in balanced development of communicative skills and linguistic systems among L2 learners.

Strategies that are compatible with the dual approach are by no means confined to the three—i.e., input enhancement, processing instruction, and narrow reading—described above. In the chapter by Freeman and Freeman, the strategy used by Mr. Roberts is also in line with the dual approach, as is the strategy Cobb suggested in his chapter concerning choice of texts from the canon of a single writer (see also Doughty & Varela, 1998; Doughty & Williams, 1998; Leeman et al., 1995; Rodgers, 2006). What is important to keep in mind is that these strategies are not identical in serving the dual purpose; rather, they are complementary. On the premise of a good understanding of the dual approach, teachers should by all means feel free to create their own strategies to promote comprehension, i.e., creating meaning from the propositional content of the texts for the purpose of interpreting a message (Lee, 2002), and acquisition, i.e., making form-meaning connections from the linguistic data in the texts for the purpose of constructing a linguistic system (Lee, 2002), among their own students, insofar as the strategies created adhere to two principles: (a) that semantic processing tasks precede syntactic processing tasks and (b) that they separately aim at enhancing development of a communicative reading ability and acquisition of form-meaning connections, nevertheless within the same meaningful context as provided by the reading texts.

Reflection Questions

Reflection Questions

1. Why is a comprehension-exclusive approach to teaching L2 reading inadequate?

2. The dual approach stresses the primacy of meaning-based processing of text. Can the dual components, comprehension and acquisition, be reversed? Why or why not?

3. This chapter introduces three pedagogical strategies for integrating a focus on form in a comprehension-based approach to teaching reading. Can you think of other strategies that might achieve the dual purpose of fostering comprehension and acquisition?

4. Is it true that all L2 learners, regardless of proficiency, assume a meaning-based approach to processing L2 texts? Under which circumstances may the processing of form and meaning occur simultaneously?

Epilogue: Reflections on Second Language Reading Research and Instruction

William Grabe, Northern Arizona University

If you, the reader, have gotten to this concluding chapter, you have learned a lot about L2 reading and about various components of L2 reading ability, including how research can be employed to argue for various perspectives on reading, how vocabulary and extensive reading support reading development, how text can influence the reader, and, most importantly, how various reading skills can be taught to improve L2 students' reading abilities. All chapters present ways to understand important components of reading ability, linking research to instruction.

The chapters in this volume raise important issues that need to be considered by anyone interested in how a student becomes a reader in a second language. While the chapters are not intended to provide general overviews of how reading develops over an extended period of time, or how reading abilities combine to bring about comprehension of a text, they do offer many insights into the reading process and many possibilities for future exploration.

Each chapter explores a set of specific areas associated with L2 reading, including word recognition, vocabulary learning, extensive reading, or reading strategies. For example, for L2 readers, it is clear from research that word recognition skills are essential for reading, no matter what first language and L2 are involved, but that these skills vary from L1 to L2. Students bring their L1 perspectives to L2 reading and need appropriate assistance in moving toward fluent word recognition abilities in the L2. This is a generally recognized perspective among L2 reading researchers (Bernhardt, 2005; Cook, 2005; Koda, 2005). Similarly, reading strategies are essential for L2 reading, and there are key strategies that assist L2 readers, yet there is no one set formula for what represent the two or three most effective strategies to be used at all times and for all students (Anderson, N., 2005; Ediger, 2006; Grabe, 2006; Taylor, Stephens, & Asher, 2006).

What is especially important about the contributions to this volume are the efforts made to connect theory and instruction and to move beyond implications to applications. Of course, the theory-instruction application cycle does not end with applications; we need to assess the applications to observe the extent to which instruction made a difference in learning to read. Determining if applications have been beneficial or not then leads directly back to theory. Improvements in reading can be linked back to specific teaching practices that can inform and alter the theories that drive the instructional implications in the first place. Relations between learning theory and instructional practice should be synergistic—theory without effective translation into practice is potentially wasteful; practice without explanatory theory represents guessing what to do with curricular and instruction planning. However, this mutually supporting process between theory and practice is neither simple nor obvious in many L2 settings. A real strength of this volume is that the chapters succeed in linking theory and practice, though they also reveal some of the difficulties in building theory and practice connections.

In order to contextualize my comments, and lend some coherence to them, I first outline a framework for reading comprehension that can be used to interpret the relationship between L2 reading comprehension and reading instruction. Then I highlight some of the key themes running across multiple chapters in the book and consider further issues raised by this volume that might be addressed more systematically in a companion volume.

How READING COMPREHENSION WORKS

A simple sketch of reading comprehension is first needed to outline the components of reading comprehension abilities, to recognize some of the major differences between L1 and L2 reading comprehension skills, and to interpret my comments on the volume. An examination of the components of reading ability highlights various ways in which L1 reading and L2 reading abilities differ, particularly at less than advanced levels. The component abilities outlined below are all critical for the development of reading comprehension. How they work together in real time processing goes beyond the purpose of this concluding chapter (but see Grabe & Stoller, 2002; Perfetti, Landi, & Oakhill, 2005; Pressley, 2006).

Letter-Sound Correspondences

At beginning stages of reading in English, learners need to develop knowledge of letter-sound correspondences. This ability includes phonological awareness of how sounds pattern to form words, knowledge of the alphabet letter names, and the ability to match letters to sounds appropriately. This knowledge is essential to learn to read an alphabetic script, and it needs to be taught formally, especially in English (Ehri, Nunes, Stahl, & Willows, 2001; Ehri, Nunes, Willows et al., 2001; Pressley, 2006; Snow & Juel, 2005). With respect to letter-sound correspondences, L2 learners come with a wide assortment of language and literacy backgrounds: They may begin to read English as children, adolescents, adults; they may have prior L1 literacy experience or not; or they may come from alphabetic or non-alphabetic L1s. These differences influence patterns of L2 reading development, including knowledge of letter-sound correspondences. Not all L2 readers learn to read in exactly the same way, and they most often need to read the L2 in some ways that are different from L1 reading experiences (Cook, 2005; Frost, 2005; Koda, 2005). If L2 students have had prior L1 experience with learning to read an alphabetic script, this experience greatly simplifies the process of accessing letter-sound correspondences in English. If learners do not have this prior experience, then instruction must address this need explicitly and immediately.

Lexical Access

Fluent reading requires accurate and automatic lexical access of the word meanings stored in the reader's long-term memory. While reading comprehension entails more than simply accessing words quickly and accurately, comprehension cannot be maintained successfully without accurate and automatic lexical access (Perfetti & Hart, 2001). Moreover, developing automatic lexical access for a large number of words requires a lot of reading practice over a long period of time (Pressley, 2006). In L2 contexts, automatic lexical access for most words in a text develops late, at advanced stages of L2 reading abilities, and many L2 readers never achieve automatic lexical access in ways that approach L1 reader skills (Segalowitz, 2003). The skills of fluent word reading and lexical access represents a major difference between L1 and L2 readers. Most L1 English learners develop automatic word recognition skills for 98–99 percent of the words they encounter in grade-appropriate texts by the end of fourth grade (Carver, 1994; Pressley, 2006). L2 readers almost never have a comparable reading experience.

A Large Vocabulary

The larger a reader's vocabulary, the more efficient will be a reader's comprehension processing, particularly with texts at or above ability level. In English L1 contexts, word knowledge is seen as comprising 5,000–7,000 words at age five, and averaging 40,000 words for high school graduates (with a wide range of variation). Average word knowledge grows by approximately 3,000–4,000 words per year for each year of schooling (again, with wide variation). While some L2 vocabulary researchers consider L1 reader word knowledge as comprising approximately 17,000–20,000 word families, and L2 students as needing 5,000 word families for comprehension of most texts (Nation 2001; cf. Hazenburg & Hulstijn, 1996), these views contrast with English L1 vocabulary researchers, who are more comfortable with fluent adult readers knowing 40,000 to 60,000 words (Anglin, 1993; Graves, 2004; Scott, 2005; Stahl & Nagy, 2006). Aside from the competing views on reader word knowledge, it should be obvious that L2 readers generally do not reach a recognition vocabulary of 40,000 words in English, suggesting a major difference between L1 and L2 readers. Cobb (this volume) provides an excellent review and discussion of these issues from an L2 perspective.

Morphological Information

Over the past decade, much more emphasis has been given to the role of morphological knowledge in L1 reading comprehension (Carlisle, 2003;

Edwards et al., 2004; Scott, 2005). Knowing how words are put together to form derived words and how morphology signals part-of-speech and syntactic information contributes to vocabulary growth and indirectly to reading comprehension abilities (Carlisle, 2003). L1 researchers state that more than 60 percent of English school words have a transparent morphology for word learning (Nagy & Anderson, 1984), and derived words represent 40 percent of learners' word knowledge by fifth grade (Anglin, 1993). L2 learners have much less exposure to English morphological knowledge and this difference influences L2 reading in ways distinct from L1 reading (see Anderson, this volume).

Syntactic Processing

The role of syntactic processing is generally not discussed as a factor related to reading comprehension, but the role of syntax in L2 comprehension has been clearly demonstrated (Fender, 2001; Grabe, 2004, 2005b; Urquhart & Weir, 1998). In fact, L1 researchers are coming to recognize that syntactic factors influence comprehension (particularly in disability studies), though not nearly as obviously as in L2 contexts. The ability to process clausal and phrasal information while reading is a skill that develops through considerable time engaged in reading (i.e., amount of exposure to print). It is straightforward that this ability differs for L1 and L2 readers and this difference suggests distinct ways of reading for L2 learners until they are very advanced readers.

Forming Meaning Units

The skills of lexical access and syntactic processing allow the reader to form semantic meaning units (almost simultaneously with the phrasal and clausal processing of linguistic information). The skills involved in semantic meaning unit formation are automatic from early L1 (listening) comprehension. Moreover, the abilities to form meaning units are basically the same across L1 and L2 processing and across reading and listening. What distinguishes L1 and L2 readers is the limited linguistic skills of lexical access and syntactic parsing that provide the input for generating meaning units (see Grabe & Stoller, 2002).

Models of Reading Comprehension

Connecting Main Ideas to Build a Text Model of Reading

The basic building block of reading comprehension is the formation of a "text model of reading." As clausal semantic units are processed and combined, related items get linked across these units. As linked items are reinforced across units, these ideas become thematic main ideas of the text. Non-repeated items are deleted. Information is restructured to reflect these main ideas and supporting ideas. Inferences are used primarily to create additional relevant links to maintain coherence (Grabe & Stoller, 2002; Kintsch & Rawson, 2005; Perfetti, 1999; Pressley, 2006). Readers' abilities to comprehend are also related to the degree of effort assigned to understanding the text, establishing "the standard of coherence" (Linderholm, Virtue, Tzeng, & van den Broek, 2004; Perfetti, Landi, & Oakhill, 2005). Differences between L1 and L2 reading do emerge as a result of limited linguistic input, varying background knowledge, and social and cultural purposes for reading. These same factors also apply to the three following processing mechanisms and limit all three during L2 reading.

Building a Situation Model of the Text (What We Learn and Store from the Text)

Fluent readers are fully able to re-interpret the text model into a more elaborate "situation model of reading" and do so automatically. The situation model adds reader attitudes, evaluations, personal elaborative inferences, and strong linkages to background knowledge. This view of parallel developing text and situation models of comprehension has been developed for over twenty years among reading researchers and cognitive psychologists (Kintsch, 1998; Perfetti, 1999; Pressley, 2006; van Dijk & Kintsch, 1983). The situation model also provides direct links back to the initial set of goal-setting processes. The emerging situation model must reflect not only the reader's goals and attitudes (about the author, for example), but it must also connect the background information, expectations, and goals generated at the outset of the reading to the information produced by the text model. Effective reading comprehension does this well.

Directing Attention and Executive Control

All discourse comprehension researchers recognize that reading comprehension incorporates attentional mechanisms, particularly when reading difficult materials and when learning goals (as opposed to enjoyment goals) are primary. Such executive control processes (a) respond to reading goals and purposes, (b) apply strategies appropriately, (c) engage metacognitive awareness, (d) draw on background knowledge as appropriate, and (e) form inferences for text processing. How such conscious processing is carried out as part of reading comprehension is less clearly understood in terms of cognitive models, but all agree that such processing does in fact occur on a continual basis. Instructional research on reading strategy development and metacognitive awareness demonstrates consistently that these factors influence reading comprehension (Baker, 2002; Guthrie, 2004; Guthrie, Wigfield, & Perencevich, 2004; Pressley, 2006).

Processing Concepts

For the above components to work together in reading comprehension, a number of processing mechanisms are essential and they impact reading comprehension when they are not functioning effectively. Fluent readers have extraordinarily fast word recognition skills, recognizing a word at between 50 and 100 milliseconds. They have automatized the processes of word recognition, initial syntactic parsing, initial semantic unit formation, and text model formation. The ability to automatize many processes is what allows a good reader to carry out many processes simultaneously and what permits the appropriate timing to integrate information from multiple sources. The several processes that are automatic during fluent reading may not be directly observable or accessible to reflection on the reader's part. But this non-accessability does not mean that these processes are "not occurring" continually; in fact, they are continuously occurring. For example, it is not true that fluent readers no longer use grammatical information while reading. Rather, fluent readers have become very good at using this information automatically.

Good readers are also able to engage attentional processes selectively to ensure an appropriate "standard of coherence," and they can suppress irrelevant information efficiently (see Leow, this volume, for a discussion of attentional processes). All of these processes are active as part of working memory (Grabe & Stoller, 2002; Perfetti, 1999; Stanovich, 2000).

This sketch of reading comprehension processes and their interactions provides a framework for interpreting themes that run through multiple chapters in this volume. Reflecting back on the chapters of this volume, it is interesting to see how they address various components of reading, providing important evidence and insights into how L2 reading develops and how instruction can support and accelerate this development.

COMMON THEMES ACROSS MULTIPLE CHAPTERS

Several themes run across many chapters. I highlight eight in this section to show how the chapters work together to build a larger view of L2 reading comprehension. The first is the need to understand the specific situation of *the L2 reader* and how that reader deals with a learning situation that is different from the L1 student learning to read. In fact, almost every student learns basic L1 reading skills in the context of a stable L1 educational system, even though they may not develop the level of advanced critical reading skills that are valued by educational systems. The same certainly cannot be said of L2 readers. L2 readers must learn to read in ways somewhat different from L1 learners, and some reading processes (e.g., word recognition, morphological processing) vary between L1 and L2 processes. Many L2 learners never become fluent at what might be considered basic L1 reading tasks. Both Shiotsu and Cobb address this issue.

Second, most chapters support or assume a view of L2 reading that requires a set of critical *components skills for reading*. A component skills orientation is widely accepted among L2 reading researchers (Alderson, 2000; Anderson, N., 1999; Bernhardt, 2005; Koda, 2005), and most chapters reinforce this orientation, either explicitly or implicitly (see Horst, Shiotsu, Pulido, Leow, Anderson, Cobb, and Han & D'Angelo, this volume). Shiotsu provides an excellent review of L2 word recognition skills and demonstrates clearly that better L2 readers have more developed word recognition skills, particularly greater orthographic awareness and better lexical-semantic knowledge. Cobb also notes the importance of rapid word recognition as a critical component of reading ability. Pulido emphasizes the interaction between skills involving background knowledge use and vocabulary knowledge on further vocabulary growth (and implicitly as supports for L2 reading ability). Han and D'Angelo argue that instruction needs to reflect a dual commitment to linguistic knowledge resources and the processing needs of the L2 reader.

Third, L2 students need to acquire *a large recognition vocabulary*. The relationship between vocabulary and reading comprehension is an important one that is emphasized in multiple chapters. While the mechanisms by which a learner acquires a large vocabulary are not straightforward, thus the source of some debate, there are still important research findings that are highlighted in multiple chapters. Cobb presents an excellent analysis of L2 reader needs for vocabulary and examines the difficulties involved in learning a large recognition vocabulary.

From a learning perspective, the general principle that learners best acquire vocabulary through both extensive reading (or extensive exposure to print) over a long period of time and specific types of effective instructional practices is now emerging as an important insight. Anderson makes a strong argument for this combined perspective on vocabulary learning. Several vocabulary instruction activities carried out consistently over time can support and accelerate the vocabulary that is learned through extensive exposure to print. Pulido focuses directly on the importance of vocabulary learning from reading and offers many suggestions for how to support vocabulary growth in the classroom context. Leow highlights the possible benefits of glossing as an aid to comprehension.

Fourth, *extensive reading* is a critical curricular support for reading development. Carried out appropriately and for a long period of time, extensive reading gives students practice with texts that are challenging but not too difficult; it provides extended practice that automatizes basic recognition and parsing processes; it builds text reading fluency with easier texts; it supports vocabulary learning; it motivates students to read more; and it allows learners to apply a range of comprehension strategies on a regular basis. Given this list of benefits, it is hard to argue against the efficacy of extensive reading practice in L2 reading instruction. These points are persuasively argued by Horst (this volume), and the two experiments she reports provide helpful models for future research efforts (see also Shiotsu, Pulido).

In her chapter on extensive reading, Horst raises a number of additional key points that need to be highlighted. Horst points out that written texts (as opposed to spoken texts) provide many more opportunities for new word learning because written texts are more complex linguistically and have much more less-common vocabulary (see also Cunningham, 2005; Stahl & Nagy, 2006; Stanovich, 2000). This view is extended by Anderson's discussion of the differing types of linguistic input arising from differing types of texts, and emphasizes the need to think carefully about text selection in a reading course. Horst also identifies frequency of repetition for vocabulary learning as a critical feature of language development. She notes that eight to ten repetitions may be a critical number; her study explored words encountered more than fifteen times. These ideas are supported by Cobb's analysis of L2 vocabulary learning, and they match up well with other L1 and L2 views on word repetition frequency and vocabulary learning (Pigada & Schmitt, 2006; Scott, 2005).

Fifth, a number of chapters emphasize *fluency and automaticity of processing* as crucial for L2 reading abilities. In some cases, these skills focused on word-level processing for speed and accuracy (Horst, Shiotsu, Pulido, Cobb); in other cases, the fluency emphasis also extended to passage fluency skills. Freeman and Freeman suggest that rereading familiar texts and reading along with audio tapes are helpful activities that build reading fluency. Anderson is emphatic about the importance of passage reading fluency and recommends repeated reading, class-paced reading, and self-paced reading as practices to build fluency.

Sixth, several chapters emphasize the importance of *strategy instruction and the importance of the strategic reader* (see Anderson, N., 2005; Ediger, 2006; Grabe, 2006). Pulido focuses on inferencing skills, previewing, summarizing, creating graphic organizers, and monitoring comprehension. Both Anderson and Freeman and Freeman emphasize the importance of predicting future directions in a text. Anderson adds the importance of teaching for main idea recognition, summarizing, and text structure awareness as further strategic goals for reading comprehension.

Anderson also raises the important issue of metacogntive awareness as a strategic goal for readers. Students learning to read need to develop their abilities to monitor their comprehension, set and adjust reading goals as appropriate, repair loss of comprehension, and evaluate the relationship between their understanding of the text and their purposes for reading. Metacognitive awareness is not, in itself, a strategy; rather, it is a heightened awareness of how to use strategies most effectively for comprehension and learning purposes. Suggestions for developing these abilities include raising awareness of text structure, questioning the text and intentions of the author, introducing and discussing strategy use with students, and having students provide think-aloud verbal reports of strategy uses while reading.

Seventh, *background knowledge* and the role of familiar reading content also play a role in reading abilities. Both Anderson and Freeman and Freeman argue that activating student background knowledge is a critical component of effective instruction and improved comprehension. Pulido notes that topic familiarity leads to better vocabulary learning while reading. Building background knowledge can be established also through thematic instruction that allows content to become both more familiar and also more complex—promoting reader engagement. At the same time, Pulido points out that background knowledge can sometimes mislead L2 readers, especially lower-ability readers (see also Anderson, this volume; Bernhardt, 2005).

Eighth, multiple chapters address explicitly the need to move beyond implications from research and *address instructional applications* that fit the L2 reading context (Bernhardt, 2005). Often, research studies make general recommendations about instruction, but these recommendations tend to remain generic and somewhat abstract. When research offers implications for teaching, these implications need to be explored explicitly and actual practices should be suggested that can be acted upon and evaluated by teachers as action research. Anderson is very direct about the need to extend beyond implications and develop applications that are supported by both reading research indirectly and instructional training research more directly. He provides an extensive set of effective instructional practices that are well grounded in research evidence but also that can be easily articulated into a coherent and extended curricular framework (see Anderson, 2002–2003; 2007/2008/2009).

Pulido, Freeman and Freeman, Leow, and Cobb, while adopting differing orientations to reading, all make specific teaching suggestions for enhancing reading instruction. Pulido provides a number of specific instructional recommendations for pre-reading activities as well as suggestions for building new vocabulary knowledge. She also emphasizes the need for extensive reading as part of reading instruction. Freeman and Freeman provide many good instructional suggestions focusing on thematic instruction, project work, and teacher practices to promote student engagement with texts. Leow suggests that learners should engage in awareness raising tasks after exposure to key forms or key vocabulary as a good way to focus selective attention. Getting students to think aloud about what they are doing or what they are noticing might also prove useful (and is consistent with L1 reading research; Pressley, 2006).

Cobb argues persuasively that computer applications effectively support vocabulary development and indirectly support reading comprehension. They also offer a number of helpful specific instructional options. One particularly useful suggestion involving computer applications is a program for collecting and saving all new words that a group or the teacher feel should be stored. These words then create a vocabulary resource, almost like an electronic word wall, from which many types of activities, exercises, re-arrangements, and re-uses can be developed.

ISSUES TO CONSIDER FURTHER

The themes that run through multiple chapters in this volume deserve careful reflection. At the same time, other themes related to L2 reading were addressed in a very limited way and require additional research and research-to-practice exploration. Several issues that are essential for L2 reading development and instructional practice did not recur across multiple chapters. In a number of cases, issues are only raised in a single chapter, indicating that they are not yet recognized generally as goals for reading instruction.

Among issues needing to be addressed more generally as crucial in reading and reading instruction are the roles of fluency development (Anderson), motivation (Freeman & Freeman), and content and language integrated instruction (Freeman & Freeman). It is surprising that these issues only arise in two chapters. There is also relatively little on evaluation and assessment of learning improvement (Anderson) and computer applications to support reading instruction (Cobb). Finally, although the present volume focuses on the learning processes of students, there is, nonetheless, surprising little on issues of teacher training and teacher development (Cobb). It is understandable that authors would focus on specific topics and issues and that gaps would emerge. However, these minimally treated topics suggest that there are more chapters and edited volumes waiting to be written on L2 reading development.

Another issue emerging from the chapters is the need for additional research of various types, including well-controlled longitudinal studies that involve instructional training with well-controlled experimental and control groups, studies that include introspective and retrospective input from participants, and studies that can be compared for varying student populations. Too often in L2 settings, a single study can take on too much significance because there are no comparable studies involving similar methods and research questions but with differing learner groups. A related observation concerning research is the need for cautious interpretation of results (Leow). A number of chapters have noted some of the limitations of existing research in L2 reading and Leow, in particular, makes a number of recommendations in this regard.

Multiple chapters offer excellent descriptions and guidelines for further research. Horst provides a clear illustration of how to pursue and overcome constraints associated with research on extensive reading. Shiotsu presents an excellent explanation for how to carry out word recognition research and use response-time measures effectively. Leow makes a persuasive argument for incorporating think-aloud data collection as part of any extended research agenda.

A final issue central to this volume is the relationship between reading comprehension and second language acquisition (SLA). More specifically, a number of chapters explore the relationship between reading comprehension as a language skill and SLA, which more typically focuses on the acquisition of specific language structures, whether through explicit instruction or implicit processing. While it is true that reading requires knowledge of language, and SLA analyzes how language knowledge is acquired, it is nonetheless difficult to build strong linkages between the development of reading comprehension as a skill and SLA with its strong emphasis on linguistic representation (theories of language knowledge and language structures). In multiple chapters, evidence for reading is drawn from studies of comprehensible input, input enhancement, modified interaction, grammar learning as a proxy for reading development, language uptake, and communicative competence. In the large majority of the SLA studies referred to, successful learning is typically not measured in terms of reading comprehension test outcomes but rather in terms of successful learning and use of linguistic forms.

Typically SLA orientations to L2 reading abilities use reading as an input resource and examine the extent to which some lexical knowledge or grammatical systems have been learned. Most reading research is focused on how other factors (e.g., vocabulary and grammar knowledge) enhance reading development. The tension that results from these different orientations is evident in this volume, with Pulido, Leow, and Han and D'Angelo taking a stronger formal SLA slant in their chapters. Han & D'Angelo also seek to address the tension between SLA and reading orientations to language development by arguing for instruction that emphasizes both form-based tasks and meaning-based tasks. However, for both types of tasks, studies tend to focus on language knowledge and language uptake outcomes.

The continued exploration of the relationships between SLA and reading comprehension development remains important. As multiple chapters in this volume indicate, vocabulary learning may be a crucial juncture that brings together SLA theories and reading comprehension research. However, the relationship is not straightforward as two distinct foundations generally inform each of these research areas—linguistic theory for SLA and cognitive psychology for comprehension research. Furthermore, research methodologies and specific research goals are distinct, and measurements of successful outcomes are generally different. Nonetheless, the goal to examine these relationships, despite problems, is necessary, and this volume will contribute strongly to future explorations.

Each chapter makes important contributions to how we should understand L2 reading ability and effective reading instruction. I have sought to highlight some of the ways that the chapters mutually reinforce major themes and issues for L2 reading. Of course, there are additional issues that could, and should, be explored further. After all, one volume cannot offer definitive analyses to all the issues associated with L2 reading. At the same time, this volume is an invaluable collection, taking us far along the right path.

REFERENCES

Adams, S. (1982). Scripts and the recognition of unfamiliar vocabulary: Enhancing second language reading skills. *The Modern Language Journal, 66,* 155–159.

Aebersold, J., & Field, M. (1997). *From reader to reading teacher.* Cambridge, UK: Cambridge University Press.

Afflerbach, P., Pearson, P., & Paris, S. (2008). Skills and strategies: Their differences, their relationships, and why it matters. In K. Mokhtari & R. Sheorey (Eds.), *Reading strategies of first- and second-language learners: See how they read* (pp. 11–24). Norwood, MA: Christopher-Gordon.

Akamatsu, N. (1999). The effects of first language orthographic features on word recognition processing in English as a second language. *Reading and Writing: An Interdisciplinary Journal, 11*(4), 381–403.

———. (2003). The effects of first language orthographic features on second language reading in text. *Language Learning, 53*(2), 207–231.

———. (2005). Effects of second language reading proficiency and first language orthography on second language word recognition. In V. Cook & B. Bassetti (Eds.), *Second language writing systems.* Clevedon, UK: Multilingual Matters.

Alanen, R. (1995). Input enhancement and rule presentation in second language acquisition. In R. W. Schmidt (Ed.), *Attention and awareness in foreign language learning* (Technical Report #9) (pp. 259–302). Honolulu: University of Hawaii, Second Language Teaching & Curriculum Center.

Alderson, C. (1984). Reading in a foreign language: A reading problem or a language problem? In J. Alderson & A. Urquhart (Eds.), *Reading in a foreign language* (pp. 1–24). London: Longman.

Alderson, J. C. (2000). *Assessing reading.* New York: Cambridge University Press.

Al-Hamly, M., & Coombe, C. (2005). Self-assessment accuracy revisited: The Arab EFL context. In P. Davidson, C. Coombe, & W. Jones (Eds.), *Assessment in the Arab world.* Dubai, UAE: TESOL Arabia.

Aliki (1998). *Painted words/Spoken memories.* New York: Greenwillow Books.

Allport, A. (1988). What concept of consciousness? In A. Marcel & E. Bisiach (Eds.), *Consciousness in contemporary science* (pp. 159–182). London: Clarendon Press.

Al-Seghayer, K. (2001). The effect of multimedia annotation modes on L2 vocabulary acquisition: A comparative study. *Language Learning & Technology, 5,* 202–232.

Anderson, N. (1991). Individual differences in strategy use in second language reading and testing. *The Modern Language Journal, 75*, 460–472.

———. (1993a). Reading rate: Pump it up. In R. Day (Ed.), *New ways in teaching reading* (pp. 188–189). Alexandria, VA: TESOL.

———. (1993b). Repeated reading. In R. Day (Ed.), *New ways in teaching reading* (pp. 190–191). Alexandria, VA: TESOL.

———. (1999). *Exploring second language reading: Issues and strategies.* Boston: Heinle.

———. (2002). The role of metacognition in second/foreign language teaching and learning. *ERIC Digest.* Retrieved from www.cal.org/ericcll/digest/0110anderson.html

———. (2002/2003). *Active skills for reading: Books 1–4.* Boston: Heinle.

———. (2004). Developing metacognitive awareness. In J. Bamford & R. Day (Eds.), *Extensive reading activities for teaching language* (pp. 175–180). Cambridge, UK: Cambridge University Press.

———. (2005). L2 strategy research. In E. Hinkel (Ed.), *Handbook of research in second language teaching and learning* (pp. 757–772). Mahwah, NJ: Lawrence Erlbaum.

———. (2007/2008/2009). *Active skills for reading: Intro, Books 1–4* (2nd ed.). Boston: Heinle.

———. (2008). *Practical English language teaching: Reading.* New York: McGraw Hill.

Anderson, N., & Vandergrift, L. (1996). Increasing metacognitive awareness in the L2 classroom by using think-aloud protocols and other verbal report formats. In R. Oxford (Ed.), *Language learning strategies around the world: Cross-cultural perspectives* (pp. 3–18). Manoa: University of Hawaii Press.

Anderson, R., & Freebody, P. (1981). Vocabulary knowledge. In J.T. Guthrie (Ed.), *Comprehension and teaching: Research reviews* (pp. 77–117). Newark, DE: International Reading Association.

Anderson, R. C. (1996). Research foundations to support wide reading. In V. Greaney (Ed.), *Promoting reading in developing countries* (pp. 55–77). Newark, DE: International Reading Association.

Anglin, J. (1993). Vocabulary development: A morphological analysis. *Monographs of the Society of Research in Child Development, 58*(10), Serial No. 238.

August, D., & Shanahan, T. (Eds.). (2006). *Developing literacy in second-language learners: Report of the National Literacy Panel on Language Minority Children and Youth.* Mahwah, NJ: Lawrence Erlbaum.

Baddeley, A. (1998). *Human memory: Theory and practice.* Needham Heights, MA: Allyn & Bacon.

Baker, L. (2002). Metacognition in comprehension instruction. In C. Block & M. Pressley (Eds.), *Comprehension instruction: Research-based best practices* (pp. 77–95). New York: Guilford Press.

Bardovi-Harlig, K. (1995). The interaction of pedagogy and natural sequences in the acquisition of tense and aspect. In F. Eckman, D. Highland, J. Lee, & R. Weber (Eds.), *Second language acquisition theory and pedagogy* (pp. 151–168). Mahwah, NJ: Lawrence Erlbaum.

Barry, S., & Lazarte, A. (1998). Evidence for mental models: How do prior knowledge, syntactic complexity, and reading topic affect inference generation in a recall task for nonnative readers of Spanish? *The Modern Language Journal, 82,* 176–193.

Baumann, J. (1984). The effectiveness of a direct instruction paradigm for teaching main idea comprehension. *Reading Research Quarterly, 20,* 27–55.

Beck, I., McKeown, M., Hamilton, R., & Kucan, L. (1997). *Questioning the author: An approach for enhancing student engagement with text.* Newark, DE: International Reading Association.

Bell, J. (1995). The relationship between L1 and L2 literacy: Some complicating factors. *TESOL Quarterly, 29,* 687–704.

Bell, T. (2001). Extensive reading: Speed and comprehension. *The Reading Matrix, 1*(1), April 2001. Retrieved from www.readingmatrix.com/journal.html

Bengeleil, N., & Paribakht, S. (2004). L2 reading proficiency and lexical inferencing by university EFL learners. *Canadian Modern Language Review, 61,* 225–249.

Bernhardt, E. (1991). *Reading development in a second language: Theoretical, empirical, and classroom perspectives.* Norwood, NJ: Ablex.

———. (2005). Progress & procrastination in second language reading. In M. McGroarty (Ed.), *Annual review of applied linguistics, 25,* 133–150. New York: Cambridge University Press.

Blau, E. (1982). The effect of syntax on readability for ESL students in Puerto Rico. *TESOL Quarterly, 16,* 517–527.

Bley-Vroman, R. (1989). What is the logical problem of foreign language learning? In S. G. A. J. Schachter (Ed.), *Linguistic perspectives on second language acquisition* (pp. 41–68). Cambridge, UK: Cambridge University Press.

Bowles, M. (2003). The effects of textual enhancement on language learning: An online/offline study of fourth-semester students. In P. Kempchinsky & C. Piñeros (Eds.), *Theory, practice, and acquisition: Papers from the 6ᵗʰ Hispanic Linguistics Symposium and the 5ᵗʰ Conference on the Acquisition of Spanish & Portuguese* (pp. 395–411). Somerville, MA: Cascadilla Press.

———. (2004). L2 glossing: To CALL or not to CALL. *Hispania, 87,* 543–555.

Bowles, M., & Leow, R. (2005). Reactivity and type of verbal report in SLA research methodology: Expanding the scope of investigation. *Studies in Second Language Acquisition, 27,* 415–440.

Brown, T., Carr, T., & Chaderjian, M. (1987). Orthography, familiarity, and meaningfulness reconsidered: Attention strategies may affect the lexical sensitivity of visual code formation. *Journal of Experimental Psychology: Human Perception and Performance, 13*(1), 127–139.

Brown, T., & Haynes, M. (1985). Literacy background and reading development in a second language. In T. Carr (Ed.), *The development of reading skills.* San Francisco: Jossey-Bass.

Carlisle, J. (2003). Morphology matters in learning to read: A commentary. *Reading Psychology, 24,* 291–322.

Carr, T., & Curran, T. (1994). Cognitive factors in learning about structured sequences: Applications to syntax. *Studies in Second Language Acquisition, 16,* 205–230.

Carrell, P. (1983a). Background knowledge in second language comprehension. *Language Learning and Communication, 2,* 25–34.

———. (1983b). Some issues in studying the role of schemata, or background knowledge, in second language comprehension. *Reading in a Foreign Language, 1,* 81–92.

———. (1984). The effects of rhetorical organization on L2 readers. *TESOL Quarterly, 18,* 441–469.

———. (1985). Facilitating L2 reading by teaching text structure. *TESOL Quarterly, 19,* 727–752.

———. (1987). Content and formal schemata in ESL reading. *TESOL Quarterly, 21,* 461–481.

———. (1991). Second language reading: Reading ability or language proficiency? *Applied Linguistics, 12,* 159–179.

Carrell, P., Devine, J., & Eskey, D. (1988). *Interactive approaches to second language reading.* Cambridge, UK: Cambridge University Press.

Carrell, P., & Eisterhold, J. C. (1983). Schema theory and L2 reading pedagogy. *TESOL Quarterly, 17,* 553–573.

Carrell, P., Pharis, B. G., and Liberto, J. C. (1989). Metacognitive strategy training for L2 reading. *TESOL Quarterly, 23,* 647–678.

Carroll, J., Davies, P., & Richman, B. (1971). *The American heritage word fluency book.* New York: Houghton Mifflin.

Carver, R. (1994). Percentage of unknown vocabulary words in text as a function of the relative difficulty of the text: Implications for instruction. *Journal of Reading Behavior, 26,* 413–437.

Chamot, A.U., & O'Malley, J. M. (1994). *The CALLA handbook: Implementing the cognitive academic language learning approach.* White Plains, NY: Addison-Wesley Longman.

Chang, Y. C. (2005). The effects of prompting on EFL college students use of a mapping strategy and their recall of expository texts. *Dissertation Abstracts International, 66*(3), 936A–937A.

Chaudron, C. (1985). Intake: On models and methods for discovering learners' processing of input. *Studies in Second Language Acquisition, 7,* 1–14.

Chen, H.-C., & Graves, M. (1995). Effects of previewing and providing background knowledge on Taiwanese college students' comprehension of American short stories. *TESOL Quarterly, 29,* 663–686.

Chen, Q., & Donin, J. (1997). Discourse processing of first and second language Biology texts: Effects of language proficiency and domain-specific knowledge. *The Modern Language Journal, 81,* 209–227.

Cheng, A. (2002). The effects of processing instruction on the acquisition of *ser* and *estar. Hispania, 85,* 308–323.

Chern, C. (1993). Chinese students' word-solving strategies in reading in English. In T. Huckin, M. Haynes, & J. Coady (Eds.), *Second language reading and vocabulary learning* (pp. 67–82). Norwood, NJ: Ablex.

Chun, D., & Plass, J. (1996). Effects of multimedia annotations on vocabulary acquisition. *The Modern Language Journal, 80*(2), 183–198.

Chung, J. (2000). Signals and reading comprehension—theory and practice. *System, 28,* 247–259.

Clark, R. (1983). Reconsidering research on learning from media. *Review of Educational Research, 53,* 445–459.

———. (Ed.). (2001). *Learning from media: Arguments, analysis, evidence.* Greenwich, CT: Information Age Publishing.

Clarke, M., & Silberstein, S. (1977). Toward a realization of psycholinguistic principles in the L2 reading class. In R. Mackay, B. Barkman, & R. Jordan (Eds.), *Reading in a second language* (pp. 48–65). Rowley, MA: Newbury House.

Coady, J. (1979). A psycholinguistic model of the L2 reader. In R. Mackay, B. Barkman, & R. Jordan (Eds.), *Reading in a second language* (pp. 5–12). Rowley, MA: Newbury House.

Coady, J., Magoto, J., Hubbard, P., Graney, J., & Mokhtari, K. (1993). High frequency vocabulary and reading proficiency in L2 reading. In T. Huckin, M. Haynes, & J. Coady (Eds.), *Second language reading and vocabulary learning* (pp. 217–228). Norwood, NJ: Ablex.

Cobb, T. (1997). Cognitive efficiency: Toward a revised theory of media. *Educational Technology Research & Development, 45*(4), 21–35.

———. (1999). Applying constructivism: A test for the learner as scientist. *Educational Technology Research & Development, 47*(3), 15–33.

———. (2008a). On chalkface & interface: A developer's take on the classroom distance metacomparison. Response to Bernard et al. comparison of effectiveness of classroom vs. distance education. Manuscript submitted for review.

———. (2008b). *Toward a practical methodology of reaction time testing: How and why.* Manuscript in preparation.

Cobb, T., Greaves, C., & Horst, M. (2001a/2001b). Peut-on augmenter le rythme d'acquisition lexicale par la lecture? Une expérience de lecture en français appuyée sur une série de ressources en ligne [Can the rate of lexical acquisition from reading be increased? An experiment in reading French with a suite of on-line resources]. In P. Raymond & C. Cornaire (Eds.), *Regards sur la didactique des langues secondes* (pp. 131–153). Outremont, Quebec. English available at www.lextutor.ca/cv/BouleE.htm

Cobb, T., & Horst, M. (2001). Reading academic English: Carrying learners across the lexical threshold. In J. Flowerdew & M. Peacock (Eds.), *The English for academic purposes curriculum* (pp. 315–329). Cambridge, UK: Cambridge University Press.

Cohen, A. (1990). *Language learning: Insights for learners, teachers, and researchers.* New York: Newbury House.

Cohen, J., MacWhinney, B., Flatt, M., & Provost, J. (1993). PsyScope: A new graphic interactive environment for designing psychology experiments. *Behavioral Research Methods, Instruments, and Computers, 25*(2), 257–271.

Collier, V. (1995). Acquiring a second language for school. *Directions in Language and Education, 1*(4). Retrieved from www.ncela.gwu.edu/pubs/directions/04.htm

Collier, V., & Thomas W. (2004). The astounding effectiveness of dual language education for all. *NABE Journal of Research and Practice, 2*(1), 1–19.

Cook, V. (1997). *Second language learning and language teaching.* London: Arnold.

———. (2005). An introduction to researching second language writing systems. In V. Cook & B. Bassetti (Eds.), *Second language writing systems* (pp. 1–67). Clevedon, UK: Multilingual Matters.

Cook, V., & Bassetti, B. (2005). An introduction to researching second language writing systems. In V. Cook & B. Bassetti (Eds.), *Second language writing systems.* Clevedon, UK: Multilingual Matters.

Coxhead, A. (2000). A new academic word list. *TESOL Quarterly, 23*(2), 213–238.

Craik, F., & Tulving, E. (1975). Depth of processing and the retention of words in episodic memory. *Journal of Experimental Psychology, 104,* 268–294.

Crawford, M. (2005). Adding variety to word recognition exercises. *English Teaching Forum, 43*(2), 36–41.

Cummins, J. (1978). Bilingualism and the development of metalinguistic awareness. *Journal of Cross-Cultural Psychology, 9*(2), 131–149.

———. (1981). The role of primary language development in promoting educational success for language minority students. In *Schooling and Language Minority Students: A Theoretical Framework* (pp. 3–49). Los Angeles: California State University, Evaluation, Dissemination and Assessment Center.

———. (2000). *Language, power and pedagogy: Bilingual children in the crossfire.* Clevedon, UK: Multilingual Matters.

Cunningham, A. (2005). Vocabulary growth through independent reading and reading aloud to children. In E. Hiebert & M. Kamil (Eds.), *Teaching and learning vocabulary* (pp. 45–68). Mahwah, NJ: Lawrence Erlbaum.

Curran, T., & Keele, S. (1993). Attentional and nonattentional forms of sequence learning. *Journal of Experimental Psychology: Learning, Memory, and Cognition, 19,* 189–202.

Davey, E. (1983). Think aloud—Modeling the cognitive processes of reading comprehension. *Journal of Reading, 27,* 44–47.

Davies, A. (1984). Simple, simplified and simplification: What is authentic? In J. Alderson & A. Urquhart (Eds.), *Reading in a foreign language* (pp. 181–195). New York: Longman.

Davis, J. (1989). Facilitating effects of marginal glosses on foreign language reading. *The Modern Language Journal, 73,* 41–48.

Day, R. (1993). *New ways in teaching reading.* Alexandria, VA: TESOL.

Day, R., & Bamford, J (1998). *Extensive reading in the second language classroom.* Cambridge, UK: Cambridge University Press.

Day, R., Omura, C., & Hiramatsu, M. (1991). Incidental EFL vocabulary learning and reading. *Reading in a Foreign Language, 7*(2), 541–551.

de Bot, K., Paribakht, T., & Wesche, M. (1997). Toward a lexical processing model for the study of second language vocabulary acquisition. *Studies in Second Language Acquisition, 19,* 309–329.

DeKeyser, R. (2000). The robustness of critical period effects in second language acquisition. *Studies in Second Language Acquisition, 22,* 499–533.

de Ridder, I. (2002). Visible or invisible links: Does the highlighting of hyperlinks affect incidental vocabulary learning, text comprehension, and the reading process? *Language Learning & Technology, 6,* 123–146.

Diaz-Rico, L., & Weed, K. (2002). *The cross-cultural, language, academic development: A complete K–12 reference guide.* Boston: Allyn and Bacon.

Doddis, A. (1985). La cohesion textual en un discurso expositivo auténtico simplificado y en sus correspondientes recreaciones. *Lenguas Modernas, 12,* 136–148.

Doughty, C. (1991). Second language instruction does make a difference. *Studies in Second Language Acquisition, 13,* 431–469.

———. (2004). Effects of instruction on learning a second language: A critique of instructed SLA research. In B. VanPatten, J. Williams, S. Rott, & M. Overstreet (Eds.), *Form-meaning connections in second language acquisition* (pp. 181–202). Mahwah, NJ: Lawrence Erlbaum.

Doughty, C., & Varela, E. (1998). Communicative focus on form. In C. Doughty & J. Williams (Eds.), *Focus on form in classroom second language acquisition* (pp. 114–138). Cambridge, UK: Cambridge University Press.

Doughty, C., & Williams, J. (1998). Pedagogical choices in focus on form. In C. Doughty & J. Williams (Eds.), *Focus on form in classroom second language acquisition* (pp. 197–261). Cambridge, UK: Cambridge University Press.

Dubin, F., & Bycina, D. (1991). Academic reading and the L2/EFL teacher. In M. Celce-Murcia (Ed.), *Teaching English as a second or foreign language* (2nd ed.), (pp. 195–215). New York: Newbury House.

Ediger, A. (2006). Developing strategic L2 readers...by reading for authentic purposes. In E. Uso-Juan & A. Martinez-Flor (Eds.), *Current trends in the development and teaching of the four language skills* (pp. 303–328). New York: Mouton de Gruyter.

Edwards, E., Font, G., Baumann, J., & Boland, E. (2004). Unlocking word meanings: Strategies and guidelines for teaching morphemic and contextual analysis. In J. Baumann & E. Kame'enui (Eds.), *Vocabulary instruction: From research to practice* (pp. 159–176). New York: Guilford Press.

Ehri, L., Nunes, S., Stahl, S., & Willows, D. (2001). Systematic phonics instruction helps student learn to read: Evidence from the National Reading Panel's meta-analysis. *Review of Educational Research, 71,* 393–447.

Ehri, L., Nunes, S., Willows, D., Schuster, B., Yaghoub-Zadeh, Z., & Shanahan, T. (2001). Phonemic awareness instruction helps children learn to read: Evidence for the National Reading Panel's meta-analysis. *Reading Research Quarterly, 36*, 250–287.

Elley, W. (1991). Acquiring literacy in a second language: The effect of book-based programs. *Language Learning, 41*, 375–411.

Ellis, N. (1994). Vocabulary acquisition: The implicit ins and outs of explicit cognitive mediation. In N. Ellis (Ed.), *Implicit and explicit learning of languages* (pp. 211–282). London: Academic Press.

———. (1995). The psychology of foreign language vocabulary acquisition: Implications for CALL. *Computer Assisted Language Learning, 8*, 103–128.

———. (2001). Memory for language. In P. Robinson (Ed.), *Cognition and second language instruction* (pp. 33–68). Cambridge, UK: Cambridge University Press.

———. (2002). Reflections on frequency effects in language processing. *Studies in Second Language Acquisition, 24*(2), 297–339.

Ellis, R. (1994). A theory of instructed second language acquisition. In N. Ellis (Ed.), *Implicit and explicit learning of languages*. New York: Academic Press.

Ericsson, K., & Simon, H. (1984). *Protocol analysis: Verbal reports as data.* Cambridge: MIT Press.

Eskey, D. (1988). Holding in the bottom: An interactive approach to the language problems of second language readers. In P. Carrell, J. Devine, & D. Eskey (Eds.), *Interactive approaches to second language reading* (pp. 93–100). Cambridge, UK: Cambridge University Press.

Faerch, C., Haastrup, K., & Phillipson, R. (1984). *Learner language and language learning.* Clevedon, UK: Multilingual Matters.

Faerch, C., & Kasper, G. (1986). The role of comprehensible input in second-language acquisition. *Applied Linguistics, 7*(3), 257–273.

Fang, Z. (2008). Going beyond the Fab Five: Helping students cope with the unique linguistic challenges of expository reading in intermediate grades. *Journal of Adolescent and Adult Literacy, 51*, 470–497.

Fang, Z., & Schleppegrell, M. (2008). *Reading in secondary content areas: A language-based pedagogy.* Ann Arbor: The University of Michigan Press.

Favreau, M., & Segalowitz, N. (1982). Second language reading in fluent bilinguals. *Applied Psycholinguistics, 3*(4), 329–341.

Fender, M. (2001). A review of L1 and L2/ESL word integration skills and the nature of L2/ESL word integration development involved in lower-level text processing. *Language Learning, 51*, 319–396.

Fitzgerald, J. (1993). Literacy and students who are learning English as a second language. *The Reading Teacher, 46*(8), 638–647.

———. (1995). English-as-a-second-language reading instruction in the United States: A research review. *Journal of Reading Behavior, 27*(2), 115–152.

Flurkey, A. (1997). Reading as flow: A linguistic alternative to fluency. Unpublished doctoral dissertation, University of Arizona–Tucson.

Folse, K. S. (2004). *Vocabulary myths: Applying second language research to classroom teaching.* Ann Arbor: The University of Michigan Press.

———. (2007). *Rapid reading practices: Developing word automaticity in reading.* Ann Arbor: The University of Michigan Press.

Fraser, C. (1999). Lexical processing strategy use and vocabulary learning through reading. *Studies in Second Language Acquisition, 21,* 225–41.

Freeman, Y., Freeman, A., & Freeman, D. (2003). Home run books: Connecting students to culturally relevant texts. *NABE News, 26*(3), 5–8, 11–12.

Freeman, Y., Freeman, D., & Mercuri, S. (2005). *Dual language essentials for teachers and administrators.* Portsmouth, NH: Heinemann.

Freeman, Y., & Freeman, D. (1998). *ESL/EFL teaching: Principles for success.* Portsmouth, NH: Heinemann.

Frost, R. (2005). Orthographic systems and skilled word recognition processes in reading. In M. Snowling & C. Hulme (Eds.), *The science of reading: A handbook* (pp. 272–295). Malden, MA: Blackwell.

Fukkink, R., Hulstijn, J., & Simis, A. (2005). Does training in second-language word recognition skills affect reading comprehension? An experimental study. *The Modern Language Journal, 89,* 54–75.

Gardner, D. (2004). Vocabulary input through extensive reading: A comparison of words found in children's narrative and expository reading materials. *Applied Linguistics, 25,* 1–37.

Gass, S. (1988). Integrating research areas: A framework for second language studies. *Applied Linguistics, 9,* 198–217.

———. (1999). Incidental vocabulary learning. *Studies in Second Language Acquisition, 21,* 319–333.

Gass, S., & Selinker, L. (2001). *Second language acquisition* (2nd ed.). Mahwah, NJ: Lawrence Erlbaum.

Gee, J. (1992). *The social mind: Language, ideology, and social practice.* New York: Bergin and Garvey.

Genesee, F. (1987). *Learning through two languages: Studies of immersion and bilingual education.* Rowley, MA: Newbury House.

Gettys, S., Imhof, L., & Kautz, J. (2001). Computer-assisted reading: The effect of glossing format on comprehension and vocabulary retention. *Foreign Language Annals, 34,* 91–106.

Gilman, P. (1992). *Something from nothing.* New York: Scholastic.

Goodman, K. (1967). Reading: A psycholinguistic guessing game. *Journal of Reading Specialist, 6,* 126–135.

———. (1973). Psycholinguistic universals of the reading process. In F. Smith (Ed.), *Psycholinguistics and Reading* (pp. 177–182). New York: Holt, Rinehart, and Winston.

———. (1976). Reading: A psycholinguistic guessing game. In H. Singer, & R. Ruddell (Eds)., *Theoretical models and processes of reading* (2nd ed.) (pp. 497–508). Newark, DE: International Reading Association.

————. (1984). Unity in reading. In A. Purves & O. Niles (Eds.), *Becoming readers in a complex society: Eighty-third yearbook of the National Society for the Study of Education* (pp. 79–114). Chicago: University of Chicago Press.

Goodman, Y., Watson, D., & Burke, C. (1987). *Reading miscue inventory: Alternative procedures.* New York: R.C. Owen.

Goswami, U., & Bryant, P. (1990). *Phonological skills and learning to read.* Hove, UK: Lawrence Erlbaum.

Gough, P., & Hillinger, M. (1980). Learning to read: An unnatural act. *Bulletin of the Orton Society, 30,* 179–190.

Grabe, W. (1991). Current developments in second language reading research. *TESOL Quarterly, 25,* 375–406.

————. (2004). Research on teaching reading. *Annual Review of Applied Linguistics, 24,* 44–69.

————. (2005a, July). Research on reading instruction: Advances, issues, and possibilities. Paper presented at the 14th World Conference of Applied Linguistics, Madison, WI.

————. (2005b). The role of grammar in reading development. In. J. Frodesen & C. Holten (Eds.), *The power of context in language teaching and learning* (pp. 129–139). Boston: Thompson Heinle.

————. (2006). Areas of research that influence L2 reading instruction. In E. Uso-Juan & A. Martinez-Flor (Eds.), *Current trends in the development and teaching of the four language skills* (pp. 280–301). New York: Mouton de Gruyter.

Grabe, W., & Stoller, F. (2002). *Teaching and researching reading.* Harlow, UK: Pearson.

Graesser, A., Singer, M., & Trabasso, T. (1994). Constructing inferences during narrative text comprehension. *Psychological Review, 101,* 371–395.

Graves, M. (2004). Teaching prefixes: As good as it gets. In J. Baumann & E. Kae'enui (Eds.), *Vocabulary instruction: Research to practice* (pp. 81–99). New York: Guilford.

Graves, M. F., & Watts-Taffe, S. M. (2002). The place of word consciousness in a research-based vocabulary program. In A. Farstrup & S. Samuels (Eds.), *What research has to say about reading instruction* (pp. 140–165). Newark, DE: The International Reading Association.

Greenslade, T. (2000). *The effects of syntactic simplification on adult learners' intake, textual comprehension, and sentence interpretation and production.* Unpublished doctoral dissertation, Georgetown University.

Gross, K. H. (2005). The influence of background knowledge for reader response to foreign language literary texts: Student responses in oral and written forms. *Dissertation Abstracts International, 65(9),* 3380A.

Gu, Y., & Johnson, R. (1996). Vocabulary learning strategies and language learning outcomes. *Language Learning, 46,* 643–679.

Guthrie, J. (2004). Teaching for literacy engagement. *Journal of Literacy Research, 36,* 1–30.

Guthrie, J., Wigfield, A., & Perencevich, K. (Eds.). (2004). *Motivating reading comprehension: Concept-oriented reading instruction*. Mahwah, NJ: Lawrence Erlbaum.

Haastrup, K. (1989). The learner as word processor. *AILA Review, 6*, 34–46.

Han, Z. H. (2004). *Fossilization in adult second language acquisition*. Clevedon, UK: Multilingual Matters.

Han, Z. H., Park, E., & Combs, C. (2008). Textual input enhancement: Issues and possibilities. *Applied Linguistics, 29*(4), 597–618.

Hardcastle, V. (1993). The naturalists versus the skeptics: The debate over a scientific understanding of consciousness. *Journal of Mind and Behavior, 14*, 27–50.

Harley, B. (1998). The role of focus-on-form tasks in promoting child L2 acquisition. In C. Doughty & J. Williams (Eds.), *Focus on form in classroom second language acquisition* (pp. 156–174). Cambridge, UK: Cambridge University Press.

Harley, B., & Swain, M. (1984). The interlanguage of immersion students and its implications for second language teaching. In A. Davies, C. Criper, & A. P. R. Howatt (Eds.), *Interlanguage* (pp. 291–311). Edinburgh: Edinburgh University Press.

Hatch, E. (1983). Simplified input and second language acquisition. In R. Anderson (Ed.), *Pidginization and Creolization as language acquisition* (pp. 64–86). Rowley, MA: Newbury House.

Hauptman, P. (2000). Some hypotheses on the nature of difficulty and ease in second language reading: An application of schema theory. *Foreign Language Annals, 33*, 622–631.

Haynes, M., & Baker, I. (1993). American and Chinese readers learning from lexical familiarizations in English text. In T. Huckin, M. Haynes, & J. Coady (Eds.), *Second language reading and vocabulary learning* (pp. 130–150). Norwood, NJ: Ablex.

Haynes, M., & Carr, T. (1990). Writing system background and second language reading: A component skills analysis of English Reading by native speaker-readers of Chinese. In T. Carr & B. Levy (Eds.), *Reading and its development: Component skills approaches* (pp. 375–421). San Diego, CA: Academic Press.

Hazenburg, S., & Hulstijn, J. (1996). Defining a minimal receptive second-language vocabulary for non-native university students: An empirical investigation. *Applied Linguistics, 17*, 145–163.

Higgins, J., & Wallace, R. (1989). Hopalong: A computer reader pacer. *System, 17*, 389–399.

Hill, D., & Prowse, P. (2001). *How I met myself: Cambridge English readers*. Cambridge, UK: Cambridge University Press.

Hirsh, D., & Nation, P. (1992). What vocabulary size is needed to read unsimplified texts for pleasure? *Reading in a Foreign Language, 8*(2), 689–696.

Holm, A., & Dodd, B. J. (1996). The effect of first written language on the acquisition of English literacy. *Cognition, 59*, 119–147.

Horst, M. (2005a). Learning L2 vocabulary through extensive reading: A measurement study. *Canadian Modern Language Review, 61,* 355–382.

———. (2005b, March). Vocabulary development and extensive reading in a second language. Paper presented at the University of Alberta, Edmonton, Canada.

Horst, M., Cobb, T., & Meara, P. (1998). Beyond A Clockwork Orange: Acquiring second language vocabulary through reading. *Reading in a Foreign Language, 11,* 207–223.

Horst, M., Cobb, T., & Nicolae, I. (2005). Expanding academic vocabulary with a collaborative on-line database. *Language Learning & Technology, 9*(2), 90–110.

Horst, M., & Meara, P. (1999). Test of a model for predicting second language lexical growth through reading. *Canadian Modern Language Review, 56*(2), 308–328.

Hu, M., & Nation, P. (2000). Unknown vocabulary density and reading comprehension. *Reading in a Foreign Language, 13,* 403–430.

Hudson, T. (1982). The effects of induced schemata on the 'short circuit' in L2 reading: Non-decoding factors in L2 reading performance. *Language Learning, 32,* 3–31.

Hulstijn, J. (2001). Intentional and incidental second language vocabulary learning: A reappraisal of elaboration, rehearsal and automaticity. In P. Robinson (Ed.), *Cognition and second language instruction* (pp. 258–286). Cambridge, UK: Cambridge University Press.

———. (2003). Incidental and intentional learning. In C. Doughty & M. Long (Eds.), *The handbook of second language acquisition* (pp. 349–381). Oxford, UK: Blackwell.

Hulstijn, J., Hollander, M., & Greidanus, T. (1996). Incidental vocabulary learning by advanced foreign language students: The influence of marginal glosses, dictionary use, and reoccurrence of unknown words. *The Modern Language Journal, 80*(3), 327–339.

Hunt, A., & Beglar, D. (2005). A framework for developing EFL reading vocabulary. *Reading in a Foreign Language, 17,* 23–59.

Hyland, K., & Tse, P. (2007). Is there an "academic vocabulary"? *TESOL Quarterly, 41,* 235–253.

Institute of International Education. (2003). *Open doors: Report on international student exchange.* New York: Author.

Issidorides, D., & Hulstijn, J. (1992). Comprehension of grammatically modified and non-modified sentences by second language learners. *Applied Psycholinguistics, 13*(2), 147–161.

Irwin, J. W. (1991). *Teaching reading comprehension processes* (2nd ed.). Englewood Cliffs, NJ: Prentice Hall.

Izumi, S. (2002). Output, input enhancement, and the noticing hypothesis: An experimental study on ESL relativization. *Studies in Second Language Acquisition, 24,* 541–577.

Jacobs, G., Dufon, P., & Hong, F. (1994). L1 and L2 glosses in reading passages: Their effectiveness for increasing comprehension and vocabulary knowledge. *Journal of Research in Reading, 17*(1), 19–28.

Jensen, L. (1986). Advanced reading skills in a comprehensive course. In F. Dubin, D. Eskey, & W. Grabe (Eds.), *Teaching second language reading for academic purposes* (pp. 103–124). Reading, MA: Addison-Wesley.

Johnson, K., & Johnson, H. (1998). *Encyclopedic dictionary of applied linguistics.* Oxford, UK: Blackwell.

Johnson, P. (1982). Effects on reading comprehension of building background knowledge. *TESOL Quarterly, 16*(3), 503–516.

Jourdenais, R. (1998). *The effects of textual enhancement on the acquisition of the Spanish preterit and imperfect.* Unpublished doctoral dissertation, Georgetown University.

Jourdenais, R., Ota, M., Stauffer, S., Boyson, B., & Doughty, C. (1995). Does textual enhancement promote noticing?: A think aloud protocol analysis. In R. Schmidt (Ed.), *Attention and awareness in foreign language learning* (pp. 183–216). Honolulu: University of Hawaii, Second Language Teaching and Curriculum Center.

Just, M., & Carpenter, P. (1992). A capacity theory of comprehension: Individual differences in working memory. *Psychological Review, 99*, 122–149.

Karlsen, B., & Gardner, F. (1990). *Adult basic learning examination.* San Antonio, TX: The Psychological Corporation.

Kawai, Y., Oxford, R., & Iran-Nejad, A. (2000). Sources of internal self-regulation with a focus on language learning. *The Journal of Mind and Behavior, 21*, 45–60.

Kelch, K. (1985). Modified talk in the classroom. *International Review of Applied Linguistics, 17*, 159–165.

Kintsch, W. (1998). *Comprehension: A paradigm for cognition.* Cambridge, UK: Cambridge University Press.

Kintsch, W., & Rawson, K. (2005). Comprehension. In M. Snowling & C. Hulme (Eds.), *The science of reading: A Handbook* (pp. 209–226). Malden, MA: Blackwell.

Koda, K. (1989). The effects of transferred vocabulary knowledge on the development of L2 reading proficiency. *Foreign Language Annals, 22*, 529–540.

———. (2005). *Insights into second language reading: A cross-linguistic approach.* Cambridge, UK: Cambridge University Press.

Kost, C., Foss, P., & Lenzini, J. (1999). Textual and pictorial glosses: Effectiveness on incidental vocabulary growth when reading in foreign language. *Foreign Language Annals, 32*(1), 89–113.

Kowal, M., & Swain, M. (1997). From semantic to syntactic processing: How can we promote it in the immersion classroom? In R. Johnson & M. Swain (Eds.), *Immersion eEducation: International perspectives* (pp. 284–309). Cambridge, UK: Cambridge University Press.

Krashen, S. (1981). The case for narrow reading. *TESOL Newsletter, 12*, 23.

————. (1982). *Principles and practice in second language acquisition*. New York: Pergamon Press.

————. (1985). *The input hypothesis*. Oxford, UK: Pergamon Press.

————. (1989). We acquire vocabulary and spelling by reading: Additional evidence for the input hypothesis. *The Modern Language Journal, 73,* 440–464.

————. (1993). *The power of reading: Insights from the research*. Englewood, CA: Libraries Unlimited.

————. (2003). *Explorations in language acquisition and use: The Taipei lectures*. Portsmouth, NH: Heinemann.

Kucer, S. & Tuten, J. (2003). Revisiting and rethinking the reading process. *Language Arts, 80*(4), 284–290.

Kucera, H., & Francis, W. (1967). *Computational analysis of present day American English*. Providence, RI: Brown University Press.

Lado, R. (1964). *Language teaching: A scientific approach*. New York: McGraw-Hill.

Larsen-Freeman, D. (1975). The acquisition of grammatical morphemes by adult ESL students. *TESOL Quarterly, 9,* 409–420.

Laufer, B. (1989). What percentage of text-lexis is essential for comprehension? In C. Lauren & M. Nordman (Eds.), *Special language: From humans thinking to thinking machines*. Clevedon, UK: Multilingual Matters.

————. (1992). How much lexis is necessary for reading comprehension? In P. Arnaud & H. Bejoint (Eds.), *Vocabulary and applied linguistics* (pp. 126–132). London: Macmillan.

————. (1997). The lexical plight in second language reading: Words you don't know, words you think you know, and words you can't guess. In J. Coady & T. Huckin (Eds.), *Second language vocabulary acquisition: A rationale for pedagogy* (pp. 20–33). Cambridge, UK: Cambridge University Press.

Laufer, B., & Hulstijn, J. (2001). Incidental vocabulary acquisition in a second language: The construct of task-induced involvement. *Applied Linguistics, 22,* 1–26.

Laufer, B., & Nation, P. (1995). Vocabulary size and use: Lexical richness in L2 written production. *Applied Linguistics, 16,* 307–322.

Laufer, B., & Sim, D. (1985). Measuring and explaining the threshold needed for English for Academic Purposes tests. *Foreign Language Annals, 18,* 405–413.

Lawson, M., & Hogben, D. (1996). The vocabulary-learning strategies of foreign-language students. *Language Learning, 46,* 101–135.

Lee, J. (1998). The relationship of verb morphology to second language reading comprehension and input processing. *The Modern Language Journal, 82*(i), 33–48.

————. (2002). The initial impact of reading as input for the acquisition of future tense morphology in Spanish. In S. Gass, K. Bardovi-Harlig, S. Magnan, & J. Walz (Eds.), *Pedagogical norms for second and foreign language learning and teaching* (pp. 119–140). Amsterdam: John Benjamins.

Lee, J., & Schallert, D. (1997). The relative contribution of L2 language proficiency and L1 reading ability to L2 reading performance: A test of the threshold hypothesis in an EFL context. *TESOL Quarterly, 31*(4), 713–739.

Lee, J., & Valdman, A. (2000). Introduction. In J. Lee & A. Valdman (Eds.), *Form and meaning: Multiple perspectives* (pp. ix-xx). Boston: Heinle.

Lee, J., & VanPatten, B. (2003). *Making communicative language teaching happen.* New York: McGraw Hill.

Lee, J., & Wolf, D. (1997). A quantitative and qualitative analysis of the word-meaning inferencing strategies of L1 and L2 readers. *Spanish Applied Linguistics, 1,* 24–64.

Leech, G., Rayson, P., & Wilson, A. (2001). *Word frequencies in written and spoken English: Based on the British national corpus.* London: Longman.

Leeman, J., Arteagoitia, I., Fridman, B., & Doughty, C. (1995). Integrating attention to form with meaning: Focus on from in content-based Spanish instruction. In R. Schmidt (Ed.), *Attention and awareness in foreign language learning (Technical Report #9)* (pp. 217–258). Honolulu: University of Hawaii, Second Language Teaching & Curriculum Center.

Leow, R. (1993). To simplify or not to simplify. *Studies in Second Language Acquisition, 15,* 333–355.

———. (1995). Modality and intake in SLA. *Studies in Second Language Acquisition, 17,* 79–89.

———. (1997a). Attention, awareness, and foreign language behavior. *Language Learning, 47,* 467–506.

———. (1997b). Simplification and second language acquisition. *World Englishes, 16,* 291–296.

———. (1997c). The effects of input enhancement and text length on adult L2 readers' comprehension and intake in second language acquisition. *Applied Language Learning, 8,* 151–182.

———. (1998). The effects of amount and type of exposure on adult learners' L2 development in SLA. *The Modern Language Journal, 82,* 49–68.

———. (1999). Attention, awareness, and focus on form research: A critical overview. In J. F. Lee & A. Valdman (Eds.), *Meaning and form: Multiple perspectives* (pp. 69–98). Boston: Heinle & Heinle.

———. (2000). A study of the role of awareness in foreign language behavior: Aware vs. unaware learners. *Studies in Second Language Acquisition, 22,* 557–584.

———. (2001a). Attention, awareness and foreign language behavior. *Language Learning, 51,* 113–155.

———. (2001b). Do learners notice enhanced forms while interacting with the L2?: An online and offline study of the role of written input enhancement in L2 reading. *Hispania, 84,* 496–509.

Leow, R., Egi, T., Nuevo, A.-M., & Tsai, Y. (2003). The roles of textual enhancement and type of linguistic item in adult L2 learners' comprehension and intake. *Applied Language Learning, 13,* 93–108.

Leow, R., & Morgan-Short, K. (2004). To think aloud or not to think aloud: The issue of reactivity in SLA research methodology. *Studies in Second Language Acquisition, 26*, 35–57.

Lewis, R. (1971). *Reading for Adults*. London: Longman.

Li, X. (1988). Effects of contextual cues on inferring and remembering meanings of new words. *Applied Linguistics, 9*(4), 402–413.

Lightbown, P. (1992). Can they do it themselves? A comprehension-based ESL course for young children. In R. Courchêne, J. John, C. Thérien, & J. Glidden (Eds.), *Comprehension-based second language teaching: Current trends* (pp. 353–370). Ottawa, Canada: University of Ottawa Press.

———. (2000). Classroom SLA research and second language teaching. *Applied Linguistics, 21*(4), 431–462.

Lightbown, P., Halter, R., White, J., & Horst, M. (2002). Comprehension-based learning: The limits of "Do it yourself." *Canadian Modern Language Review, 58*, 427–464.

Lightbown, P., & Spada, N. (1990). Focus on form and corrective feedback in communicative language teaching: Effects on second language learning. *Studies in Second Language Acquisition, 12*(4), 429–448.

———. (2006). *How languages are learned* (3rd ed.). Oxford, UK: Oxford University Press.

Lindholm-Leary, K. J. (2001). *Dual language education*. Clevedon, UK: Multilingual Matters.

Lomicka, L. (1998). To gloss or not to gloss: An investigation of reading comprehension online. *Language Learning & Technology, 1*, 41–50.

London, J. (1903). *Call of the wild*. Retrieved December 20, 2005, from www.archive.org/details/callw10

Long, M. (1983). Native speaker/non-native speaker conversation and the negotiation of comprehensible input. *Applied Linguistics, 4*(2), 126–141.

———. (1985). Input and second language acquisition theory. In. S. Gass & C. Madden (Eds.), *Input in second language acquisition* (pp. 377–393). Rowley, MA: Newbury House.

———. (1991). Focus on form: A design feature in language teaching methodology. In K. de Bot, D. Coste, C. Kramsch, & R. Ginsberg (Eds.), *Foreign language research in a cross-cultural perspective* (pp. 39–52). Amsterdam: John Benjamins.

———. (1996). The role of the linguistic environment in second language acquisition. In W. Ritchie & T. Bhatia (Eds.), *Handbook of second language acquisition* (pp. 413–468). New York: Academic Press.

Long, M., & Robinson, P. (1998) Focus on form: Theory, research, and practice. In C. Doughty & J. Williams (Eds.), *Focus on form in classroom second language acquisition* (pp. 16–41). Cambridge, UK: Cambridge University Press.

Loschky, L. (1994). Comprehensible input and second language acquisition: What is the relationship? *Studies in Second Language Acquisition, 16*(3), 303–323.

Lyman-Hager, M., Davis, J., Burnett, J., & Chennault, R. (1993). Une Vie de Boy: Interactive reading in French. In F. Borchardt & E. Johnson (Eds.), *Proceedings of the CALICO 1993 Annual Symposium on "Assessment"* (pp. 93–97). Durham, NC: Duke University.

Lyster, R., & Ranta, L. (1997). Corrective feedback and learner uptake. *Studies in Second Language Acquisition, 19*, 37–66.

Maclean, M., & D'Anglejan, A. (1986). Rational cloze and retrospection: Insights into first and second language reading comprehension. *Canadian Modern Language Review, 42*, 814–826.

Macnamara, J. (1970). Comparative studies of reading and problem solving in two languages. *TESOL Quarterly, 4*, 107–116.

Mason, B., & Krashen, S. (1997). Extensive reading in English as a foreign language. *System, 25*, 91–102.

McLaughlin, B. (1987). *Theories of second language learning.* London: Edward Arnold.

McLaughlin, B., Rossman, T., & McLeod, B. (1983). Second language learning: An information-processing perspective. *Language Learning, 33*(2), 135–158.

Meara, P. (1996). The dimensions of lexical competence. In G. Brown, K. Malmkjaer, & J. Williams (Eds.), *Performance and competence in second language acquisition* (pp. 35–53). New York: Cambridge University Press.

Meara, P., & Buxton, B. (1987). An alternative to multiple-choice tests. *Language Testing, 4*(2), 142–154.

Meara, P., Lightbown, P. M., & Halter, R. H. (1997). Classrooms as lexical environments. *Language Teaching Research, 1*, 28–47.

Mezynski, K. (1983). Issues concerning the acquisition of knowledge: Effects of vocabulary training on reading comprehension. *Review of Educational Research, 53*(2), 253–279.

Milton, J., & Meara, P. (1995). How periods abroad affect vocabulary growth in a foreign language. *ITL Review of Applied Linguistics, 107/108*, 17–34.

Mokhtari, K., & Sheorey, R. (2002). Measuring ESL students' awareness of reading strategies. *Journal of Developmental Education, 25*(3), 2–10.

Mondria, J. (2003). The effects of inferring, verifying, and memorizing on the retention of L2 word meanings: An experimental comparison of the "meaning-inferred method" and the "meaning-given method." *Studies in Second Language Acquisition, 25*, 473–499.

Mondria, J., & Wit-de Boer, M. (1991). The effects of contextual richness on the guessability and retention of words in a foreign language. *Applied Linguistics, 12*, 249–267.

Montgomery, L. M. (2002). *Anne of Green Gables* (simplified ESL version). Harlow, UK: Pearson.

Morgan-Short, K., & Wood Bowden, H. (in press). Processing instruction and meaningful output-based instruction: Effects on second language development. *Studies in Second Language Acquisition, 28*.

Morris, C., Bransford, J., & Franks, J. (1977). Levels of processing versus transfer appropriate processing. *Journal of Verbal Learning and Verbal Behavior, 16,* 519–533.

Morrow, K. (1980). *Skills for Reading.* Oxford, UK: Oxford University Press.

———. (1981). Principles of communicative methodology. In K. Johnson & K. Morrow (Eds.), *Communication in the classroom.* London: Longman.

Morrow, K., & Schocker, M. (1987). Using texts in a communicative approach. *ELT Journal, 41*(4), 248–256.

Mountain, L. (2005). ROOTing out meaning: More morphemic analysis for primary pupils. *The Reading Teacher, 58,* 742–749.

Muljani, D., Koda, K., & Moates, D. R. (1998). The development of word recognition in a second language. *Applied Psycholinguistics, 19,* 99–113.

Nagata, N. (1999). The effectiveness of computer-assisted interactive glosses. *Foreign Language Annals, 32,* 469–479.

Nagy, W. (1997). On the role of context in first-and second-language vocabulary learning. In N. Schmitt, & M. McCarthy (Eds.), *Vocabulary: Description, acquisition and pedagogy* (pp. 64–83). Cambridge, UK: Cambridge University Press.

Nagy, W., & Anderson, R. (1984). How many words are there in printed school English? *Reading Research Quarterly, 19,* 304–330.

Nagy, W., Herman, P., & Anderson, R. (1985). Learning words from context. *Reading Research Quarterly, 20,* 233–253.

Nassaji, H. (2002). Schema theory and knowledge-based processes in second language reading comprehension: A need for alternative perspectives. *Language Learning, 52,* 439–481.

———. (2003). L2 vocabulary learning from context: Strategies, knowledge sources, and their relationship with success in L2 lexical inferencing. *TESOL Quarterly, 37,* 645–70.

———. (2004). The relationship between depth of vocabulary knowledge and L2 learners' lexical inferencing strategy use and success. *Canadian Modern Language Review, 61,* 107–134.

Nassaji, H., & Geva, E. (1999). The contribution of phonological and orthographic processing skills to adult ESL reading: Evidence from native speakers of Farsi. *Applied Psycholinguistics, 20,* 241–267.

Nation, P. (1990). *Teaching and learning vocabulary.* New York: Newbury House.

———. (2001). *Learning vocabulary in another language.* Cambridge, UK: Cambridge University Press.

National Institute of Child Health and Human Development. (2000). Report of the National Reading Panel. Teaching children to read: An evidence-based assessment of the scientific research literature on reading and its implications for instruction. Washington, DC: National Reading Panel.

Nikolov, M. (2006). Test-taking strategies of 12- and 13-year-old Hungarian learners of EFL: Why whales have migraines. *Language Learning, 56*(1), 1–51.

Nunan, D. (1997). Does learner training make a difference? *Lenguas Modernas, 24,* 123–142.

Nuttall, C. (1982). *Teaching reading skills in a foreign language.* Oxford, UK: Heinemann.

———. (1996). *Teaching reading skills in a foreign language. New edition.* Oxford, UK: Heinemann.

Ogden, C. (1930). *Basic English: A general introduction with rules and grammar* London: Kegan Paul.

O'Malley, J., & Valdez Pierce, L. (1996). *Authentic assessment for English language learners.* Reading, MA: Addison-Wesley.

Overstreet, M. (1998). Text enhancement and content familiarity: The focus of learner attention. *Spanish Applied Linguistics, 2,* 229–258.

Oxford, R. (1990). *Language learning strategies: What every teacher should know.* New York: Newbury House.

Palincsar, A., & Brown, A. (1984). Reciprocal teaching of comprehension-fostering and monitoring activities. *Cognition and Instruction, 1,* 117–175.

Paran, A. (1996). Reading in EFL: Facts and fictions. *ELT Journal, 50*(1), 25–33.

Paribakht, T., & Wesche, M. (1993). The relationship between reading comprehension and second language development in a comprehension-based ESL program. *TESL Canada Journal, 2,* 9–29.

———. (1999). Reading and "incidental" L2 vocabulary acquisition. An introspective study of lexical inferencing. *Studies in Second Language Acquisition, 21,* 195–224.

Park, E. S. (2004). Constraints of implicit focus on form: Insights from a study of input enhancement. *Teachers College, Columbia University Working Papers in TESOL & Applied Linguistics, 4*(2), 1–30. Retrieved from journals. tc-library.org/index.php/tesol

Parry, K. (1997). Vocabulary and comprehension: Two portraits. In J. Coady, & T. Huckin (Eds.), *Second language vocabulary acquisition: A rationale for pedagogy* (pp. 55–68). Cambridge, UK: Cambridge University Press.

Paulson, E. (2002). Are oral reading word omissions and substitutions caused by careless eye movements? *Reading Psychology, 23*(1), 45–66.

———. (2005). Viewing eye movements through the lens of chaos theory: How reading is like the weather. *Reading Research Quarterly, 40*(3), 338–358.

Paulson, E., Flurkey, A., Goodman, Y., & Goodman, K. (2003). Eye movements and miscue analysis: Reading from a constructivist perspective. *The Yearbook of the National Reading Conference, 52,* 345–355.

Paulson, E., & Freeman, A. (2003). *Insight from the eyes: The science of effective reading instruction.* Portsmouth, NH: Heinemann.

Perfetti, C. (1985). *Reading ability.* New York: Oxford University Press.

———. (1999). Comprehending written language: A blueprint for the reader. In C. Brown & P. Hagoort (Eds.), *Neurocognition of language* (pp. 167–208). Oxford, UK: Oxford University Press.

Perfetti, C., & Hart, L. (2001). The lexical basis of comprehension skill. In D. Gorfien (Ed.), *On the consequences of meaning selection.* Washington, DC: American Psychological Association.

Perfetti, C., Landi, N., & Oakhill, J. (2005). The acquisition of reading comprehension skill. In M. Snowling & C. Hulme (Eds.), *The science of reading* (pp. 227–247). Malden, MA: Blackwell.

Perfetti, C. A., & Roth, S. (1981). Some of the interactive processes in reading and their role in reading skill. In A. Lesgold & C. Perfetti (Eds.), *Interactive processes in reading* (pp. 269–297). Hillsdale, NJ: Lawrence Erlbaum.

Peters, A. (1985). Language segmentation: Operating principles for the perception and analysis of language. In D. I. Slobin (Ed.), *The cross-linguistic study of language acquisition. Volume 2: Theoretical issues* (pp. 1029–1068). Mahwah, NJ: Lawrence Erlbaum.

Pigada, M., & Schmitt, N. (2006). Vocabulary acquisition from extensive reading: A case study. *Reading in a Foreign Language, 18,* 1–28.

Pitts, M., White, H., & Krashen, S. (1989). Acquiring second language vocabulary through reading: A replication of the Clockwork Orange study using second language acquirers. *Reading in a Foreign Language, 5,* 271–275.

Pressley, M. (2006). *Reading instruction that works* (3rd ed.). New York: Guilford Press.

Pritchard, R. (1990). The effects of cultural schemata on reading processing strategies. *Reading Research Quarterly, 25,* 273–295.

Pulido, D. (2000). *The impact of topic familiarity, L2 reading proficiency, and L2 passage sight vocabulary on incidental vocabulary gain through reading for adult learners of Spanish as a foreign language.* Unpublished doctoral dissertation, University of Illinois–Urbana-Champaign.

———. (2003). Modeling the role of second language proficiency and topic familiarity in second language incidental vocabulary acquisition through reading. *Language Learning, 53,* 233–284.

———. (2004a). The relationship between text comprehension and second language incidental vocabulary acquisition: A matter of topic familiarity? *Language Learning, 54,* 469–523.

———. (2004b). The effect of cultural familiarity on incidental vocabulary acquisition through reading. *The Reading Matrix: An Online International Journal, 4,* 20–53.

———. (2005, October). Reader-based factors influencing L2 lexical input processing during strategic tasks. Paper presented at the Second Language Research Forum, Teachers College, Columbia University, New York.

———. (2007). The effects of topic familiarity and passage sight vocabulary on L2 lexical inferencing and retention through reading. *Applied Linguistics, 28*(1), 66–86.

Purcell-Gates, V., Duke, N., & Martineau, J. (2007). Learning to read and write genre-specific text: Roles of authentic experience and explicit teaching. *Reading Research Quarterly, 42,* 8–45.

Richards, J. C. (2006). Materials development and research—Making the connection. *RELC Journal, 37*, 5–26.

Robinson, H., Faraone, V., Hittleman, D. R., & Unruh, E. (1990). *Reading comprehension instruction 1783–1987: A review of trends and research.* Newark, DE: International Reading Association.

Robinson, P. (1995). Attention, memory, and the 'noticing' hypothesis. *Language Learning, 45*, 283–331.

———. (2003). Attention and memory. In C. Doughty & M. Long (Eds.), *The handbook of second language acquisition* (pp. 631–678). Oxford, UK: Blackwell.

Rodgers, D. (2006). Developing content and form: Encouraging evidence from Italian content-based instruction. *The Modern Language Journal, 90*(3), 373–386.

Rolstad, K., Mahoney, K., & Glass, G. (2005). A meta-analysis of program effectiveness research on English language learners. *Educational Policy, 19*(4), 572–594.

Rosa, E., & Leow, R. (2004). Computerized task-based exposure, explicitness and type of feedback on Spanish L2 development. *The Modern Language Journal, 88*, 192–217.

Rosa E., & O'Neill, M. (1999). Explicitness, intake, and the issue of awareness: Another piece to the puzzle. *Studies in Second Language Acquisition, 21*, 511–556.

Rott, S. (2000). Relationships between the process of reading, word inferencing, and incidental word acquisition. In J. Lee & A.Valdman (Eds.), *Form and Meaning: Multiple Perspectives* (pp. 255–282). Boston: Heinle & Heinle.

Rubin, J., Chamot, A., Harris, V., & Anderson, N. J. (2007). Intervening in the use of strategies. In A. Cohen & E. Macaro (Eds.), *Language Learner Strategies: 30 Years of Research and Practice* (pp. 141–160). Oxford, UK: Oxford University Press.

Rumelhart, D. (1980). Schemata: The building blocks of cognition. In R. Spiro, B. Bruce, & W. Brewer (Eds.), *Theoretical issues in reading comprehension* (pp. 33–58). Hillsdale, NJ: Lawrence Erlbaum.

Samuda, V. (2001). Guiding relationships between form and meaning during task performance: The role of the teacher. In M. Bygate, P. Skehan, & M. Swain (Eds.), *Researching pedagogic tasks, second language learning, teaching, and testing* (pp. 119–140). Harlow, UK: Longman.

Samuels, S. J. (1979). The method of repeated readings. *The Reading Teacher, 32*, 403–408.

Saragi, T., Nation, P., & Meister, G. (1978). Vocabulary learning and reading. *System, 6*, 72–80.

Sasaki, M. (2005). The effect of L1 reading processes on L2: A crosslinguistic comparison of Italian and Japanese users of English. In V. Cook & B. Bassetti (Eds.), *Second language writing systems.* Clevedon, UK: Multilingual Matters.

Schank, R., & Abelson, R. (1977). *Scripts, plans, goals, and understanding.* Hillsdale, NJ: Lawrence Erlbaum.

Schmidt, R. (1990). The role of consciousness in second language learning. *Applied Linguistics, 11*, 129–158.

———. (1993). Awareness and second language acquisition. *Annual Review of Applied Linguistics, 13*, 206–226.

———. (1995). Consciousness and foreign language learning: A tutorial on the role of attention and awareness in learning. In R.W. Schmidt (Ed.), *Attention and awareness in foreign language learning* (pp. 1–63). Honolulu: University of Hawaii, Second Language Teaching and Curriculum Center.

———. (2001). Attention. In P. Robinson (Ed.), *Cognition and second language instruction* (pp. 3–32). Cambridge, UK: Cambridge University Press.

Schmitt, N. (1997). Vocabulary learning strategies. In N. Schmitt & M. McCarthy (Eds.), *Vocabulary: Description, acquisition, and pedagogy* (pp.199–227). Cambridge, UK: Cambridge University Press.

———. (2000). *Vocabulary in language teaching*. Cambridge, UK: Cambridge University Press.

Schmitt, N., & Schmitt, D. (2005). *Focus on vocabulary: Mastering the academic word list*. White Plains, NY: Longman.

Schmitt, N., & Zimmermann, C. (2002). Derivative word forms: What do learners know? *TESOL Quarterly, 36*, 145–171.

Schouten-van Parreren, C. (1989). Vocabulary learning through reading: Which conditions should be met when presenting words in texts? *AILA Review 6*, 75–85.

Scott, J. (2005). Creating opportunities to acquire new word meanings from text. In E. Hiebert & M. Kamil (Eds.), *Teaching and leaning vocabulary: Bringing research to practice* (pp. 69–91). Mahwah, NJ: Lawrence Erlbaum.

Segalowitz, N. (1986). Second language reading. In. J. Vaid (Ed.), *Language processing in bilinguals: Psycholinguistic and neuropsychological perspectives* (pp. 3–19). Hillsdale, NJ: Lawrence Erlbaum.

———. (2003). Automaticity and second language development. In C. Doughty & M. Long (Eds.), *The handbook of second language acquisition* (pp. 382–408). Oxford, UK: Blackwell.

Segalowitz, N., Poulsen, C., & Komoda, M. (1991). Lower level components of reading skill in higher level bilinguals: Implications for reading instruction. In J. H. Hulstijn (Ed.), *Reading in second languages: AILA review, 8* (pp. 5–14). Amsterdam: Free University Press.

Segalowitz, N., Watson, V., & Segalowitz, S. (1995). Vocabulary skill: Single-case assessment of automaticity of word recognition in a timed lexical decision task. *Second Language Research, 11*, 121–136.

Segalowitz, S., & Segalowitz, N. (1993). Skilled performance, practice, and the differentiation of speed up from automatization effects: Evidence from second language word recognition. *Applied Psycholinguistics, 14*, 369–385.

Segalowitz, S., Segalowitz, N., & Wood, A. (1998). Assessing the development of automaticity in second language word recognition. *Applied Psycholinguistics, 19*(1), 53–68.

228

Sevier, M. (2004). Review of the compleat lexical tutor. *TESL-EJ 8*(3). Retrieved December 20, 2005, from www-writing.berkeley.edu/TESL-EJ/ej31/m2.html

Sharwood Smith, M. (1981). Consciousness-raising and the second language learner. *Applied Linguistics, 2,* 159–168.

———. (1986). Comprehension versus acquisition: Two ways of processing input. *Applied Linguistics, 7*(3), 239–256.

———. (1991). Speaking to many minds: On the relevance of different types of language information for the L2 learner. *Second Language Research, 7*(2), 118–132.

———. (1993). Input enhancement in instructed SLA: Theoretical bases. *Studies in Second Language Acquisition, 15,* 165–179.

Shen, Z. H. (2004). Effects of previewing and providing background knowledge on EFL reading comprehension of American documentary narratives. *TESL Reporter, 37,* 50–63.

Sheorey, R., & Mokhtari, K. (2001). Differences in the metacognitive awareness of reading strategies among native and non-native readers. *System, 29,* 431–449.

Shizuka, T. (2000). *The validity of incorporating reading speed and response confidence in measurement of EFL reading proficiency.* Unpublished doctoral dissertation, University of Reading, UK.

———. (2004). *New horizons in computerized testing of reading.* Suita, Japan: Kansai University Press.

Shook, D. (1994). FL/L2 reading, grammatical information, and the input-to-intake phenomenon. *Applied Language Learning, 5,* 57–93.

———. (1999). What foreign language reading recalls reveal about the input-to-intake phenomenon. *Applied Language Learning, 10,* 39–76.

Simard, D., & Wong, W. (2001). Alertness, orientation, and detection: The conceptualization of attentional functions in SLA. *Studies in Second Language Acquisition, 23*(1), 103–124.

Skehan, P. (1998). *A cognitive approach to language learning.* Oxford, UK: Oxford University Press.

Snellings, P., van Gelderen, A., & de Glopper, K. (2002). Lexical retrieval: An aspect of fluent second language production that can be enhanced. *Language Learning, 52*(4), 723–754.

Snow, C., & Juel, C. (2005). Teaching children to read: What do we know about how to do it? In M. Snowling & C. Hume (Eds.), *The science of reading: A handbook.* Malden, MA: Blackwell.

Spada, N., & Lightbown, P. (1993). Instruction and development of questions in L2 classrooms. *Studies in Second Language Acquisition, 15,* 205–224.

Stahl, S. (1998). Four questions about vocabulary. In C. Hynd (Ed.), *Learning from text across conceptual domains* (pp. 73–94). Mahwah, NJ: Lawrence Erlbaum.

———. (2004). What do we know about fluency? In P. McCardle & V. Schhabra (Eds.), The voice of evidence in reading research (pp. 187-211). Baltimore: Brookes.

Stahl, S., & Nagy, W. (2006). *Teaching word meanings*. Mahwah, NJ: Lawrence Erlbaum.

Stanovich, K. (1980). Toward an interactive-compensatory model of individual differences in the development of reading fluency. *Reading Research Quarterly, 16,* 32–71.

———. (1986). Matthew effects in reading: Some consequences of individual differences in the acquisition of literacy. *Reading Research Quarterly, 21,* 360–400.

———. (1991). Word recognition: Changing perspectives. In R. Barr, M. Kamil, P. Mosenthal, & P. Pearson (Eds.), *Handbook of reading research, Vol. 2* (pp. 418–452). Mahwah, NJ: Lawrence Erlbaum.

———. (1998). Twenty-five years of research on the reading process: The grand synthesis and what it means for our field. In T. Shanahan & F. Rodriguez-Brown (Eds.), *Forty-seventh yearbook of the National Reading Conference* (pp. 44–58). Chicago: National Reading Conference.

———. (2000). *Progress in understanding reading: Scientific foundations and new frontiers*. New York: Guilford.

Sternberg, R. (1987). Most vocabulary is learned from context. In M. McKeown & M. Curtis (Eds.), *The nature of vocabulary acquisition* (pp. 89–105). Hillsdale, NJ: Lawrence Erlbaum.

Stoller, F. (1986) Reading lab: developing low-level reading skills. In F. Dubin, D. Eskey, & W. Grabe (Eds.) Teaching second language reading for academic purposes (pp. 51–76). Reading, MA: Addison-Wesley.

Strong-Krause, D. (2000). Exploring the effectiveness of self-assessment strategies in ESL placement. In G. Ekbatani & H. Pierson (Eds.), *Learner-directed assessment in ESL* (pp. 49–73). Mahwah, NJ: Lawrence Erlbaum.

Sutarsyah, C., Nation, P., & Kennedy, G. (1994). How useful is EAP vocabulary for ESP? A corpus based case study. RELC Journal, 25(2), 34–50.

Swaffar, J., Arens, K., & Byrnes, H. (1991). *Reading for meaning: An integrated approach to language learning*. Englewood Cliffs, NJ: Prentice Hall.

Swain, M. (1985). Communicative competence: Some roles of comprehensible input and comprehensible output in its development. In S. Gass, & C. Madden (Eds.), *Input in second language acquisition* (pp. 235–253). Rowley, MA: Newbury House.

———. (1991). French immersion and its offshoots: Getting two for one. In B. Freed (Ed.), *Foreign language acquisition: Research and the classroom* (pp. 91–103). Lexington, VA: Heath.

Taylor, A., Stevens, J., & Asher, J. W. (2006). The effects of explicit reading strategy training on L2 reading comprehension. In J. Norris & L. Ortega (Eds.), *Synthesizing research on language learning and teaching* (pp. 213–244). Philadelphia: John Benjamins.

Terrell, T. (1991). The role of grammar instruction in a communicative approach. *The Modern Language Journal, 75,* 52–63.

Thomas, W., & Collier, V. (2001). A national study of school effectiveness for language minority students' long-term academic achievement: Final report. Berkeley, CA: Center for Research on Education, Diversity & Excellence.

———. (2002). A national study of school effectiveness for language minority students' long-term academic achievement, 2002. Berkeley, CA: Center for Research on Education, Diversity & Excellence.

Tindale, J. (2003). *Teaching reading*. Sydney, Australia: National Centre for English Language Teaching and Research.

Tomlin, R., & Villa, V. (1994). Attention in cognitive science and second language acquisition. *Studies in Second Language Acquisition, 16*(2), 183–203.

Truscott, J. (1998). Noticing in second language acquisition: A critical review. *Second Language Research, 14*(2), 103–135.

Ulijn, J., & Strother, J. (1990). The effect of syntactic simplification on reading EST texts as L1 and L2. *Journal of Research in Reading, 13*, 38–54.

Urquhart, S., & Weir, C. (1998). *Reading in a second language: Process, product and practice*. New York: Longman.

U.S. Census Bureau. (2000). Census 2000: Language use. Retrieved from www.census.gov/population/www/socdemo/lang_use.html

van Dijk, T., & Kintsch, W. (1983). *Strategies of discourse comprehension*. New York: Academic Press.

van Gelderen, A., Schoonen, R., de Glopper, K., Hulstijn, J., Simis, A., Snellings, P., et al. (2004). Linguistic knowledge, processing speed, and metacognitive knowledge in first- and second-language reading comprehension: A componential analysis. *Journal of Educational Psychology, 96*(1), 19–30.

VanPatten, B. (1990). Attention to form and content in the input. *Studies in Second Language Acquisition, 12*, 287–301.

———. (1996). *Input processing and grammar instruction: Theory and research*. Norwood, NJ: Ablex.

———. (2004). *Processing Instruction*. Mahwah, NJ: Lawrence Erlbaum.

VanPatten, B., & Cadierno, T. (1993). Input processing and second language acquisition: A role for instruction. *The Modern Language Journal, 77*, 45–57.

VanPatten, B., & Oikkenon, S. (1996). The causative variables in processing instruction: Explanation vs. structured input activities. *Studies in Second Language Acquisition, 18*, 495–510.

VanPatten, B., & Sanz, C. (1995). From input to output: Processing instruction and communicative tasks. In F. Eckman, D. Highland, P. Lee, J. Mileham, & R. Weber (Eds.), *Second language acquisition theory and pedagogy* (pp. 169–185). Mahwah, NJ: Lawrence Erlbaum.

Velmans, M. (1991). Is human information processing conscious? *Behavioral and Brain Sciences, 14*, 651–669.

Waber, B. (1972). *Ira sleeps over*. Boston: Houghton Mifflin.

Wade-Woolley, L. (1999). First language influences on second language word reading: All roads lead to Rome. *Language Learning, 49*(3), 447–471.

Walczyk, J. (2000). The interplay between automatic and control processes in reading. *Reading Research Quarterly, 35,* 554–566.

Wang, M., & Koda, K. (2005). Commonalities and differences in word identification skills among learners of English as a second language. *Language Learning, 55*(1), 71–98.

Wang, M., Koda, K., & Perfetti, C. A. (2003). Alphabetic and nonalphabetic L1 effects in English word identification: A comparison of Korean and Chinese English L2 learners. *Cognition, 87*(2), 129–149.

Waring, R. (2001). Research in extensive reading. *Studies in Foreign Languages and Literature, 25,* 1–15. Okayama, Japan: Notre Dame Seishin University.

Waring, R., & Takaki, M. (2003). At what rate do learners learn and retain new vocabulary from reading a graded reader? *Reading in a Foreign Language, 15,* 130–163.

Watanabe, Y. (1997). Input, intake, and retention: Effects of increased processing on incidental learning of foreign language vocabulary. *Studies in Second Language Acquisition, 19,* 287–307.

Weber, R. (1991). Linguistic diversity and reading in an American society. In R. Barr, P. Kamil, P. Mosenthal, & D. Pearson (Eds.), *Handbook of reading research, Vol. 2* (pp. 97–119). New York: Longman.

Wesche, M., & Paribakht, T.S. (1996). Assessing vocabulary knowledge: Depth versus breadth. *Canadian Modern Language Review, 53,* 13–39.

West, C., Hedge, T., & Bronte, E. (2000). *Wuthering heights.* Oxford, UK: Oxford University Press.

West, M. (1953). *A general service list of English words.* London: Longman.

White, J. (1998). Getting the learners' attention. In C. Doughty & J. Williams (Eds.), Focus on form in classroom second language acquisition (pp. 85–113). Cambridge, UK: Cambridge University Press.

White, L. (1987). Against comprehensible input: The input hypothesis and the development of second-language competence. *Applied Linguistics, 8,* 95–110.

White, L., Spada, N., Lightbown, P. & Ranta, L. (1991). Input enhancement and L2 question formation. *Applied Linguistics, 12*(4), 416–432.

White, T., Sowell, J., & Yanagihara, A. (1989). Teaching elementary students to use word part clues. *The Reading Teacher, 42,* 302–308.

Wholey, M (2000). *Reading matters 1.* New York: Houghton Mifflin.

Wickens, C. (1989). Attention and skilled performance. In D. H. Holding (Ed.), *Human skills* (pp. 71–105). New York: John Wiley.

Wilheim, J. (2001). *Improving comprehension with think-aloud strategies.* New York: Scholastic.

Williams, J. (2001). Learner-generated focus on form. *Language Learning, 51*(1), Supplement 1, 303–345.

Wilson, J., & Prowse, P. (2001). *Staying together: Cambridge English readers.* Cambridge, UK: Cambridge University Press.

Winograd, P., & Hare, V. C. (1988). Direct instruction of reading comprehension strategies: The nature of teacher explanation. In C. Weinstein, E. Goetz, & P. Alexander (Eds.) *Learning and study strategies: Issues in assessment, instruction, and evaluation* (pp. 121–139). San Diego, CA: Academic Press.

Wong, W. (2003). Textual enhancement and simplified input: Effects on L2 comprehension and acquisition of non-meaningful grammatical form. *Applied Language Learning, 13,* 109–132.

Yang, H., & Weir, C. (1998). *Validation study of the college English test.* Shanghai: China National College English Testing Committee.

Young, D. (1999). Linguistic simplification of SL reading materials: Effective instructional practice? *The Modern Language Journal, 83,* 350–366.

Zahar, R., Cobb, T., & Spada, N. (2001). Acquiring vocabulary through reading: Effects of frequency and contextual richness. *Canadian Modern Language Review, 57*(4), 541–572.

SUBJECT INDEX

AUTHOR INDEX

Willows, D., 194
Wilson, J., 47, 149
Winograd, P., 136–137
Wit-de Boer, M., 70–71, 74
Wolf, D., 69, 77
Wong, A., 85
Wood, A., 17, 155
Wood Bowden, H., 90

Yanagihara, A., 123
Yang, H., 28
Young, D., 88–89

Zahar, R., 151, 154
Zimmerman, C., 154